BETWEEN GOOD
AND EVIL

BETWEEN GOOD AND EVIL

A MASTER PROFILER'S HUNT FOR SOCIETY'S MOST VIOLENT PREDATORS

BY ROGER L. DEPUE

WITH SUSAN SCHINDEHETTE

WARNER BOOKS

NEW YORK   BOSTON

Warner Books

Time Warner Book Group
1271 Avenue of the Americas, New York, NY 10020
Visit our Web site at www.twbookmark.com.

Printed in the United States of America

First Edition: February 2005
10   9   8   7   6   5   4   3   2   1

Library of Congress Cataloging-in-Publication Data
Depue, Roger L.
    Between good and evil : a master profiler's hunt for society's most violent
predators / Roger L. Depue with Susan Schindehette.
        p. cm.
    Includes index.
    ISBN 0-446-53264-9
    1. Depue, Roger L. 2. Police—United States—Biography. 3. United States.
Federal Bureau of Investigation—Biography. 4. Serial murder investigation—
United States. 5. Good and evil. I. Schindehette, Susan. II. Title.
    HV7911.D47 A3 2005
    363.2.'092—dc22   2004017363

DEDICATION

To my wife, Joanne, who put the smile back on my face.

TABLE OF CONTENTS

BETWEEN GOOD
AND EVIL

CHAPTER ONE

TESTAMENT

SHE WAS SOMEONE'S DAUGHTER, fifteen years old, found lying on a mound of earth just off a desolate country road, with frosted pink polish on her fingernails and a gaping wound where her throat had been cut. As I surveyed the scene, surrounded in stillness, I studied the details of this tableau—little girl's hands, clothing missing below the waist, bruises circling the fragile neck. But beyond the obvious evidence of violence, there was something jarring about the way the killer had left her here.

She was on her back, arms straight down at her sides. Yet after a brutal sexual assault, her legs were together now at knees and ankles, drawn up and tipped, almost demurely, to one side. Her killer had left her in a position of peaceful repose. Gently, it seemed. Tenderly. As if she were a sleeping child.

For ten years beginning in 1979, I was chief of the FBI's Behavioral Science Unit, at a time when its pioneering work in the field of criminal profiling first came to prominence, thanks in part to author Thomas Harris, who picked the brains of our profilers in conjuring up the character of Dr. Hannibal Lecter for his novel *The Silence of the Lambs*.

Today, in a related incarnation, I am the founder of The Academy Group, an elite international crime consulting firm whose half dozen members, all FBI, CIA, or Secret Service veterans, constitute a brain trust of the world's top forensic behavioral science experts in their respective fields: from sexual homicide and child predation, to international terrorism and espionage.

In that role I have listened to tapes of the Columbine school shootings, studied the rage wounds inflicted with a golf club on Martha Moxley's skull, analyzed the JonBenet Ramsey ransom note, and helped a colleague plan his approach in debriefing the notorious FBI agent-turned-traitor Robert Hanssen. I am summoned to cases when all other investigations have failed, when law firms, police jurisdictions, or the emotionally devastated families of victims have nowhere else to turn. It is work that calls on me to be an advocate, a father confessor, and, sometimes, even a bit of the diviner.

In the course of my career I have seen horrible things—cruelty and human depravity in every imaginable permutation. In the 1980s I supervised agents investigating a series of bizarre homicides in California, in which the killer not only eviscerated his victims, but lingered at the scene while blood pooled in their abdominal cavities. Only after carefully studying the crime scene did we recognize the special proclivity of twenty-seven-year-old Richard Trenton Chase, whom the press later christened the Vampire Killer. It was revealed in the odd ring marks found on the floor next to victims, the kind that might be left by someone drinking from a blood-filled plastic yogurt cup.

A decade later, reviewing the murder of a housebound elderly woman, I noted the tremendous amounts of blood—sprays of darkening crimson on the walls, ceiling, and floors in the room where she was killed. But I was also struck by something that had not been given much significance by local police—the fact there was no blood at all on any of the room's baseboards. The killer, I realized, must have wiped them down afterward.

Even after forensic lab tests confirmed that scenario, there was still no obvious message, of the kind left as a taunt by the seasoned serial killer at a crime scene. This was evidence of a disordered perpetrator clinging to the control afforded by familiar routine. Of someone, I thought, who might recently have left a psychiatric facility. Ultimately, investigation did indeed bear out that theory—the perpetrator was a young man just released from a California state mental hospital, whose job had been cleaning the baseboards on his ward.

Now, at a rural crime scene near a farmer's field, I was trying to solve the brutal murder of an innocent fifteen-year-old girl. And I began to try to decipher what our killer had written with his savagery.

Bloodstains pointed to the precise location of the murder, a dense wood thick with stands of evergreen and maple, fifty feet from the side of the road. But the killer had chosen not to leave his victim there, and I knew what that meant. Any subject with normal human response—one who had, say, raped this young girl and then, in a panic, killed her—would have done all he could to hide his crime and avoid detection. He would have left her in the woods, perhaps in a shallow grave, or at least made some effort to hide her corpse in the brush. But this killer followed a different imperative. He had deposited his victim where he was certain she would be found.

Why would he do such a thing? Was he a braggart, a provoca-teur? I didn't think so. I have seen sexual predators make un-speakable displays of their victims, violating them with gun barrels and broom handles in what hardened investigators refer to as "stick jobs." But this killer had shown no such contempt. It seemed to me that there was only one plausible explanation: He had moved his victim because he did not want to leave her in the woods, unseen, where she might be vulnerable to insects or ani-mals. He wanted whoever found her to appreciate her—as he had—with her freshness and beauty still intact.

Even so, he might have dragged her by the hair, or simply dumped her body. Instead, he had gone to the trouble of laying her carefully on a raised berm, higher than the surrounding ground. And then I began to understand. This killer did what human beings have done with objects of veneration since time immemorial. He had placed his victim on an altar.

Quickly, the pieces began to fit. After he had brutalized her, he felt remorse, very nearly a tenderness toward her. He treated her gently after he killed her, and I knew now exactly how he had transported her to this resting place. He had carried her from the spot where he had killed her the way a parent would a sleeping child—slipping one hand beneath her back, and the other under her knees. Then, when he laid her down softly on the ground, as if not to wake her, her knees had rolled gently to one side. What did this mean?

It meant that he knew her. Finally, it was clear to me. Who-ever killed this young girl had also, in his own evil way, loved her.

How can those two things—love and hate—exist together in a person? In the same way, I believe, that good and evil exist in the world. In a constant state of tension, fighting each other for dominance. I know something about that struggle. I believe that

I have a deeper understanding of these things than most people do.

My work has given me a profound respect for what humans suffer at the hands of evil, and a particular sensitivity for what its victims endure. During every investigation that I participate in, there is always an invisible observer at my shoulder, whose presence I never forget. Regardless of the circumstances of a case, I am always giving voice to its silent victim.

What must this young girl's final minutes have been like? Did she cry out while he was repeatedly stabbing her, or keep silent, breathing like a wounded animal, watching for the next glint of a blade? Did her thoughts turn to her parents in those final seconds, when she was overwhelmed by the deepest loneliness she had ever known? Did she experience a dissociative response, the sense of drifting upward and watching her own death as if from above? Or did she sink mercifully into unconsciousness, and feel nothing as her life ebbed away?

The most difficult part of solving a case is the fathoming of it, the understanding of the measure of evil that produced it. The rest—the legwork and interrogation—come only after the intuiting, as the means of proving an investigative hypothesis. In this instance, once I had a clear picture of how the crime had occurred, the rest was not difficult. Investigators narrowed their focus to a relatively short list of potential suspects, questioned them thoroughly, and ultimately charged and convicted an obsessive young man—the young girl's neighbor.

When I was a young man, a friend taught me the ancient art of dowsing, and after a time, I became something of a practitioner myself, finding water underground as a kind of parlor trick for friends. It might seem odd that a man so rooted in grim reality would take an interest in something so ethereal. In fact, I'm fascinated by the unseen forces at play in the lives of human beings.

Still, I'm sometimes challenged by abstract intellectual discussion about the nature of evil. If Hitler genuinely believed that he was carrying out a noble mission by exterminating Jews, some wonder, was he truly evil? Were there mitigating factors, others ask, for the genocide of his countrymen carried out by Cambodia's Pol Pot? What exactly runs through the mind of an Osama bin Laden? I've never had the time to engage in such armchair dialectics. My job has been to try to stop human predators before they kill again, and after studying them so closely over so many years, to me their traits seem clearly recognizable.

They are rational, sadistic, often intelligent, and almost invariably narcissistic. They see themselves as living in a realm somewhere above the rest of us, in a place where the rules of normal society do not apply. Over the years, I've drawn up a list of their common operating principles, something that I call the Anti-Commandments: "That which you love is what I most seek to destroy." "Life is as meaningless as death." "There are few things more pleasurable than hurting someone who is trying to help me." "People die too easily. It should be more painful, and take longer."

The depth of this psychopathic evil is beyond the comprehension of most normal people. I have seen it many times: a pedophile is arrested, a man from a comfortable, upper-class neighborhood. Suddenly, all of his neighbors express shock and disbelief. "He was such a fine, upstanding man, a doting father. Why, he even coached Little League. He can't possibly have done what he's accused of."

What those good people don't fully comprehend is that, as a pedophile, this man is, above all, a sexual abuser of children. That is what he is at his core. He hurts children because, to him, their suffering is of no consequence. It is a meaningless by-product of behavior that makes him feel good, and his own pleasure is more important to him than anything, or anyone, else. Invariably, even from behind prison bars, he will never concede that what he did was damaging to a child. No, he insists, what he did was done out of love. It's the rest of the world that doesn't understand.

The reality is that this man's wife, his nice house in the suburbs, his coaching job, even his own children, are props—the artifice that covers up, and facilitates, what he truly is. He continues to do what he does because that is what he cherishes above all else. What is most real about him is his evil.

Evil is more than a vague notion. It is an entity, and it is manifest on the earth. It has reflexes and intuition, senses vulnerability, and changes its form to adapt to its surroundings. Those who do not believe the Devil walks this earth have not seen the things that I have seen.

The stories I will relate are not fabrications. I have witnessed the unbelievable. Eviscerated children. Mothers who have sold their own toddlers into prostitution, and profited from the videotapes of them being victimized by strangers. Fathers who sleep with their daughters, and their daughter's daughters. A man who, because a six-year-old girl doesn't know her spelling words, binds her with duct tape and pierces her with an embroidery needle more than two hundred times.

Evil is not a discrete entity that springs forth fully formed. It is born in the mind, takes root there as fantasy, and prospers when normal human restraint can no longer contain it. I have seen it devour the personalities of men like Richard Speck,

Jeffrey Dahmer, and Ted Bundy, turning them into blank-faced sociopaths who clearly know right from wrong, but choose, time and again, to follow their own base urges, with complete disregard for the terrible human suffering they cause.

I believe that every act of homicide causes a slight unbalancing in the world, and that it diminishes life's universal equation. In the interest of justice, it is imperative that someone try to right that imbalance. But the task of fighting evil can take a terrible toll on the people who are charged with it. It can cost them their families, their equilibrium, their capacity for joy.

A relentless diet of human misery and sadistic violence can bring any human being—even those armored by years of experience in a law enforcement career—to the brink of despair. I once came to that place myself. But I returned from it, because, along with the evil, I have also come to know something about the redemptive power of good.

A decade ago, I lost the person who embodied most of what was true and worthwhile in my life, and the tragedy of her death caused a grief so great that I came to question God's very existence. I made a decision to leave the world for a holy place, one that, I hoped, would be untouched by evil. I did my searching there, and made my peace. But ultimately, I came to understand that it was only by returning to the world that I would find redemption.

I have stood at the edge of the abyss and peered down into the darkest things that human beings are capable of, at times feared that evil, and very nearly seen it bring me to my knees. But, always, I have tried to conquer it, or at least to force it into submission. In the final accounting, I am a man of faith, in spite of the work that I have done. Or, perhaps, because of it.

How is it that a human being can dwell in the midst of such

depravity, be reminded every day of the suffering of victims, and emerge from it intact? Is the path of evil irrevocable, or do we have the power to change it? It's not for me to preach or posture. I can only bear witness to what I have seen.

I believe that we are all players in an ongoing battle, one that is both larger and more subtle than we often realize. What follows is a dispatch from the front lines of that war—a cautionary tale. It is the story of one man's travels through darkness and redemption, a testament to the belief that in the unending struggle between God and the Devil, evil prevails in this world mostly when we, through apathy, fear, or indifference, allow it to.

In the fall of 1990 a phone call came to my Virginia consulting firm, The Academy Group, from a law firm in Bucks County, Pennsylvania, requesting our help with a cold case robbery-homicide that had taken place some six years before. Its victim, a young woman in her twenties, had been found early one morning, stabbed to death, in the kitchen of the fast food restaurant where she worked. Her name was Terri Brooks.

The attorney, Greg Sturn, with the firm of Harris and Harris, told me that despite a lengthy investigation, local police had never been able to solve the case. But since money was missing from the restaurant safe, and similar fast food robberies had been common in the early 1980s, the consensus was that this must have been the same thing—an armed robbery gone bad.

Now, said Sturn, the dead girl's father and stepmother, George Brooks and his wife, Betty, intended to file a wrongful death suit against the Marriott Corporation, owner of the restaurant chain where Terri had worked. Since Terri's death occurred while she was on the job, state law dictated the case be filed as a workmen's compensation claim; that was the sole legal remedy available to the Brookses.

And that presented a problem. Under workmen's comp rules, the only parties eligible for a monetary award were the victim's dependents, and Terri, who was single and childless at the time of her death, had none. Which meant that her only living survivors—her parents and siblings—could file a claim, but weren't eligible to collect a financial settlement.

It seemed like a cruel catch-22. But there was an alternative, said Sturn. Pennsylvania law allowed one exception to the workmen's comp provision: If a plaintiff could prove that something called "personal animus"—malevolent ill will—had existed between killer and victim, then Terri's parents could step outside the workmen's comp restriction and take their case to civil court. Of course, the idea that Terri's killer knew her might well make a negligence case against the corporation more difficult to prove, but Sturn wasn't worried about that. Marriott company policy clearly stated that employees weren't supposed to work alone at night. And on the night she was murdered, Terri had been closing up the restaurant alone.

That was the financial issue, but of course, it wasn't the only one. After George Brooks and his first wife—Terri's biological mother—had divorced, he went on to raise Terri and her three brothers and sisters by himself, and it was obvious he had loved his daughter deeply. He managed to survive in the wake of her murder, as the parents of many murdered children do. But it hadn't been easy. George Brooks did the best he could to carry on with his life. But six long years after Terri's death, he was still grieving. He needed to know who had killed his little girl.

After talking it over with my colleague, Ken Baker, we agreed to take on the case, and I asked the law firm to send us what information they had. A few days later, it arrived—a large manila envelope of investigative reports, depositions, police reports, autopsy information, and crime scene photographs. I poured myself a cup of coffee, we closed the door behind us, and sat down at the table in our conference room to begin reconstructing what had happened to Terri Brooks in the final hour of her life.

Just after 6:00 a.m. on the foggy morning of February 4, 1984, the general manager of a Roy Rogers restaurant at Oxford Valley Road and Route 1 in Falls Township, in Bucks County, came to work. He found the outer restaurant doors unlocked, the inner doors locked, and immediately became suspicious. He went inside, and was heading for the kitchen when he saw shoes and a set of store keys on the floor. Then he discovered Terri Brooks, twenty-five, his assistant manager, lying on the floor. She had been brutally murdered, and $2,579 was missing from the office safe.

When Terri didn't return home that morning, her father, George, called the restaurant to see if she was there. He was told Terri had been taken to the hospital. "Is she all right?" he asked. "Is she all right?" Finally, they gave him the terrible news: Terri was dead.

All murder cases are tragic in their own way, but this one broke your heart. George Brooks was working class, and he had helped put Terri through college at the University of Maryland. She hoped to have a career in restaurant management, and she often stayed after closing at the restaurant, finishing up the paperwork. She was also engaged to be married that coming summer. In fact, two days before her death, she and her fiancé had put down a deposit on a honeymoon trip to Hawaii. Later that week, Terri was going to pick out her wedding dress.

A good investigator can tell a lot about a killer by studying evidence at the scene of the crime—blood splatter, the position of the body, the pattern of wounds. But the killer isn't the only one to leave telling information. Sometimes, the victim leaves a message, too. And as I looked at the horrific murder scene photographs, I felt it: Terri herself was trying to tell us something.

She was found lying in a pool of blood on a dark industrial tile floor, on her back, not far from the restaurant's office, still wearing her winter jacket. Her shoes, keys, and cigarettes were lying nearby. Her face was cut and badly bruised. The hyoid bone in her throat was fractured, which meant she had been strangled. A clear plastic trash bag liner was wrapped around her neck, covering her head. And a butcher knife was protruding from her throat, lodged with such force it couldn't be pulled out from between the vertebrae of the spinal column.

In all of my years of law enforcement, I had never before seen anything quite like it: beating, strangulation, stabbing, and suffocation—four distinct modes of death. At that moment, I had no idea who had taken this young woman's life so brutally, or why. But I did know that whoever murdered Terri Brooks had killed her four times.

We began to piece together a hypothetical sequence of events. It was a Friday night, and the kitchen had been cleaned and prepped for the morning shift, and Terri was ready to go home. She had her coat on and her purse, cigarettes, and keys with her. She was closing up when someone came to the door. Whether she knew the person or didn't, she let him in. Then something began to go horribly wrong. It was as if she had suddenly said to herself,

"I've got to get out of here." She bolted for the door, and if it had only opened outward instead of inward, she might have made it.

He hit her like a football player, tackling her so hard she was literally knocked out of her shoes. Her purse, keys, and cigarettes flew onto the floor. She was stunned, but after taking a moment to recover, she started to fight back. She had played intramural sports in college. She was young and athletic, and fought with all her strength. They exchanged blows. He punched her in the face repeatedly, hitting her as hard as he could.

At some point, he dragged her across the tile floor, causing holes in her nylons on the top of her feet, worn away by the friction. There was a tremendous bruise line across her upper chest, from where she was slammed into the stainless steel counter. He started to strangle her, with such force he fractured the hyoid bone, just below the larynx. But she continued to fight.

Then came the butcher knife. Maybe the killer was the one who took it first, from the rack above the oven. Maybe it was Terri who grabbed it in an effort to defend herself, in which case he would have wrested it away from her. She had defensive wounds on her hands, which meant that as he was trying to cut her throat, she put her hands up to keep the blade away. Finally, perhaps holding her around the neck from behind, he plunged the knife into the front of her throat, where it partially cut her spinal cord. Still, she struggled. He pulled the knife out, but only partway, and then plunged it in again, harder. This time, the blade entered between the sixth and seventh vertebrae, and severed the other half of her spinal cord.

Now she was paralyzed from the neck down, and she went limp, slipping to the floor. When she was found, her arms and legs were not cocked or bent, but extended straight out. At that point, she would have offered no resistance.

The knife was still protruding from her throat, lodged tightly between the vertebrae of the spine. As she struggled before she was stabbed, her neck had been extended, and the blade was thrust into her with such force that when she dropped to the floor, her head snapped forward, wedging the blade between her vertebrae. Even after all that, she was still alive. The blade had not severed her jugular vein or carotid artery. Her assailant realized she was still breathing. So he went to a storage area where the supplies were kept, and found a plastic trash bag. He wrapped it around her neck and head and, in one final spasm of violence, asphyxiated her.

There are many ways to kill a human being. If the perpetrator uses a gun, it is a more distanced act, cold and impersonal. But this killer wanted the pleasure of using his hands. He wanted to see his victim's face, to look her in the eye as she died. One thing was clear. No matter what the local police had concluded, this was no simple robbery. Terri Brooks had not been fighting for the money, or even for her virtue. This young woman had been fighting for her life.

After I examined the file and talked it over with Ken, we found that we both had the same reaction. The Academy Group had been hired by a law firm to make a determination on a legal technicality in this case—the existence of personal animus—which was very different from being assigned as a homicide investigator to find the killer. Strictly speaking, it was not our job to provide a definitive resolution to the crime.

But after seeing how Terri Brooks had met her end, Ken and I looked at each other and said, "Let's solve the damn thing anyway."

After all these years, it wasn't about the accolade. I'd had plenty of recognition by that time—citations and promotions, moments in the limelight, the respect of my peers. This was about something deeper, about knowing that the person who'd killed this young woman was still out there somewhere, living his life, as if it were the natural order of things. He'd done something unspeakable, and he was smug in the knowledge that he'd gotten away with it. There was no one to fight on Terri's behalf. No one but us.

It wasn't going to be easy to solve this crime, but I knew what it would take. Working along with Ken, I'd have to tap into everything I'd learned in forty years of law enforcement. Still, wasn't that the value of the past—its bearing on the future? The search for Terri Brooks's killer would mark a chapter in a journey that had begun many years before. It would serve as a clear reminder of where I had come from, and how far I had already gone.

CHAPTER TWO

IN THE BEGINNING

WHEN FIRST THEY SAW IT on that summer evening in the early 1930s, wandering through the neighborhood, it didn't look like anyone's idea of danger. A small brown and white dog, short-haired, tent-shaped ears, and a looped, shaggy tail. But there was something about the way it walked, front paws crossing over each other as it took odd sidesteps, angling down the street. That, and the strange slope of its neck as it meandered, head down, peering up almost quizzically from heavy eyes. It stumbled a few times, but never stopped moving, without any clear direction or intent. When they tried to holler it out of the yard, it didn't even cock an ear. Finally, through the screen door, a woman spotted the frothy, telltale saliva on its muzzle. "My God," she said, almost in a whisper. "That's a mad dog."

Even in that hard, asphalt-edge Detroit neighborhood, the first thing they did was call my father. And in the same way he always did, he figured out how best to respond. Sometimes, he knew, a kind word was what was called for, or the offer of a seat on the stoop for a long talk on a hot summer night. This time, what was needed was the gun.

He went into his lockbox, drew out his .32 caliber special, and went out searching for the animal. A half hour later, he spotted it, twenty yards away in an open field, covering ground at a trot, listing to one side. Yes, he thought to himself, they were right: This was a rabid creature if ever there was one.

Moving insistently, in fits and starts, the dog wasn't easy to draw a bead on. But that did not deter my father. He knew this animal was in the final stage of its disease, still fighting the strange force that had come to inhabit its body. It would be able to maintain its equilibrium for a time. But then, as the virus flowered in the bloodstream and entered its brain, there would come the death throes. That was when it could turn lethal on a dime, breaking into a run and snapping its jaws at anything in its path. He did not dare move closer. He would have to keep his distance.

My father took aim, steadied his hand, shuttered down his eyelids to a squint, and squeezed one off. "Boom!" The animal crumpled, dead by the time it hit the ground—out of its misery, and now in a place where it could do no harm. Forever after in our neighborhood, Alvoy Depue was known for his reputation as a sharpshooter. But to hear him tell the story, which happened not long after I was born, that was just the luckiest shot he ever made.

My father was a police officer.

As a boy, I had very little understanding of what being a law enforcement officer meant, except that my father worked long hours, and after he came home, tired, he would sometimes have to talk on the phone until late at night settling what seemed to be other people's problems. On the rare occasions he showed up late for Mass on Sunday and the kids at school tried to make an issue of it, the nuns always set them straight. The cause for Alvoy Depue's tardiness must have been a police emergency, they said, because he was the kind of man who would never put business before God.

What I did know was that whenever I came home, walked up those back steps and through the door, the first thing I did was to look off toward the living room, to see if my father was in his chair. If he was sitting there, reading the paper, all was right with the world. I was safe, secure, and there was no way anyone could hurt me. I took that feeling as much for granted as I did the nightly ritual I most associated with his job. That was when, as soon as he set foot in the house, the first thing he did was to take his .32 revolver out of his holster and lock it up in a metal cabinet in the kitchen. He always liked that gun best, even when he later got a bigger, fancier gun—a pearl-handled .357 Magnum.

My brothers and I learned early on that guns were serious business, they weren't toys, and if we ever happened to find one lying around, we were not to touch it, but to run to tell the nearest grown-up. We always obeyed that rule, but in time it took on a special meaning. That was because of what happened to Tommy Cunningham.

When I was eight, the Cunninghams lived right around the corner from us. Tommy, who was a couple of years older than I was, was in my brother Ken's class, and Tommy's older brother Billy was the same age as my big brother, Gordon. We weren't best friends necessarily, but we all hung around together the way neighborhood kids do, and we all went to Sacred Heart elementary school together, where we were all taught by the nuns of the Immaculate Heart of Mary. Tommy was your basic all-American boy—blue, blue eyes, light brown hair, and freckles, a happy kind of kid. And Tommy's dad, like almost everybody in the neighborhood, was a big deer hunter. Along with thousands of other guys, every fall hunting season he would head to northern Michigan with his buddies in the hopes of bagging a deer, heading home with his trophy in one of the monumental Sunday night traffic jams comprised of an endless procession of gutted, glassy-eyed deer carcasses strapped to family station wagons.

Then one fall when Tommy's dad came home from one of his hunting trips, he put his stuff down in the living room, and went out in the backyard to clean his guns. He must have had to leave for a minute to do something else, and Billy must have forgotten what all of us were told, over and over. Because he evidently picked up his father's deer rifle and started fooling around with it, unlocking it, and pointing it at Tommy and saying, "Bang, you're dead." Only this time, for some reason, the gun was loaded, and when Billy pulled the trigger, it kicked back and fired, and killed his little brother instantly.

The whole neighborhood was different afterward, and so was Billy. He grew sad and quiet, and he started keeping to himself in a way he never did before. There were no psychiatrists and counselors for kids in those days, and people didn't talk much about their problems, let alone a tragedy of this size. Left to his own devices, Billy was trying to cope with things the only way he could. It took me a while to realize I would never see Tommy Cunningham again, and what happened to him was the biggest shock of my early years. It was my first real experience with death, and, in its own way, a great revelation. It made me realize there were things in this world even my father's strong, broad shoulders could not protect me from.

The week I was born, *Life* magazine ran a full-page advertisement for Lucky Strikes on its back cover, showing the movie star Dolores del Rio, standing like an empress wrapped in chiffon and diamonds, a wisp of smoke rising from a cigarette in the elegant fingers of her right hand. The headline read: "Her Throat Insured For $50,000," a sum that was, as del Rio explained in the accompanying text, actually "a studio precaution against my holding up a picture. So I take no chances on an irritated throat. No matter how much I use my voice in acting, I always find Luckies gentle."

That same week, in February of 1938, the magazine also had a photo of actor Gary Cooper on its cover, an article on the popular new sport of "surf-riding" in California, and a blurb about a country doctor who traveled by snowshoe to his patients through a fierce winter blizzard in Stillwater, Minnesota. Also, toward the back, was an article on how some of the smaller countries in Europe were beginning to flirt with the Fascist powers, along with a picture of the Yugoslavian premier strolling next to a plump man in a sweater vest, identified as "Germany's No. 2 man, jubilant Hermann Göring."

Those may have been more innocent times; then again, maybe they weren't innocent at all. Maybe we were just standing on the edge of a precipice that we couldn't see. As a kid, I, like the rest of the country, had no inkling of what twenty years of smoking cigarettes could do to the human lung, or how that happy guy in the sweater vest could conjure up something called Auschwitz, let alone help push the buttons to start the Second World War. What little I knew of global events was what I heard at the dinner table about how assembly line workers at the Ford auto plant in Dearborn were trying to organize themselves so they could make more money, and about how, a few years before I was born, four of them had gotten themselves shot for doing it.

Detroit in those days was flooded with the energy of hopeful émigrés from the South seeking assembly line work at the auto plants, and still three decades away from its sad notoriety as a decaying urban shell and home to some of the worst race riots in the country's history. For now, the strife of the world seemed far away from our house on Meier Road in the blue-collar suburb of Roseville, on the city's east side. Seven of us—me, my parents, and my four brothers—lived in a small, square 1930s bungalow covered in the kind of ugly red fiber siding that cracked and split with age, and didn't look so great even when it was new.

Standing at the far end of a narrow cinder driveway that left permanent tattoos if you fell and cut your knees on it, the house had two bedrooms and a front porch big enough to hold four rocking chairs and any number of neighbors. The yard, the biggest on our street because my father had the foresight to buy three lots, later helped to set it off from the rows of cookie-cutter houses that would eventually sprout up all around us to make homes for returning GIs. But in my boyhood, its two greatest assets were a pair of trees for climbing, and a field out back my brothers and I used for building forts and playing football.

There wasn't a lot of money when I was growing up. We didn't even have an indoor bathroom until the day my parents added one between their bedroom and the one where my brothers and I slept, crowded into two side-by-side bunk beds. Our laundry water came from a cistern, and the coal we used to heat our house was stored in a bin that took up a good part of the basement. The guy who drove the coal truck looked to us like a pretty scary character. He was always black from being covered with coal dust, and you'd better get out of his way when he dropped the coal chute from his truck right through the basement window and, in a haze of dust, let those black clumps roll straight down and into the bin. We watched my father stoke the furnace when the fire got low. And on Saturday mornings it was our job to dump the spent ashes into buckets and spread them out in the back lot where my mother kept a vegetable garden and grew cucumbers, tomatoes, and green string beans for canning.

Other kids may have tried to make the claim, but my father really *was* the toughest guy in the neighborhood. He'd started out his adult working life hauling heavy metal milk cans for Borden's Dairy, but when the opportunity presented itself to sign up as an auxiliary police officer, he ran with it, working his way up through the ranks from patrolman to city police inspector, which made pretty much the whole police department his deputy. It was quite an accomplishment for a strapping Frenchman who'd never finished high school.

As a boy, he'd grown up in hard surroundings. When he was two years old, his mother died in childbirth, and after his father remarried, his stepmother died, too. When my grandfather married for the third time, his new wife already had two young daughters of her own, and she wasn't very happy about suddenly being saddled with three rowdy boys. After a while, to settle the friction in the household, my father was sent out to work as a farm hand, in exchange for room and board.

The way he coped with the hardship was to exercise and become physically strong. At five-foot-nine and two hundred and twenty pounds, he was solid muscle, built like a tree trunk, and in my eyes, indestructible. He could pick up a square, fifty-pound weight with his little finger and hoist it over his head, and he'd do it if you coaxed him.

My father used the same approach in handling bad guys. He could be intimidating without ever drawing his gun. We lived just a few blocks from the local police station where he worked, but because we didn't have a garage, he parked in one up the road, offered by a fellow officer. That meant my father had to walk home late at night when he came off duty, and once I overhead him dressing down a bunch of toughs who had been giving him a hard time. "If you guys think you're such bad-asses, why don't you come back when I finish my shift at eleven p.m.," he said. "I park my car on the corner of Martin and Tighe, and there aren't any streetlights on that stretch of block, so it's pretty dark around here that time of night. I walk home alone, so if you guys think you're so tough, you wait for me, and I'll show you what tough is all about." They never did, but that kind of thing worried me. I used to be afraid for my father, wondering if they might decide to jump him, or even shoot him. Anything could happen.

It was important that his sons be as strong as he was. He even tried to teach my oldest brother, Gordon, how to box, but when he saw Gordon starting to turn into a bully, he stopped, and he never taught the rest of us. When he was a kid, Gordon could build anything, even pirate muskets from parts of an old rocking chair. But my brother Ken was the one I was closest to. When I was in early elementary school, a kid in the neighborhood started beating me up regularly, and I was afraid to fight him. Ken was the one who said, "Go on, Rog. You can take that guy. You can whip him. Why don't you?"

So I started doing push-ups, and one day when the kid started shoving me again, I finally started wrestling back. The two of us wound up in a ditch, and it just so happened that as we rolled in, he wound up on the bottom. That was the first fight I ever won, and it certainly wasn't because of my superior skills. But it did mark the end of me tolerating being pushed around, or having kids pick on me. It gave me a kind of confidence, and I realized that sometimes, you just had to fight. As regrettable as it might be, this was the way you had to deal with the world, especially in a rough neighborhood. I learned there were times in life when it was important to stick up for yourself, to defend your honor, and sometimes, if you did that just once, it was enough to head off more trouble in the long run.

The tough-guy routine wasn't the sum total of my father's role as a policeman, though. I remember how the telephone used to ring at the house, sometimes late, on some kind of police business, and how often we'd overhear him giving advice to someone about some problem, and how it seemed as if he was always on-call. It gave me the impression he was a very important person, not only for the way patrol cars would sometimes pick him up at the house on the weekends to go work on a case, but also for the number of ordinary people who came to the house to ask for some help with their marital problems, or their father's alcoholism, or their delinquent kids. He'd go out and sit with them in the car, or on one of the picnic tables he put in the vacant lot next to our house, and just talk to them.

Maybe because of all the hours he'd put in to feed his family, my father didn't get to spend as much time with us as he might have liked. When I got a little older, we went out a couple of times on Lake St. Clair in his friend's fishing boat, but when I was small, I missed doing things with him. My father wasn't the type to go out and throw the football around. He was stern, and sometimes even more than harsh. My brother Ken was the one who taught me how to ride on the handlebars of his bike and play sports and build forts. I don't think my father had much experience with those kinds of things, and if it sometimes seemed he didn't know about being in a family, it was because he'd never really had one. "But I intend to give him one," my mother would tell us. "And you're it."

My mother, Viola Westrick, had grown up on a one-hundred-sixty-acre farm in St. Clair, about thirty miles outside Detroit. She never worked outside our home, probably because, with five boys, there was enough inside it to keep her plenty busy. Ken says that when he was a teenager and had a few too many beers, he always knew he could wake my mother up by throwing a pebble at her window, because she was such a light sleeper, and she would be the one to come down and unlock the back door to sneak him in without my father hearing. If my father had been too hard on us about something, my mother was the one who would come in and sit on the side of the bed at night, reach over and brush the hair out of our eyes. She did what mothers are supposed to do. She was the one who explained the world to you.

It was a big event whenever my mother's oldest sister, Aunt Rose, drove up to see us from Ohio in her big green Buick. She was a very pretty lady and worked as a beautician, so her hair was always fixed up, and she wore powder and lipstick and wonderful perfume. Once, she arrived to take care of us because my mother was going into the hospital to have a baby. Two, actually—twin little girls who died right after they were born. My brothers and I never had the chance to see them, and nothing was ever really explained to us about what happened, or why. Asking questions was frowned upon, but we overheard things and tried to piece them together. What I remember most about that particular trip of Aunt Rose's was how quiet my mother was when she came home from the hospital empty-handed. In time, my parents had two more kids after me—Duane, and then Gary. But never another little sister.

In the world beyond our own were the people next door, who lived in a house my father always described with a single word: "Trouble." Someday, he said, when he got enough money, "I'm going to buy that house and burn it to the ground. Burn it, and tear it down." The adults talked about how there was too much alcohol in that house, which to me meant you'd hear fights and screaming and dishes breaking, and sometimes the police would come. At the time when I was seven or eight, the people who lived there had three little girls—a baby in diapers, a two-year-old, and a little girl about four years old, whose name was Sara Rose.

The mother was a gaunt, hollow-eyed redhead who always seemed to be wearing a faded floral housecoat with a torn pocket or a three-corner tear, and she and her kids looked like they never had enough to eat. Her husband was a skinny guy with sharp features and a mustache, and whenever the loud, angry sounds started up, my father would shake his head and say, "Aw, they're drinking again." In the middle of all that was Sara Rose.

She had brown hair, kind of curly but usually too messed up to tell. Her nose was runny, and she never looked very clean. And she had a sad kind of look about her, especially when she'd come over to our back steps on summer nights, standing in the porch light and watching us through the screen door while we ate dinner at the kitchen table. Sometimes my mother would get up and give her food to take home. But other times she'd say, "Now Sara Rose, you mustn't stand out there and watch people eat their dinner. That's not polite. It's time for you to go on back to your own house now." And she would. She'd go away for a little while, and then she'd come back.

At the time, we had a dog we loved a lot, a collie-husky mix named Rex. Once, Sara Rose came over, and as she was going down the five steps off the back porch, she must have stepped on Rex's tail by accident, because he swung around and hit her with his jaw. I don't think he meant to bite her, I think he was just startled, but when they collided, he split her lip. That was all the opportunity her father needed. He was a housepainter who was always out of work, and he sued my father, and made us put Rex to sleep. It was an awfully sad thing, because we were crazy about that dog.

Afterward, my father put up a fence between our houses, and there was a lot of animosity on both sides. Even then Sara Rose would come over to the edge of our property and hang on to the fence posts, trying to see through the slats. I felt sorry for her, and it made me feel bad to see the little scar on her lip. Then, one day her mother died after swallowing a can of Drano, the father and his three little girls moved away, and I never saw them again.

I used to wonder whatever happened to those people next door, especially Sara Rose. I guess in a way I was like her big brother, because I wanted to take care of her. I somehow got the idea it was my job to protect her, and for the rest of my life, I always remembered her. Not because we ever kept in touch, or ran into each other later and became friends. It was because, as I would come to learn, the world was full of people like Sara Rose.

By sixth grade I was performing in school plays, and the high point of that year was when I won the part of Jesus in the Easter Passion Play. My big scene was the Agony in the Garden, where

Christ was anticipating his death and all his friends fell asleep, leaving him deserted and alone. My line was, "Father, if it be possible, let this chalice pass from me. But if that cannot be, Your will be done, not mine." Then, in the Crucifixion scene, I hung from the Cross with my arms outstretched, from nails made to look as if they'd pierced my hands. Even as a little kid, that had quite an effect on me. I may not have understood the full theological significance of what I was doing, but I started thinking Jesus was quite a hero. The way I saw it, he was certainly powerful enough to have stopped all the suffering he was going through if he wanted to, but he didn't. Instead, he endured it. Bravery in action, I thought. Sacrifice for the greater good.

Not long after, I decided I'd heard all my father's stories about growing up on the farm, and my life to date was pretty dull by comparison. What I needed was some adventure. The opportunity for it came in the form of a brand-new school forty miles away, on Washtenaw Avenue between Ypsilanti and Ann Arbor— the Holy Ghost Fathers Mission Seminary. Its vocation director came to our school one day, and afterward, I stuck around to ask him some questions. How many kids would be there, and what would we do during the day? What kind of classes did you have to take, and how much did it cost to go there? The more I turned it over in my mind, the more I was convinced this was exactly what I needed—living away from home and trying something totally different. I made the announcement to my parents at the dinner table one night. "I want to go to school at the seminary," I said.

"Fine," said my father. "If you can save half the tuition, you can." That meant half of three hundred dollars, which was a staggering amount of money to us at the time. But between odd jobs and my paper route, I eventually saved up the requisite one hundred fifty-five dollars and thirty-seven cents.

The Holy Ghost Fathers Mission Seminary was basically a religious boarding school where I took college prep courses in Latin, French, chemistry, and the classics. For the first time in my life I learned about real literature. I even started writing poems. One, for English class, was a fifteen-stanza epic about St. Christopher that turned out to be so much more involved than what had originally been assigned, my teacher seriously thought I must have plagiarized it from a book in the library. Which was pretty flattering, since I knew I hadn't.

In short, the world began to open up for me, the world of the mind. Until that time, I'd been preoccupied with the same things the rest of the kids my age were: sports, other kids, and, to a lesser degree, school. But after two and a half years of religious high school, I realized there was something else I was beginning to be preoccupied with. Girls. More specifically, Sharon Endres, a little dark-haired number who was four years younger than I was, and lived up the street from us in Roseville. The Endreses had five kids, just like we did, and I used to deliver the *Detroit News* to her house on my paper route. Her father, Walt, who worked for Holly Carburetor, was a nice guy, and a great tipper. Even though the *News* was forty-five cents a week, Walt would give me fifty and say, "Keep the change, kid."

I'd known Sharon almost since I could remember, and for a long time she was just another person on my paper route. But now, whenever I went home for vacations, I began to see her, as they say, with different eyes. I thought long and hard about how to express my intentions, dazzling her with my newfound worldliness and savoir faire. Finally, I decided to send her a note: "Je pense vous êtes très jolie," I wrote. *Très debonair.*

By the end of the year, I'd come to the conclusion that the Holy Ghost Fathers weren't for me, and I wanted out. My mother wasn't too happy about it, but there was no changing my mind, so I switched for senior year to St. Gertrude's High School in St. Clair Shores, and began my turnaround. I started to drink beer, raise hell, and catch it from my father for things like getting into a fistfight on the first day of school. I don't really know why all of this happened. I was angry, I suppose, although even in retrospect, I'm not sure at what.

In any case, things got worse as the year went on. My grades fell. I became cockier, and more of a wise-ass. But on the plus side, I was extremely popular. Just one month after I landed at St. Gertrude's, in fact, I was elected senior class president, but when one of the nuns sidled up to me and said, "Someone who's been here four years deserves that. Not you," I realized she was right, and declined the honor.

This was the 1950s, and Roseville was a rough neighborhood. Kids in those days didn't yet have Glocks and Uzis, but they fought with chains, knives, shivs, baseball bats, and, if nothing else was available, their fists. Onscreen, there was Marlon Brando in *The Wild One* and James Dean in *Rebel Without a Cause*. In Roseville, the Cobras, the Sharks, and the Spades were our street gangs, which were all about being cool, and not taking any crap off anybody. Six of my friends and I wore exactly the same style of mint green jacket, with black elastic cuffs and waistband, from the Roseville Department Store. Nothing written on the back, like the Detroit motorcycle gang jackets, but still enough to get the message across: "There are six of us. We hang together. And it would be in your best interest not to mess with us."

Thanks to my time with the Holy Ghost Fathers, I'd gotten

way ahead in my studies. Now, I was bringing home Bs and Cs without ever even cracking a book. I was coasting. Also, by that time I'd gone from being a soft little kid, to six feet and 170 pounds. I was fooling around with boxing and working out with weights. I wanted more than anything to join the football team, and the coach wanted to have me, but my father nixed the idea. "Get a job," he said. "You're old enough to be helping out around here." So, following in the footsteps of my brothers Gordon and Ken, I became the third Depue kid to stand behind the counters of the Roseville Department Store. I wasn't a good salesperson, though, the way they were. I wasn't interested in trying to sell open-toed pumps to a bunch of old ladies in hats.

What I was interested in was pushing it, just for the hell of it. Once in school, a kid cut in front of me when we were standing in line to pay our book bills. A few minutes later when we passed each other in the hall, I leaned over and shoved him into the wall. "I don't know who the hell you think you are," I said, "but don't you ever cut in front of me again."

"Why don't you take it to the gym?" his friend said, and so we did. I landed five or six good punches and cleaned this kid's clock, and all of a sudden I had an instant reputation. I was the new go-to guy at St. Gertrude's. Apparently none of those kids ever had anyone to stick up for them before, so whenever punks from the public high school showed up to start a fight or cause trouble, the refrain was automatic: "Get Depue."

Sometimes, when I crossed paths with guys who, by reputation, were a lot tougher than I was, my father came in handy. Since he often had dealings with the worst kids because of his job, he could feed me critical intelligence. "Yeah, I had that guy in the station the other day," he'd tell me, "and I had him cryin' like a baby." One who never did was Bobby Hill, a well-built guy with the standard brush cut, low-slung Levi's, pack of Luckies rolled up in his T-shirt sleeve, and leather jacket with the Shark insignia on the back. The story was that he'd just gotten out of Jackson prison. One day I was at the local dairy bar when he came in and slid right next to me in a booth. "Well, well, if it isn't Depue," he said. "You know what? Your old man locked me up last night."

I was pinned against the inside wall and couldn't get out, so I braced myself. "Oh boy, here it comes," I thought.

"Yeah," Bobby said. "It was around eight o'clock when he got me in the cell, and I hadn't had anything to eat all day. He asked me if I was hungry, and I was. So he went over to the White Spot and brought back a bag of hamburgers for me. You know what I think, Depue? I think your old man is pretty cool."

I realized my father was respected in the community, and was seen as a fair man because he believed in tempering justice with mercy. Later in life, when he talked about his days as a policeman, he'd say, "I saw some pretty horrible things, Roger. Terrible. Especially the domestic calls. The worst part was while all the fighting was going on, there'd always be little kids huddled in the corner, scared to death. So I'd shame the parents, make 'em cry, and then kiss and make up before I left. And I told them I sure wasn't going to be happy about it if I got a dispatch to come back."

He didn't show much mercy three days before graduation, though, when I got into another big fight, this time with an older guy at school. Afterward, the principal called me into her office and really lit into me. "You know, there were two of us in this fight," I said, trying to defend myself. "Where's the other guy?"

"They had to take him to the hospital because his eye looked pretty bad," she said. Then she expelled me.

My father went to the school. So did my mother. And it was only after some major lobbying that I was even allowed to graduate. My hand was so busted up I could barely hold a rag, but that Saturday I washed every window in the school, which was the only thing that allowed me to get my diploma with everybody else two days later.

At the time I got out of St. Gertrude's, eighteen was the accepted age at which a young man of my social status got a job, left home, and began living as a man. I went through the motions, and that summer started looking for a job the way an eighteen-year-old does: Get up in the morning, look under the bed and in the closets. Yup, no jobs today, I guess. And then go outside and start looking for something fun to do. But by the end of the summer, I was feeling the pressure to get on with life and get out into the world. For someone like me, the solution was simple. My oldest brother, Gordon, had already gone into the Army, and so had Ken. But as far as I was concerned, the Marine Corps was the toughest, finest fighting outfit in the world. When I came home from the recruiter's office and said, "Dad, I joined the Marines today," he said, "Probably do you some good."

That year, 1956, I was sent to boot camp in San Diego—an eighteen-year-old kid who'd never been that far away from home, now living in a bare metal corrugated Quonset hut and surrounded by strangers. I'd come into the Corps as a Detroit punk with a DA haircut and a big attitude. The duck's ass was shaved off to bristle, and the ruthless drill instructors whittled down my attitude. But the Corps did teach me how to take care of myself.

One night, a guy named Mike Glaab, from River Rouge, not far from my home, just happened to be assigned to my bottom bunk. He was seventeen years old, six-foot-three and one hundred eighty-five pounds, a tough kid just like me. After lights out, I leaned over and said, "Mike, you awake?"

"Yeah."

"Well, good. Because from the looks of things around here, there are some guys who are gonna want to kick our ass. A man's gotta have a backup, you know? We're both from Detroit and all, so, if you're willing to back me up, I'll do the same for you."

"You got it," he said. "We're partners."

I don't know if I did something to offend them, or if they didn't like my attitude, or if they were just being bad-asses, but it wasn't long before some Hawaiians in the unit started to mess with me. Little things. They'd short-sheet my bed—take the top sheet and fold it so you couldn't get into the bunk when the drill instructor screamed "Get into the rack!" and gave you about five seconds to do it. If you were short-sheeted, you couldn't get your legs under the blankets, and you had to just lie there all bunched up until after the DI left at lights out, so you could hop out of bed and remake it.

After falling out in the mornings and doing calisthenics, we were assigned to work parties, one of whose tasks was to clean out the Quonset hut. It was the only time we all weren't together, and it gave the five Hawaiians on the cleaning party the time to do whatever they wanted in the huts. Sure enough, one night I got into my bunk, and it was short-sheeted. I could hear muffled laughter from somewhere down the line. The first time it happened, I figured, "I can take a joke. It's not like I didn't have four brothers." Then it happened a second time.

That night, I slipped out of my bunk and nudged Mike. "I need your backup," I said. "Right."

Then I crept over to the bed of the Hawaiian who seemed to be the leader, a big guy with a pretty scary reputation. He was sleeping, and I sneaked up and grabbed him by the throat.

"This is Depue," I whispered. "And you know what? I got short-sheeted again tonight. Now, I can take a joke and all. But I better not be short-sheeted tomorrow night. You got me? And if it is, I'd suggest you don't go to sleep. Because if you do, I'm going to kill you in your sack." Then I loosened my grip. He didn't jump out of the sack, didn't holler, didn't even move. And the next night when the DI hollered, "Get in the rack!" I didn't even bother checking. No short-sheets, and no more problems. That was the way we handled things in Detroit.

Later, I would go on to Camp Pendleton, then the high Sierras for cold weather advanced infantry training, and then to an amphibious assault vehicle—Amtrack—battalion on the White Beach Marine Base in Okinawa. There, I was assigned to the armory, where I learned to maintain everything from .50 caliber machine guns and 3.5-inch rocket launchers, to semiautomatic rifles and .45 pistols. But all the training didn't wipe the wildness out of me, and I loved to go into town and drink and raise hell in the bars. It reminded me of movies I'd seen about Tombstone, and about what it must have been like in the Old West. Okinawa was wide open. The only people we answered to were the American military police, and they couldn't be everywhere at once.

Still, one of the most formative experiences of my hitch in the Marines came when I wasn't even on duty. It was during a month's leave, for the Christmas holidays, back home in Roseville. Sharon and I—we'd been seeing each other pretty steadily—must have been on the outs or something, because I had a date with a little Italian girl for New Year's Eve. We went to a really nice party, and then, sometime after 2:00 a.m., she wanted to go, so I borrowed a car from a friend and drove her home. I had every intention of returning, since I was never one to leave a party in progress. But for some reason, I didn't bother to look at the fuel gauge, and on the way back, I ran out of gas. I was in the neighborhood of Mound Road on the east side when the car stalled at a traffic light, and wouldn't start back up. So here it was, nearly three o'clock in the morning on New Year's Eve, with no one around and nothing moving. I got out and pushed the car to the side of the road, and in the distance, saw a lighted Shell gas station sign.

I started walking toward it, and noticed a couple of guys about my age, wearing Levi's and leather jackets, standing next to an old Chevy parked on an angle, away from the pumps, over by the garage door. I started to relax, figuring the station was open. I'd get a can of gas, restart the car, and get back to the party before anyone noticed I was gone. I was on leave from the Marine Corps, I'd had a few drinks, it was the holidays, and life was sweet. So I walked up to the guys by their car and said, "Hey, is the station open?"

"We don't know," one said. "That's what we were wondering."

Still all happy, I said, "Oh yeah? You have car trouble, too?"

"Yeah," said the other. "Something with the rear tire."

I never saw it coming. Just as I turned around to look at the car's back wheel, they sucker-punched me, and the lights went out. Just like that. I don't know if they used their fists, or a club, or a tire iron, but I went down. And when I started hazing back into it, they were standing over me, kicking me in the face and groin and stomach, and it was all I could do just to try to cover up. For what seemed like a long time, as the blows kept coming, vicious and strong, I really believed I might die there on the concrete, swallowing blood in the driveway of a gas station garage. I couldn't understand where I was, or what had happened. All I could do was try to get my bearings, shield myself from the kicks, and try to get some air into my lungs so I could keep breathing. Over and over again, the only words I could get out were, "Why are you doing this to me? Why are you doing this?"

And then, I did something I'd never done before. I started begging them to stop. I pleaded for my life. At one point, with blood streaming into my eyes, I found the strength to try to pick myself up, but just as I got up onto all fours, they kicked me down again. And all the time they were working me over, they were laughing. Finally, I don't know how long later, when they decided they were finished, the first guy looked down at me on the ground and said, "Happy New Year, punk." Then he and his buddy started laughing again, got into their car and drove away.

After I was sure they were gone, I crawled over to a phone booth and called the police. Not because I wanted to report the crime, necessarily. Mainly because I needed help. After a while, two officers in a squad car arrived, and when they saw me and heard what had happened, the first thing they said was, "What's the matter with you? You new around here or something? Didn't you have enough sense to be alert about your surroundings?" The men who wore the badges were getting their licks in, too.

"I just need a gallon of gas," I said. "That's all I need." They drove me to an open station, and after I bought a can of gas, they took me back to my car. I started it up, dropped it off back at the party and, without going inside, went home. By the time my father saw me, the blood on me was drying, but his first words were, "What the hell happened to you?" and when I told him, he said, "You know, you grew up around here. What's wrong with you? How could you have let this happen?"

There was no easy way to explain it. Those cops and my father were right, I thought. Why couldn't I have been a little sharper, a little more alert? Why didn't I see it coming? I was nineteen years old, just out of boot camp, and in the best physical condition of my life. I could have licked those two guys any day of the week. I felt stupid, and guilty, and ashamed I had let myself be vulnerable. I allowed two street punks to take me to a place where I had begged them for my life.

It would be years before I began to study, in a formalized way, what happens when one human being does serious violence to another, but this was the first time I experienced it personally. I was carrying sixty bucks in my wallet, but these guys didn't rob me. They just wanted to hurt somebody. They wanted the thrill of doing that, just because they could. When they were through with me, my lips were split, my nose was bleeding, I had one eye swollen shut, and, judging from the searing pain every time I tried to take a breath, maybe cracked ribs as well. But the physical pain wasn't the worst of it. My dignity had been taken from me, for sport and amusement. It was cruelty for cruelty's sake. What these guys did to me, they did for fun.

For days afterward, every time I thought about what had happened, my eyes would well up, and I didn't speak to anyone. And then, during the last week of my leave, a kind of fury set in. It occurred to me that the guys who did this must live somewhere fairly close by, so I did the only thing available to me. I started hunting them down. I got a couple of my friends together and we started combing the part of town near where the beating took place. We went into drugstores and restaurants and gas stations.

I was looking to spot them, trying to see if I might recognize their faces on the street.

Thinking back on it, God is good for not letting me find them. If I had, I would've hurt them, badly enough to have to live with the consequences. I would've been robbed of many of the opportunities I've had in life. Instead, I finished out my two years as a Marine.

Coming back to the States from Okinawa, I was one of a few thousand Marines transferred on a huge 3,460-ton troop transport ship. I'd never been much for roller coasters and amusement park rides, but this was the real thing. We went through some breathtaking storms at thirty-six knots, and I loved it, trying to keep my footing on deck as the ship's bow rose up from the sea and then came crashing down. Waves broke over us and rolled down the deck, but I just hung on, riding with the wind in my face like a dog with its head out the window of a pickup truck.

In that huge troop transport ship, we were like a little vulnerable cork bobbing in those huge swells, so high that when we were in the wave's trough, you'd look past the gunwale and see nothing but a wall of water beside you. A lot of guys were throwing up over the side, but I was loving it, and smoking my little Between the Acts—a brand of small cigars designed to last about as long as a theater intermission. Sure, I was scared, but the exhilaration and feeling of adventure were more than the fear. To me, there was something magnificent about that roiling sea.

I saw the Marine Corps as a rite of passage, a validation of my status as an adult. Of course it didn't feel that way when I got home and, at age twenty-one, like a lot of guys in the same boat, realized I didn't have any idea where I was headed in life.

In high school, I had worked at the Roseville Department Store, but I never felt as comfortable around all those clean, well-dressed people as I did doing physical labor. So after I got home, I got a job doing heavy labor at a local factory. I'd learned a few things in the military, not least of which was the idea of the difference between the officer and the enlisted man. What they had that I didn't, was four years of college. No one in my family had ever gotten a degree, but I saw it as my ticket in life. When I asked the foreman if I could switch to the night shift so I could go to class during the day, he told me to get lost. The next day, I found a night job at a gas station and enrolled at South Macomb Community College.

At about the time I got out of the service, my mother's parents died, and she and my father bought part of the family farm. My father decided to fence in the property, so I went out and helped him. I'd been doing some boxing in the Marines, and I was in great shape. In fact, when I used the fence post hole digger, I kept jamming it into the ground too hard. "Rog," my dad said, "if you keep digging those holes so deep, we're going to have the shortest fence in the whole damn county." But he had a smile on his face when he said it.

Right around that time my father finally started seeing me as a rugged guy, someone he could pal around with, maybe even an equal. We worked together all day, and would get a six-pack and tear off big chunks of garlic ring bologna with saltines for lunch. Once, we went into a local bar for a beer, all sweaty and dirty, and a table of young farm guys started making remarks about us being riffraff from the city. I could be pretty hotheaded, and I spun around and took a couple of steps toward them. My dad was right next to me, but instead of getting threatening, he made a big dramatic gesture, looking the guys up and down. Then, in a booming voice, he said, "Come on, Rog. Let's wait until we run into some guys with a little *muscle* on 'em."

As I see it, my father never really knew what to do with my brothers and me when we were young, probably because he'd never really had the chance to be a kid himself. But size and physical strength were something he and I now had in common, and it made for a bond between us. They say the greatest compliment you can pay someone is to imitate them, and when my father began to see I wasn't so different from him after all, a lot of the distance between us somehow lessened.

That was at the time, in my early twenties, when I decided I might also like to follow in his footsteps in another way. At school, I was taking a class in psychology, and one of our assignments was to take a personal inventory assessment. I wrote down my strengths and weaknesses, made note of the things I'd been successful at, and when I looked at the results of the test, staring back at me was a policeman.

All my life I'd fought to better myself. I would never deny who I was, or where I came from, but I knew I wanted to be something more. I had been raised in innocence, hardened in the change from boy to man. And now, like my father before me, I would become an officer of the law.

CHAPTER THREE

THE BADGE

AT THE END OF THE 1950s, the town of Clare, Michigan, three hours north of Roseville, was known as "The Gateway to the North," or at least that's what the local Chamber of Commerce said in tourist brochures. In reality, tourists and deer hunters didn't have any choice but to pass through it on their way to the Upper Peninsula and points north, since the only highway ran straight through town.

The real story was that, except for Detroit, Clare was probably the closest thing Michigan had to the Wild, Wild West. There was drinking and domestic abuse and illegal gambling, along with a generally down-at-the-heels atmosphere that seeped out into the community, and even filtered into the police department. As the result of a lot of years of inattention, a lot of outstanding bench warrants had gone unserved, and summonses that were delivered were routinely ignored. The town also had a reputation for nasty bar fights, and even the local teenagers had no qualms about harassing uniformed officers—carloads of greasy-haired punks in their jalopies, looking to menace anyone in a uniform.

I knew all that because when Sharon moved to Clare after her father was transferred there, I started making the three-hundred-mile round-trip from Roseville nearly every weekend, just to see her. I'd done some looking around by that point, and Sharon was the one for me. I waited for her to graduate before we got married, which we did on August 20, 1960. Then, not long after, when Sharon got pregnant and wanted to be closer to her family, we moved from Roseville up to Clare, too.

The move derailed my immediate career plans. I'd already taken the police exam in Roseville, and placed eighth out of all prospective candidates. Now I was on a waiting list, fully expecting I'd be hired within six months. I was also in college, a real stand-out against all those sheltered, fat-faced kids in black horn-rimmed glasses. But I loved learning, and was hell-bent on getting my degree, so when we got to Clare, the first thing I did was to transfer to Central Michigan University. As for policing, I'd just have to put it on the back burner for a while.

To support us, I found construction work, pouring concrete for the city of Clare. By that time, Sharon and I were living in a little rental house on Maple Street. We were a little worried about our finances, especially with the second baby coming, so Sharon called the former tenants to see how much their utilities ran every month. It turned out the woman's husband was the town's new police chief. "Really?" said Sharon. "My husband almost went into police work. In fact, he placed eighth out of fifty applicants back in Roseville, but then we moved up here."

Sharon never mentioned the conversation, so I didn't know

what to make of it a few weeks later when Chief Milan G. "Chip" Shepherd pulled into the gas station where I was working, and started making small talk and asking a lot of questions. Did he think I was stealing from the boss or something? I told him I was studying psychology, had just gotten out of the Marines, and was really interested in police work. That's when he tipped his hand and, with a big grin, invited me down to the station to talk about a job.

It would be hard to overstate the challenges Chip faced in taking over Clare's police department—corruption, apathy, and a general disregard for what would come to be known as "quality of life" crimes. But he had charisma, drive, and a special way of dealing with kids, even the tough delinquents. What really hooked me was that Chip had a vision. More than anything, he wanted to make the police department a force that commanded respect. What cinched it was when he promised he'd work the schedule so I could keep going to college. He offered me the job, and I jumped at it.

There were only a dozen or so of us in the department, along with some auxiliary officers who worked other jobs and came in part-time. We didn't have the luxury of sending our officers to a comprehensive recruit training program, and I never did go to a police academy. Instead, our formal training came from members of the Michigan State Police who came in at Chip's request to teach us everything from lifting fingerprints and setting up roadblocks to how to conduct an interview.

Unfortunately, not everybody was on board with the new regime. One late night my partner, a veteran officer, and I responded to a call about a nasty bar fight in one of our local establishments. I wheeled up to the place in the squad car and immediately saw two bloodied, tough-looking guys slugging it out right in front of the bar, cheered on by about ten other guys. Those odds weren't particularly promising, but I bailed out of the car, charged right in, and broke things up. Then I realized something really weird: my partner wasn't there. After I managed to calm everybody down, I headed back to the patrol car, and saw him sitting in it. "Charlie, where the hell were you?" I shouted. I was pretty hot.

"You know, just as we were about to get out, we got a radio call," he said. "And after I finished with it, I saw you had the thing under control."

"Then explain to me why this door is locked," I said, yanking on the passenger side's handle. He tried to tell me he'd reached over to lock my door just before getting out himself, but the whole incident started to smell bad. When we got back to the station, I checked with the dispatcher, and as I suspected, there hadn't been any radio calls. The next morning when Chip came in, I told him about it. I learned firsthand an important lesson that would remain true throughout my entire law enforcement career: If you can't count on your partner, you are hanging in the wind. "I can't work with this guy anymore," I said. "He didn't back me up, and that's no good." The guy was a coward, and when Chip called him onto the carpet, he resigned.

Chip had leadership qualities, and before long, the ragtag Clare police force turned into a really sharp little department. I learned a lot on the job, drawing on what I knew about policing from the way my father did it. One night when a loud gang of punks was following the patrol car, for instance, I found one of the darkest streets in town, turned down it, and slowed to a crawl. The car was right behind me, mirroring every move. Then I suddenly pulled sideways, blocked the street, parked the car, and got out. I walked back to the five toughs and said, "I get the feeling you're following me." They laughed, and then I said, "You know, I've got a pretty good sense of humor, but for some reason I'm not finding this funny. So, I tell you what I'm going to do. I'm going to drive up to the next corner and turn left, and then I'm going to look in my rearview mirror. Of course, you may decide just to drive straight at that corner, and I guess that means I won't see you again.

"But if you do make the decision to hang a left at the corner, I'm going to haul all of your asses to jail, all of you, and charge you with impeding police work. You all got that?" I made my slow left turn at the corner, looked into the rearview, and watched that beat-up Chevy chug straight through the intersection and keep right on going. It was amazing to me how just a few incidents were enough to start a new momentum. Slowly but surely, things began to turn around. It was our wake-up call to the troublemakers, a signal that the days of do-as-you-please, laissez-faire policing were now over in Clare.

At the time I was earning my way toward a degree, majoring in psychology with a minor in sociology, but what I read about in the textbooks paled in comparison to what I was learning on the street. The first dead body I ever saw outside of a funeral parlor was a pale man in flannel work shirt and worn jeans, lying at the base of a grain elevator. His eyes were closed and he had a look more of puzzlement than anything else on his face, the measure of his last moments on earth. The coroner officially listed the death as an accident, the result of a fall. But even then I had my doubts.

True, the man hadn't been robbed; the worn leather wallet with pictures of his bland-looking wife and round-faced kids, along with the twenty-seven dollars and change we found in his pocket, was proof enough of that. But there was something about the ugly wound on the back of his head—the way the jagged skull edges were depressed, the irregular shape of the blood pool beneath it, the unbroken limbs lying a little too unnaturally—that made me question the verdict. I wasn't in a position to argue with the coroner. His word was gospel. But my instinct was that somebody got away with that one.

Still, that case didn't make anywhere near the impression on me that another, less sinister death did. Late one night, after the bars closed, a guy'd been walking along the shoulder of U.S. 10 at the city limits when three kids in a fast car decided to floor it. Judging by what we found, we figured they must have been going seventy miles an hour when they hit him.

Half of the poor guy's face and head came through the windshield and landed in the lap of the young girl sitting between the two boys in the front seat. The rest of his body parts were scattered over a hundred feet of roadside.

That night, in the darkness and using flashlights, we had to go out and pick up those pieces and collect them in a body bag. It was astonishing to see what was left of something that was once a person, someone with arms and legs and shoes and a life. There was no ID on him, and that night we took the remains to the coroner, whose office was located at Stephenson's Funeral Home. The next morning we unzipped the body bag and began taking out what was inside.

The coroner tried to take pieces of the face and put them together like a jigsaw puzzle. It fell to me to fish out what was left of the hands, ink the fingerpads, and try to get a serviceable print from them by rolling the fingertips onto a fingerprint sheet. The problem was there were only two fingers left on each hand. The others had been blown apart by the impact with the speeding car. What remained of the fingers was attached to cords and tendons, about twelve inches long and stripped of flesh. Other parts of him, honestly, looked like something you'd see in the window of a butcher shop. A Sunday roast. A rack of lamb. It was horrible, but those disembodied pieces of flesh were all that was left.

It was our job to identify the deceased, and the next day we did, by checking what we had against a missing person report in Loomis, a town about five miles outside Clare. As it turned out, he was a nice guy, with people who loved him. He had a drinking problem, but he wasn't a troublemaker and hadn't ever really hurt anyone. No matter what he'd done, he didn't deserve to die that way, alone at night, by the side of the road, without seeing it coming. That particular death was the most gruesome thing I'd ever seen, and I still have the images in my head of what can happen to someone who, a few hours before, was a living, breathing human being.

Other kinds of images stayed with me, for different reasons. One night during my early years on the force, I received a radio call that a car had struck a pedestrian in town, and he was down. I went to the scene of the accident, two blocks from the Greyhound bus depot, and found an elderly man in the street, surrounded by a knot of people who were trying to help him, covering him up with their coats.

The victim was conscious and, in the way people in terrible accidents often do, was trying to struggle to his feet, like a wounded deer. That was impossible, since he had what looked to me like a dislocated hip and possible leg fracture as well. I got blankets out of the patrol car trunk and covered him while we waited for the ambulance, and all the while I tried to calm him. "You're going to be all right," I told him. "The ambulance is on the way, and the hospital is close by, a really good one. This is all going to work out just fine."

The old man told me he'd just arrived in town, after taking the bus all the way from Florida to Clare to surprise his son, whom he hadn't seen in years. A few minutes later the ambulance arrived, and I helped load him onto the gurney. I don't know exactly what he said to me as the door closed, but I do remember that he thanked me. After they pulled away, I completed my accident investigation, by the book. I talked to witnesses and the shaken driver, who hadn't seen the man crossing the street midblock in the darkness.

Then I went back to the station house, turned in my paperwork, and decided to head over to the hospital to see how the man was doing. I remember walking into the emergency entrance and on into the trauma room. I was in uniform, of course, so no one stopped me or even seemed interested in the fact I was there. Everyone looked pretty busy, but I spotted one tired-looking doctor who seemed to be in charge. "I was just wondering how that pedestrian is doing, the guy who was brought in a few hours ago," I said.

"He's dead," the doctor said. "We pronounced him about an hour ago. Internal bleeding we couldn't stop."

I heard the words, but somehow they didn't quite register. I'd been talking to the guy just a few hours before, and he was talking back. I knew he'd been hurt, but when I talked to him and told him how he was going to be all right, I wasn't snowing him. That's absolutely what I thought. And then, when I started retracing my steps and putting the pieces together, I realized how much time I'd spent doing all the right bureaucratic things, crossing the T's and dotting the I's, filing my reports and following procedure. But there was one thing I hadn't done—the only thing that really needed doing.

I hadn't called the man's son to let him know his father had come to town just to see him, that he was hurt, was in the hospital, and that he was alone. The son lived only a few miles away, and could have made it to the hospital in time to see his father one last time before he died. But I hadn't called him. It didn't even cross my mind. Instead, I'd been preoccupied with the formalities and regulations.

When they heard what had happened, everyone at the station house said, "Hey, Rog, you know, you had no idea he was going to die," and, "Come on now, Rog. It wasn't your fault." But that didn't help. My priorities had been wrong, and I knew it. It was easy to get so caught up in the routine of the job that you forgot you were entering people's lives when it was important—when they were hurt, or afraid, or had witnessed violence and tragedy. In very simple ways, you could help minimize the trauma and lasting damage, if only you were aware of it. For quite a while, I felt bad about what happened. I didn't tear myself up about it. I just decided the best way to make amends was never to allow it to happen again.

By this time, I was getting more than a fair amount of experience in law enforcement, I seemed to be pretty good at it, and I really liked the work. But the best thing, to me, was seeing how the things I witnessed on the street dovetailed with what I was learning at school about human behavior. If I was interviewing a perpetrator about his crime, even after I'd pinned down all the facts, I always tried to stick around a while longer, to find out what made him tick. It used to drive some of my partners crazy, because it took up extra time. But I didn't care. I loved the study of psychology, of why people do the things they do—and of the strange, aberrant facets of the human mind. I was seeing plenty of on-the-job evidence of that.

Their family name was Punches. She was a pretty young schoolteacher in Clare, and he was a local pharmacist. They were a nice, young couple, they lived in a nice neighborhood, and there wasn't anything particularly unusual about their lives. At least until the afternoon she first noticed how, after she'd hung the laundry out on the clothesline in the backyard, some of her underthings went missing. She initially didn't think anything of it, and didn't even bother mentioning it to her husband. Maybe some kids took them, maybe the wind had blown them away.

Then, one morning after she'd put her swimsuit out on the line, it disappeared, and she started to get a little frightened. She called the police, and I responded to the call. We went over to the house, talked to her about what had happened. We canvassed the neighborhood, even hid in the garage one night after she put some nighties out to dry as a trap. But we didn't spot any sign of a suspect.

Not long after, the schoolteacher noticed one morning that someone had tried to break into her house sometime the night before. When she woke up, she saw the back screen door ajar, when she knew she'd fastened its hook-and-eye before going to bed. She called us, and when we started taking a look around, we realized someone had pulled on the door hard enough to yank the eye right out of the wood. But that was the only hard clue we found.

A few weeks later, on a Saturday night, the couple went out to a wedding and were gone for at least a few hours. When they came home, they saw the house had been broken into; someone had come through a bedroom window and stolen every item of clothing the schoolteacher owned. All of it—shoes, underwear, dresses. But nothing else was missing, not jewelry or silver, or even one of those little 1960s portable tummy TVs sitting in plain view, right on the double bed.

When I came on duty that night, I took a ride over to the house. True, proper police procedure had been followed by everyone at the scene. They'd looked around, dusted for prints, taken photographs, and asked a lot of questions. But this crime certainly wasn't the norm in this town. It was unusual, extremely frightening to the victim, and just plain creepy. Who would do such a thing? The perpetrator was obviously keeping a close eye on the house; otherwise, why would he have finally decided to enter the house, unless he knew the couple was going to be away for more than a few minutes? Did he know about the wedding? Was he watching as the schoolteacher and her husband left the house, all dressed up and carrying a wedding present to their car?

I decided to take another look around. It was wintertime, and when I got to the house, I started by walking around the yard. It had snowed the day before and there, under the window where the perp gained entry, were some footprints. At first, it wasn't easy to distinguish them, because various officers had been all over the scene. But these prints were different. They appeared to have been made by a leather-soled man's shoe, but ones with a pronounced heel, like a Beatle boot, and a long, pointed toe.

Early in my training, I'd been taught how to make plaster of paris casts for evidentiary purposes—lifting anything from tire tracks and wheel impressions to shoe prints. We were also taught to scratch the date, case number, and our initials on the casting to make a permanent record, in case you ever needed it for identification purposes in court. It was something every new officer learned, but taking the prints the right way was a pretty time-consuming process. I kept a bag of plaster of paris in the trunk of my patrol car, for starters, along with lengths of wire coat hanger that had to be set into the soft castings to stabilize them and keep them from breaking after the plaster set. But I wanted to get really good at taking impressions, and so I practiced, sometimes just for the hell of it.

Once, for instance, during a bad snowstorm, I pulled off the road near the Tobacco River, which ran through town, and noticed someone had run off the road and knocked down a few road posts, the wooden kind connected together by heavy strands of metal cable. No real harm done. But I was curious. There wasn't any paint from the vehicle on the posts, which meant the vehicle was probably big and high. But I did see an unusual tire impression—not from an ordinary passenger car, but big, wide tracks, like the kind a truck would leave. I thought, what the heck, it would be good practice, so I took my plaster of paris out of the trunk, mixed up a little batch, and made a cast of the tire track. Then, I started keeping my eyes open.

Sure enough, a few days later I was over at the Department of Public Works, and I noticed one of the tires on the trucks looked like it might be a match. I got my casting out of the trunk, and it was a dead ringer, a mirror image. I checked the logbook to see who'd had the truck on that particular night. It was Jack Bouchey, a good friend of mine, who'd actually been one of my references for getting a job at the police department. Jack had been driving one of the big snowplows the night of the storm, and didn't even realize he'd hit anything. We had a good laugh about it. Can't escape the long arm of the law, I told him. "Teach you to give *me* a job recommendation again."

But now, at the home of the Punches, I thought those unusual shoes might very well be significant, and it was important to preserve a good print of them. So I mixed up a plaster batch, found one really good full shoe and heel print from directly beneath the window, made my casts, and put them in the evidence closet. Then I started thinking about the things I was learning in my psychology classes at Central Michigan University. A lot of it, frankly, I didn't see much use for—the really abstract stuff. But the behavioral science part as it pertained to abnormal psychology was fascinating. I started to try to apply some of what I'd learned. This perp had probably started out as a peeping Tom, but now the guy was progressing. Why? And more ominously, how much further was he likely to go?

Maybe part of his attraction to this particular woman had something to do with proximity. I'd seen this guy's shoe prints, and I got the feeling he'd walked to the scene, which meant he probably lived close by. Perhaps even close enough to know when she was at home, when she hung laundry on her clothesline, or when she usually went to bed—and maybe even how dressed up she and her husband were when they left their house carrying a wedding present the Saturday night before.

I drew up a grid and began to canvass the neighborhood. I found three individuals within it who were potential suspects—all young males. One, a bit of a troublemaker, was the nephew of a wealthy resident. The second was the son of a medical doctor who exhibited some strange behavior. And the third was a local politician's son, who I knew slightly from having written him a few traffic tickets, and who seemed a little odd to me. All three were a little shaky for one reason or another, and they all lived nearby.

It was Christmastime, and it bothered me to think this guy was out there somewhere. Depressives and the mentally unstable are even more so during the holidays, and when I was at home, having a nice time with Sharon and her folks, I kept thinking some weird guy was probably keeping an eye on the school-teacher. Then one midnight, we got a report of gunshots being fired. I was on patrol and responded, cutting my lights and slipping up to the complainant's house. "Yeah, there was a guy over in the bank parking lot," she told me, still pretty excited. "I heard three shots, but I didn't see him firing. He was holding something, a gun or a stick, standing right out in the open."

"Thanks very much," I said. "You just keep your shades pulled and stay in the house. We'll find out who's doing it, ma'am, and make sure it stops. Now you have a good night."

The parking lot next to the bank was empty, so I started driving, very slowly, through the neighborhood. Soon enough, I saw him, walking down the street   the son of the local politician.

"Hey, could you jump in the car for a second," I said. "I need to talk to you." I took him down to the station and as he was getting out of the car, I heard a metallic sound from somewhere on the ground. I played it cool, acting like I hadn't heard it, and got a couple of officers in the station to hold on to him. Then I went back outside, got on my knees, peered under the car, and, right behind the wheel, found a Mauser machine pistol—an automatic weapon, still warm—the kind that fits into a wooden holster to become a shoulder weapon.

I brought it back into the station and went over to take a better look at the kid. He was sitting in a chair, not saying much. And he was wearing an expensive pair of high-style leather shoes with a high boot heel and a long, pointed toe. "Hang on a second," I said. "I'll be right back."

I went into the evidence closet, found the full shoe cast, came back with it, and said, "Let me see your foot." He put his leg out,

I held the casting up to it, and it was a perfect match. I tapped him on the knee, looked straight into his eyes and, almost in a whisper, said, "You been doing any prowling, Donnie?"

A big smile came across his face, but he didn't say anything.

"Okay, then, I guess you don't want to talk about it. But just tell me one thing. Being out alone on a night like this and all, Donnie, what the hell were you shooting at?"

For a second, he just looked at me. Then, still grinning, he took a deep breath. "Well, you know, Officer, they've got a big old lighted-up Santa Claus up on the roof of the hospital, right at the chimney top," he said. "And there was just something in me that wanted to *hit* that thing."

He was eighteen years old—legally, a keeper—so we lodged him in the county jail that night. His father, the politician, caught wind of what had happened, and was at the station by the time we got back from requesting a search warrant. He was pretty upset, but Chip talked him down, and he was cooperative. We went over to the kid's house, and in the garage found half the schoolteacher's clothes, but none of her underthings. They were all gone. "I should have shook the kid down and strip-searched him back at the station," Chip said. "He was probably wearing 'em."

In the end, I felt sorry for the kid and his family. He was obviously emotionally disturbed, and we arranged for him to get some in-patient psychiatric care. But sometime later, after I was off the force, I learned he'd committed suicide.

It was a sad ending to the story, but the case taught me something important. In any investigation, it's fine to do the basics, to note shoe prints, to measure and photograph them. But it's infinitely better to go the extra mile—to take the trouble to go into the trunk, haul out the plaster, and make the casting. That's the kind of thing that can make or break a case, and in the long run stop an innocent person from being hurt, or even killed.

It was a deceptively simple lesson, but one that would serve as the underpinning for all of the law enforcement work I'd ever do. What it taught me was that the quality of investigation is the cornerstone of solving a crime.

Even in the little burg of Clare, we handled cases whose implications stretched far beyond the town limits. Those were the days of hippies, draft dodgers, and a lot of illegal drug use, and every now and then, a couple of guys from Washington would show up in suits, with a warrant for a deserter or a dealer, and we'd help them find the suspect. I knew better than to ask questions about exactly what they were up to, but one day Chip decided to bring me a little further into the loop. He told me the out-of-town visitors were what most people called "the feds"—agents assigned out of Washington from the Federal Bureau of Investigation.

For years, there'd been rumors about organized crime's links to Clare. In fact, rightly or wrongly, a beautiful big spread near the outskirts of town, right on the Tobacco River, was referred to by locals as "the Purple Gang House." At about that time, *Life* magazine ran one of the first major national media exposés on the Mob, including the names and photographs of such key players as Joe Bonanno, Carlo Gambino, and Meyer Lansky. And that particular issue suddenly disappeared from all the newsstands in Clare. Wherever I asked for a copy, the counter clerk said, "Oh, maybe it hasn't come in yet," or, "You know, we just sold the last one."

After a while, I found out why. In Clare's ritziest section was a big, beautiful stone house with a six-hole golf course, a land-scaped swimming pool in the backyard, and a sweeping paved driveway leading up to a four-car garage. It was owned by one of the wealthiest and most prominent families in town, the Lavalles. What I soon learned was that a frequent guest at the Lavalles' was a man named Meyer Lansky—the head of the Jewish Mob.

One winter day while on patrol, I noticed a big black four-door Buick with five people in it, doing fifty in a thirty-five-mile-an-hour zone. This was right in the middle of town, so I pulled the car over at a light. When I got to the driver's window, I saw a flustered woman, Hispanic, in her midfifties. I recognized her from around town.

"Could I see your license and registration, please?" I asked.

It was obvious this was nothing more than a family get-together, so I explained how she'd been exceeding the speed limit and since we'd had several accidents in the area, I really had to write her a ticket. I could see how upset she was, perhaps embarrassed in front of her family, so when I came back to the car with the citation, I said, "I hope I didn't ruin your evening." A few days later I received a note from her at the station. "Thank you for being so courteous to me in front of my relatives," it read, and went on to say how grateful she was that I'd been so polite to her.

Over the next few weeks, I began to receive a few small gifts in the mail, rum cookies at Christmastime and that sort of thing. Then she started to send things to the house, became friendly with Sharon, and developed a soft spot for my little boy. One day a taxicab pulled up in front of the house and the driver said, "I have a package for you." Inside were four of the biggest steaks I'd ever seen—the kind of prime Texas beef that, on a forty-eight-hundred-dollar annual salary, I hadn't seen in a very long time.

At first I wondered how a woman on a limited income could

afford such an expensive present. And then I found out. She hadn't actually paid for them. She'd most likely taken them out of the well-stocked freezer of her employer, who in all likelihood would never know they were gone. That was because, as it turned out, the woman was Meyer Lansky's personal cook.

I went to Chip and told him what had happened. "First it was cookies," I said, "but now it's steaks. Really expensive ones, and I don't feel real comfortable about accepting them." By then I'd heard how the Lavalles were reported to be part owners of the Sands Hotel in Las Vegas, one of the hotels Lansky skimmed from. It made me worry that, through the cook, they were trying to make some kind of approach, and I wanted it on the table with my superior that I wasn't the type to accept any kind of bribe. I talked it over with Chip, and he checked with the FBI agents, who appreciated the tip but suggested I just let things slide.

Chip had been quietly helping the FBI with its surveillance of Lansky, and pretty soon I got an idea of my own. I had a talk with the cook and told her about how dangerous the people she was working for were. I started out by saying, "I wonder if you'd let me know from time to time who's coming to the house, and when, if you happen to know."

She thought about it for a minute, and then, without any hesitation in her voice, said, "Why, yes, I'd be willing to do that."

And she did. We became friends, and over the years this brave woman took a lot of risks for me, keeping a detailed calendar of the comings and goings of Lansky, his visitors, and their license plate numbers. It was tremendous intelligence, and it made those FBI agents think I was pretty capable and enterprising. In fact, what really made it all happen was that I'd shown a woman some respect when it was especially important to her.

The key to establishing relationships with informants, I

learned, was that in at least one way, it was no different from any other relationship. It wasn't about money, or trying to pull the wool over someone's eyes, or coercing them into cooperating. It was about honesty, and mutual respect, and letting people know that they could choose to work with you for the common good.

Chip and I were close colleagues on the force for four years, and then just as things were rolling along nicely, he came to me one afternoon in 1965 and told me he'd been offered a job in security for Dow Chemical, one of the largest employers in the state. What came next was more stunning. "I want you to know," he said, "that I'm going to recommend to the city commission that you be Clare's next chief of police."

"Chip, I'm twenty-six years old," I said. "I can't do that."

"Yes you can," he said, with such conviction I almost believed him. "You're one of the people who helped me make a turn-around in this town, and being a chief of police, especially at your age, will be an important mark in your life, no matter what you eventually do."

A month later, Chip stood before the city council and said, "We've given you a professional police department, and if you want to keep it that way, I suggest you appoint one of the key people who helped me turn it around—Roger Depue." That was how, after just turning twenty-seven, I became the youngest police chief in the state of Michigan.

As head of the department, I encouraged my people to go out to restaurants and gas stations, get to know the folks on the street. If they memorized one person's name every day, I told them, by the end of the year they'd be on a first-name basis with more than three hundred people, all of whom were potential victims, perpetrators, witnesses, or jurors. And I encouraged them to stick their necks out.

Not long after I took over the job, an anonymous call came into the station house one night. The caller, a male, reported he'd seen what he thought was a burglar in that plush neighborhood peering through windows and running in the direction of the Lavalle house. The dispatcher sent the call—"Prowler seen heading toward the Lavalle home"—and it was picked up by a squad car manned by an eager young police officer and his somewhat older partner, a sergeant named Elry Tice.

Tice pulled out all the stops, turned on the red light and siren, and came wheeling into the Lavalle driveway. His partner ran around one side of the house in the dark, Tice around the other. There was no immediate evidence of a break-in, so Tice knocked on the door and explained to the owner that a prowler was in the area and might have gained entry to the house. "Well, yes, Officer, I appreciate your letting us know," said the man who answered the door, "and please do come on in and have a look around." Which Tice did.

Apparently no one paid much attention to the mild-mannered officer with the graying hair and glasses as he snooped around the house. In fact, they had no idea that, afterward, Tice headed back to the station and drew a detailed schematic of the house's floor plan, right down to the location of bedrooms, possible hiding places, and points of egress. The other thing no one ever suspected was that the whole story about a prowler was a setup, and the anonymous caller who phoned it into the dispatcher was me.

In fact, the so-called prowler call at the Lavalle home was part of a plan I hatched to infiltrate the mobster's hideout, as advance preparation in case the FBI ever needed to conduct a raid on the place. It was that kind of enterprise on my part, I guess, that made the two visiting federal agents from Saginaw I'd gotten to know sit up and take notice. "Get that college degree," one of them said. "Because you seem like the kind of man we very well might have a place for in the FBI."

That was a pretty heady prospect for a guy like me, but there was only one problem. I still had a year of school to finish, and was at the same time trying to hold down my job and support Sharon and what by then were our three young children. "I work days and what I need for my degree are all day classes," I told the agents.

"So quit your job," they said.

Instead, I did the next best thing. Over lunch one day, I mentioned my situation to Alex Strange, the local elected juvenile court judge. He noted that I was majoring in psychology and sociology, and asked if I'd be interested in filling the opening left by the county's departing juvenile court officer.

"Would you let me finish school?" I asked.

"Work your own hours," he said. "You'll be responsible for handling neglect and abuse cases, organizing and supervising foster homes, handling delinquents and probation cases, and doing some adoption investigations. But as long as you get the work done, I don't care when you do it."

To this day, the memories that haunt me most are the ones from the child abuse cases I saw back in my days as a juvenile officer. One day, I got a call from one of the local schools, from a boy's teacher. The boy was living in a troubled home, and she was alarmed because that day, the boy, fifteen years old, had insisted on curling up in his classroom seat, with his arms wrapped around his head, refusing to sit up, even when she asked him to. Finally, she coaxed him to raise his chin, and then she saw what he was trying to hide. He had deep cuts in his scalp, bruises all over his face, and his light brown hair was clumped and tufted, as if it had been lopped off in pieces.

I made a home visit to find out what was going on, and came to a ramshackle cabin in the woods, a shack, really, with almost no furniture, and cracks between the floorboards so wide the wind blew up inside. The boy's mother was dead, and he and his three younger brothers were being raised by an abusive, alcoholic father. They all lived together in what was basically a single room. There weren't even sheets on the beds, just old woolen army blankets tossed over bare pillows and dirty mattresses.

Apparently, the boy's hair had been getting long, and the school told him he had to get a haircut. So he asked his father for the money a couple of times, and finally the old man got tired of hearing about it. "I'll cut your goddamn hair!" he screamed. In a drunken rage, he took a hunting knife from his belt and hacked his son's hair off while straddling him on the cabin floor.

Another adolescent boy—I'll call him Jesse—came to the court's attention because of his odd behavior in school. He wasn't violent or acting out, but was incredibly silent and withdrawn. We soon found out why. As it turned out, in this boy's family, his grandmother and grandfather had sexually abused their kids over the years. And now, the pattern of abuse was playing out in the third generation. The grandparents were now routinely raping this boy and his brothers and sisters, too. It was the most disturbing example of intergenerational sex abuse I'd ever seen. These kids' childhoods were being taken from them, by people who acted as if it was all a normal part of the family routine, as if it were the most ordinary thing in the world.

This sad, uncommunicative boy never talked about the abuse he'd suffered. But even so, he found a way to convey something of what was happening to him. At all times and no matter where he went, in school and even when he slept, he'd taken to wearing a crucifix around his neck. But this was no simple piece of jewelry, or a small gold cross on a slim dimestore chain. What the boy wore on his chest, hanging by a leather cord, was a six-by-ten-inch wooden cross, like the kind you'd see displayed on a bedroom wall.

As a law enforcement officer, I could handle the things adults did to other adults. But now, I just couldn't stomach seeing what they did to kids. It enraged me, and I knew, in the long run, I couldn't keep doing that kind of work. Still, after five years as a policeman and two with the juvenile court, I was determined to remain in law enforcement, but maybe shift my sights upward a bit. As soon as I got my degree, I decided to pursue my contacts with the FBI, and that meant filling out an application form. The questionnaire asked about everything I'd ever done in my life, good or bad. I told them about all the places I'd lived, how I'd gotten kicked out of high school, the scuffles I'd gotten into in the Marines, all of it. I drove down to Detroit for a battery of interviews and tests.

And then, almost when I'd forgotten about it and was thinking I maybe ought to make that run for sheriff after all, Sharon picked up the mail one morning and brought in a white envelope, addressed to me, bearing an official-looking seal. In it was a letter from J. Edgar Hoover, informing me that I was to report to the Old Post Office Building in Washington, D.C., to begin my training as a special agent of the FBI.

CHAPTER FOUR

THE BUREAU

A LOT OF PEOPLE have written about it—the Washington Monument, the Jefferson Memorial, the Reflecting Pool on the Mall that runs all the way from the statue of Lincoln down to where the Capitol stands. But on a September morning in 1968, when I arrived in Washington, D.C., and rode a bus from National Airport across the Potomac River past all of that gleaming white stone and marble, the majesty of it was beyond anything I could have pictured in my mind.

As an FBI agent in training, I was billetted two blocks from the White House at the Hotel Harrington, not far from the Old Post Office Building where we'd get most of our classroom training. We also spent three weeks at the Marine base at Quantico, Virginia, about thirty-five miles outside town, where we took firearms instruction and "defensive tactics," which was basically hand-to-hand combat, and trained at

Hogan's Alley, a stretch of fake storefronts where they taught you how to shoot bad guys without hitting innocent civilians.

Through it all, instructors drilled us on the classic principles of FBI technique: superiority of manpower, firepower, and the element of surprise. We also had to study subjects like constitutional law, including all two hundred or so federal statutes the FBI had jurisdiction over, right down to the Migratory Bird Act. Almost lost in all of that was the guy who came in to give us the obligatory one-hour lecture on the psychology of criminals. It was vague and perfunctory, and, as far as most of the students were concerned, pretty irrelevant. The class was called "Behavioral Science."

The vast majority of the forty-some recruits in my incoming new agents' class were green. They didn't come from law enforcement, and they needed to learn the basics of street-level policing. That was torture for a guy like me, who had already served as a Marine, a patrolman, and a chief of police. Three months into our sixteen-week training session, I was sent to the Bureau's Washington field office—its second largest, with around five hundred agents—to work on a squad for a week to get some real hands-on experience. Since I was already a former police chief, they put me on the number one squad, C-1, the most reactive in the field office, and the one responsible for handling bank robberies and dangerous fugitives. Every one of us was given a mentor; I was assigned to an agent named Barry Colvert.

Barry would go on to have a stellar career in the FBI and become one of the country's leading polygraph experts, examining such notorious traitors as the Walker spy family, Jonathan Pollard, and Aldrich Ames. Years later, he conducted the polygraph of Congressman Gary Condit during the Chandra Levy case. At the time I met him, Barry, a six-foot-five former Marine, was working a fugitive case, looking for an escaped federal prisoner serving time for bank robbery by the name of Harry "Rodan" Rhodes.

Rodan was a huge, hulking guy, and his nickname came from one of those awful dubbed horror movies at the time, about a monster that ate Japan. One night, after a long investigation, Barry got a tip from an informant that Rodan was working at the Shoreham, an elegant old Washington hotel on Rock Creek Park. Barry collared me and said, "I know it's late, but you're a new agent, it's time you made an arrest, and I'm taking you with me."

In the car on the way over to the hotel, he told me the Shoreham had a network of tunnels and storage rooms underneath it, so that kitchen help and the banquet staff could stay out of sight of the guests. "When we get there," he said, "I'm going to give you a clipboard to carry."

"Isn't that a little obvious?" I said.

"No, Roger," he said patiently. "We're going to pretend like we're fire inspectors." Then he showed me a picture of Rodan. "He's a big guy," Barry said. "And we don't want any trouble."

When we got to the Shoreham, we pulled into the employee entrance, made contact with management, got our clipboards, and started wandering around like we knew what we were doing. Every now and then Barry would point at something and in a loud voice say, "Look at that, Bob. Make a note of that, will you?"

Finally, we walked into a kind of locker room where the food service workers changed clothes, and there, standing right in front of us was Rodan. He glanced at us and then kept on changing. In tandem, Barry and I walked up behind him; Barry got a firm grip on one of his arms, and I took the other.

"You know, Harry, I'm afraid you're going to have to come

with us," Barry said into his ear. "Because you're supposed to be in jail, and the way I'm seeing it, you're *not*."

Then Barry click-cuffed him, just like that, with the words, "FBI. You're under arrest." No guns, no noise, no fuss. Neat, just the way the FBI likes it to be. When Barry shook him down, he found that Rodan was carrying a pretty nasty weapon, a hooked-blade linoleum cutter, all nice and sharpened. But outwardly the only aftermath of the arrest was just what Barry intended. After a while, it sort of registered with people that Rodan wasn't around anymore. "Hey, whatever happened to old what's-his-name?"

That was my first arrest as an FBI agent, and it showed me a real-life example of the element of surprise. But that wasn't the only thing Barry taught me. One day he wanted to stop to talk to one of his informants, a woman by the name of Lorraine. I'd seen Barry approach these people before. Sometimes when we pulled up, they'd take off running, and we'd have to chase some guy down an alley and throw him in the back of the car. But this time, as we drove into an alley, I saw the shadow of a woman, hunched over and in no condition to run. She was there waiting for us, and when we stopped, she got into the back seat and lay down until we drove off, so no one would see her talking to the feds.

The first thing I noticed was the terrible smell. "Lorraine, bless her heart, she'll stain the seats," Barry had told me, and he wasn't kidding. It was wintertime, but as casually as I could, I rolled down my window to let a little air in. Barry just seemed oblivious to it, exchanging pleasantries with her. Lorraine was a full-blown heroin addict. She was wearing a wig and dirty jeans, and had obviously just awakened from a nod, because there was a string of white saliva still crusted on the side of her dark face. Then, after Barry had finished talking business with her, he said,

"You know, Lorraine, it's going to be Christmas pretty soon, and I've been thinking about something."

She tried to focus. "Yeah?"

"Yeah," he said. "I was thinking it might be nice if we got you cleaned up for Christmas. What would you say to that?"

"Well, Mr. Barry, I don't know . . ." she said. "I don't know that I can do that."

"Look, Lorraine, I know some people at the hospital around here, and I can get you into a program. I really think we can get you clean. It'd be nice for your family. Get you all right for Christmas."

They went back and forth for a while, and she finally decided to take Barry up on his offer. He drove her over to Holy Cross, walked her in, had her admitted, and saw her settled. The next day, when we were in the Bureau car together, Barry pulled into a little market. "Listen, Rog," he said, "I've got to pick up a few things here. Can you go over to those magazine racks and pick out some of those Archie books, and I'll meet you back at the checkout?"

"Archie books?"

"Yeah, Archie, Jughead, Betty and Veronica," he said. "Just pick up four or five of those comics."

When I got to the register, Barry was there with a bagful of oranges, bananas, plums, cherries, and grapes. "What's all of this for?" I said. "We having a picnic or something?"

"I thought we might drop by the hospital and see how Lorraine is doing," Barry said. "You know, when they're going through withdrawal, they have a terrible thirst. It's nice for 'em to be able to have some fresh fruit."

The way Barry saw it, law enforcement was in large part public relations, the genuine kind. "We will never call them informants," he used to say. "We're making friends." If he went out of town on vacation, he sent his snitches a postcard. At Christmas, it was holiday greetings. He even got notes from Rodan's grandmother for a while because, after Rodan was back in the clink, Barry went to the trouble of picking up his last paycheck for him over at the Shoreham. And whenever someone got out of prison who Barry had locked up, he'd be on the scene to help them find a job. "If I ever need to find a bad guy in their neighborhood, I'm their best friend," he told me. "No matter what else they are, they're still human beings."

As a new agent, you remember your first informant, your first arrest, and people like Barry Colvert. They become your frame of reference for everything that follows. I said to myself, "That's the kind of agent I want to be."

After I finished my training in Washington, I received my first official assignment, to New Orleans, one of the best postings a new agent could ever hope for. It was a wild town, and the local district attorney, Jim Garrison, who went on to become well known for his work on the Kennedy assassination, had lots to keep him busy—crime, corruption, vice, narcotics and prostitution, after-hours gambling clubs, police corruption—all the good stuff. I landed right in the thick of things, working undercover with Michigan plates on my car, and staying in a little place on Canal Street, the center of a bookmaking operation. I lived there for a couple of weeks, compliments of J. Edgar Hoover, meeting my contacts, and listening in on conversations among the hoods, who called in action from the lobby of the hotel.

The techniques I'd developed as a young officer in Michigan translated pretty well to the Big Easy. Once, in connection with a federal investigation, I was assigned to question a guy by the name of Gary Eames, the leader of the Galloping Goose motorcycle gang, which, despite the name, was actually a pretty dangerous bunch of guys, who went on to become major distributors of methamphetamine throughout the whole state of Louisiana.

The agent working with me, Chris Dauwalder, and I found ourselves in a roadhouse in Orleans Parish, a rough-looking dive with a knot of Harleys parked outside. Inside, there were a few bikers at the bar, and behind it one very solid barmaid with a tattoo on one of her biceps: "Property of The Hog." Very sweet. Everyone was keeping a close eye on us, so we showed Eames's picture around and asked if anyone knew him. Chris was doing most of the talking, so I decided to take a trip to the men's room. As I was standing at the urinal, a guy walked in, right out of central casting: six-foot-two, about two hundred and ten pounds, all muscle, leather vest, no shirt, tattoos of skulls and daggers, long greasy hair. He looked at me and said, "You're FBI."

"That's right."

"You know," he said, "a few weeks ago a couple of FBI guys came in here, and our boys went over to their table, turned it over on 'em, and beat the hell out of 'em."

It was a threat, and he waited for my response. "Yeah," I said. "That's true. A few weeks ago a couple of guys did come in here, and you did think they were FBI agents, and you did kick their asses. But they weren't FBI agents."

"What are you talkin' about, man? I was here, and I saw them."

"Like I said. They weren't," I said, deliberately. "Because if they had been, my friends and I would've come down here and taken this fucking place apart, brick by brick. But you know what? It's still here. I know, because we're *pissing* in it."

There was just the hint of a smile from the guy. I had obviously passed the test. We got to talking back and forth, and it turned out he was the famous Hog, of the barmaid's tattoo. And also, for the rest of my stay, one of the best informants I had in New Orleans.

———

I worked stakeouts, which were exhilarating and challenging. But what hooked my interest in a way nothing else did was any case involving aberrant human behavior. During one homicide investigation, I interviewed the husband of a young woman who'd been murdered. He seemed appropriately devastated by the crime, and certainly wasn't a suspect himself. In fact, he told me, he had been out of state, in Texas, at the time of the murder. It seemed like an airtight alibi. But when I examined the crime scene, a few things got me thinking.

For one thing, at the time the woman's body was found, the family pet, a cute little mutt, was found in a separate, fenced-off part of the backyard, behind a closed aluminum gate. He looked like a real house pet, not the kind who was routinely kept outdoors. And there was no doghouse outside. The victim, his owner, had been brutally beaten to death in her bedroom, and forensic tests proved the crime had taken place in the middle of the night. It was odd, I thought—almost as if the dog had deliberately been put outside to keep him away from what took place in the house.

Also, at the time the crime scene was discovered, the bedroom light was off. The murder took place in predawn darkness, which meant—unless the killer had used a flashlight during commission of the crime, which seemed unlikely—the wall switch next to the door had been flipped off afterward. Furthermore, the front door wasn't locked, just pushed closed. And when we finally found the woman's car, stolen from her driveway, the keys were in the ignition, the car was locked, and it was in an airport parking lot, right between the two parallel lines.

What did all of that tell me? That whoever beat this woman's skull, repeatedly, until she bled to death, had, even in a resulting anxious and tense state, turned off the lights, put out the dog, closed the front door, and parked the family car the same way he always did. Routinely, the way a family member would've done it. I saw this as evidence of a proprietary interest on the killer's part, not only about the crime scene property, but also about his victim. It was a good hunch. When we put all the pieces together, the killer turned out to be the woman's own husband.

By that point in my career, I was pretty accustomed to crime scenes and jails. In fact, I'd seen a lot of lockups in Michigan and Washington but never anything quite like the Orleans Parish Prison. One day another agent, Chuck Harvel, and I went there to question an inmate, a six-foot-three guy nicknamed Little John, about a stolen car ring, and as we pulled up, the sight of the place struck me as medieval. It was dark and forbidding, with concrete watchtowers, stone walls ringed with razor wire, and guards with semiautomatic weapons positioned everywhere. If a building could be mean, this one was.

The interview rooms were across what was euphemistically called the prison yard. No grass, just rocks, flies, and dirt that turned to mud when it rained, which seemed about every hour or so. This was a particularly steamy day, and Chuck and I were in full regalia: Bostonian wing-tips and blue suit. J. Edgar Hoover wanted his agents to look like IBM executives, so we all had at least two suits: the one you wore while running down alleys, and the good one, which was what I was wearing that day. The only concession in New Orleans was that during the summer you were allowed to take the jacket off.

We started out across the yard, a distance of about a hundred and fifty feet. But it quickly turned into one of those weird, telescoping scenes, right out of Hitchcock's *Vertigo*. The first thing I noticed were the cells ringing the yard, two and three tiers high. As the inmates spotted us, they started to yell, just a few of them at first: "Pig!" "Cops!" "Look at the suits!" "Hey, maybe they're FBI!" And then it got worse.

From above, they started throwing things and spitting out from between the bars. I felt as though we were running a gauntlet in some movie, except this was real. The hatred was palpable, but the guard escorting us acted blasé. He didn't raise a hand or say anything in response. We were outsiders, we were vulnerable, and he wanted us to feel that. So we did the only thing we could: We met the prisoners' gaze. We didn't look away. We communicated that we weren't afraid, or if we were, we sure as hell weren't going to show it.

I was certainly no stranger to law enforcement, and I'd seen some pretty disturbing things. I won't say I was scared that day at Orleans Parish Prison. But it did underscore something I was seeing all around me. That in the Deep South of the 1960s, there were a lot of great divides.

Sharon and I had three little kids under the age of six by now, Renee, Arleen, and Steven, and we rented a house in a neighborhood of nice brick homes in Jefferson Parish, just down the river from the city. A few blocks from the house was the public elementary school where our kids might go, a modern brick building with a manicured lawn, and a high chain link fence padlocked every night to protect a big playground with swings, slides, and all kinds of sports equipment. It looked warm and welcoming.

One day as I was taking a get-acquainted walk around the neighborhood, I saw another school not far away, a run-down, ramshackle white clapboard building, a lot smaller than the first one. There was no fence and no playground, just a barren blacktop patch and a battered basketball hoop, with no net. At first I thought the place was abandoned. But the windows weren't boarded up, and there were desks and signs of life inside. Since coming to Louisiana I had seen "Colored Only" drinking fountains and "Colored Service" signs hanging above the carry-out windows at local restaurants. But those didn't have quite the same effect on me as these two schools did. If ever there was a clear symbol of the inequality between the races in the South, this was it.

When I was sixteen, I'd worked for a summer as a stock boy in the department store back in Roseville, loading trucks and stacking boxes in the stockroom. All the stock boys were white; next door were the porters—janitors and maintenance men—who all were black. Their foreman was Archie, a lanky, dark-skinned man with a wide-open smile. He didn't care much for the white foreman, Oscar, a mean-spirited German, but Archie loved us. Probably because we were cocky young kids who didn't mind working hard. One day my buddy Jim Shevela and I were told to unload some heavy boxes from an eighteen-wheeler delivery truck. The driver, a massive guy and former wrestler, started throwing them to us so hard that Jim, about five-eight, almost got knocked down a few times. We were pretty tough kids, but no match for this guy. After a while Archie saw what was going on, came over and said sternly, "You boys get off the truck."

Then we watched as he hopped up into the truck and headed for the driver. I don't know what he said, but I saw him jamming his finger at the guy and looking really serious. Then, after he delivered what looked like a pretty good dressing-down, he hopped back down. For the rest of the afternoon the wrestler handed us the boxes like a perfect gentleman.

Not long after that, one of Archie's porters accidentally broke a window in the front office. The manager was furious because some big shot from headquarters was due in town, and he was going to have to explain away the busted window. He summoned Archie to the loading dock, and right in front of everyone started really chewing him out. He stopped just short of calling Archie a nigger, but only just. That was when Archie taught something to everyone who witnessed the ugly scene.

As the boss was screaming at him, he squared his shoulders, drew himself up, threw his chin out, and said, "Sir, you may be richer than me, and you may be smarter, but I'll tell you one thing. You ain't better. You hear me? You ain't *better* than me."

All these years later, as I stood on the sidewalk looking at that dilapidated little school, I couldn't help but think of Archie. The fortunate kids, including my own, who went to the nice school in our neighborhood may have been richer. And they may even have been smarter. But they weren't better than the little black kids destined for this forlorn school. At the time, I didn't know I'd soon be assigned to the front lines of the federal government's effort to set straight that injustice.

Not long after I arrived in New Orleans, Jerris Leonard, the assistant U.S. attorney general for civil rights, came down from Washington to New Orleans for a big meeting with the special agents in charge of a number of Southern field offices, and made a pronouncement. School integration was now the law of the land, and it would be enforced in some twenty Louisiana parishes. We understood the importance of that directive, and when a superior tells FBI agents to do something, they do it. As of that day, it became our responsibility to make sure black children were allowed to enter schools unmolested, and we went about making sure they could.

Everyone hated us. Whites saw us as outside agitators who were interfering in their local affairs. Blacks thought we were making things worse for them by giving the integration effort a higher profile, and they'd get by better if only Northerners would quit making such a big deal out of it. And, perhaps worst of all, the local police didn't want us there, not only because we were infringing on their turf, but because for the most part they were all for the status quo.

If we arrested a Klansman, we put him in the back of a Bureau car and sometimes had to drive around to two or three parishes before a local sheriff would consent to let us use his jail. It was just as likely that a whole parade of rednecks in pickup trucks would be following us the whole time. Our unmarked cars were pretty obvious, and sometimes people walked over just to spit on them, or worse. One agent, a close friend of mine, had his windshield land in his lap one day when a hidden sniper fired through it with a shotgun.

By the time I was assigned to New Orleans in 1969, most of the worst violence in the school integration battle had already taken place. Our job was to exert a presence, to be the watchdogs to see things stayed on track. And we did. Once in Mississippi, a group of agents was surrounded by Klansmen, who started threatening them, screaming and training their weapons on them. Finally, they escaped, but that wasn't the end of it.

Joe Sullivan, the inspector in charge who had been sent to Mississippi by Attorney General Robert Kennedy, got ten carloads of his agents together in the town, and they all drove down and surrounded the courthouse. Sullivan kicked open the door, grabbed the sheriff by the shirt and ricocheted him off three or four walls. Then he stuck his finger in the sheriff's chest. "If you can't keep the law in this town," he said, nodding in the direction of the phalanx of agents outside, "then *they'll* do it."

That was the game we played with the Klan: "Our gang's bigger than your gang, and we've been happy to play by the rules. But if you want to play tough, we can play a helluva lot tougher than you can."

I was lucky I didn't have to work the worst of the civil rights era cases, but they were as close and familiar to me as my good friend Con Hassel. Con was assigned to Mississippi from 1964 to 1967. He was there when the bodies of civil rights workers Chaney, Goodman, and Schwerner were pulled out of an earthen dam in Neshoba County after being murdered by the Klan; he worked the investigation of the murder of Detroit civil rights worker Viola Liuzzo; and he helped provide federal protection for Martin Luther King, Jr., on the march from Selma to Montgomery.

Even in the course of their everyday work, things got so bad agents routinely took off their suit jackets so their guns and holsters were in plain view. What was most frightening about the violence was the randomness of it. One day a civil rights worker who Con knew got into his car and switched on his left-hand turn signal, which had been set to trigger an explosive device. He was killed instantly.

Con made more than one trip to the morgue in the middle of the night to view black victims who'd been beaten to death, and he took the missing persons reports on blacks who simply disappeared. He saw the way an ordinary black man walking down a street in Bellport, Mississippi, would step off the sidewalk and remove his hat whenever a white person passed.

Sometimes, if Con was out in some backwater trying to interview the relatives of some poor soul who had disappeared and was presumed executed, the victim's relatives would just shrug their shoulders and keep still. They were too intimidated to say anything, and it wasn't hard to understand why. Today, some two hundred race-related murders from that era in the South remain officially unsolved.

At the end of my New Orleans posting, I was assigned to the Washington field office and eventually landed on the C-4 criminal squad, charged with working extortion, kidnapping, fugitives, and car theft rings. I carried a .357 Magnum Model 19, which fit in a holster just above my belt, and was powerful enough to stop even the biggest guy right in his tracks. In 1973, I became a member of the FBI's first SWAT team, code-named Spider One. They taught us about a lot of things, including killing—with everything from state-of-the-art weaponry to your bare hands. Still, going in with guns blazing was for the movies. In our opinion it wasn't only stupid and dangerous, but also inelegant.

Through it all, we knew that at a crime scene things could turn on a dime. At the time, Washington was rife with bank robberies, so many that we sometimes staked out particularly vulnerable branches, putting agents armed with shotguns in unmarked cars as lookouts. A bank robbery call was one that all agents, applicants or not, were expected to respond to. One day, my partner, Joe Davis, and I received a call that a local bank branch had been hit up on Connecticut Avenue. The two robbers fled the bank, one into an alley, followed by an officer in pursuit, and the other behind the bank. When an officer came around the corner of the building, the robber raised his gun, took aim, and shot the officer in the head, killing him instantly. As we rolled up in our unmarked car, we were met by the sight of that brave man, lying motionless on the pavement.

It was a disorienting time in other ways as well. I had always been raised to respect authority and to feel a sense of patriotism toward my country and its government. But now the Watergate scandal was exploding in Washington, and it may have been even more disillusioning for us in the Bureau than it was for the rest of the country. We agents were the ones, after all, who had been taught to obey our superiors, putting our lives on the line to defend law and order, whatever the cost. And now, with the revelations about how petty political ambition had corrupted the highest levels of government, it was clear that not everyone was playing by the same rules. Of course, corruption didn't exist just within the Nixon administration. As I would soon learn, you could find bad apples in a lot of places—even the FBI.

As part of C-4, I worked a case in which the fifteen-year-old son of a wealthy local merchant was being threatened. It wasn't sophisticated extortion, just street punks trying to shake this guy down by hassling his son. The merchant received a demand for ten thousand dollars to be placed in a bag and dropped off at a storefront in a bad neighborhood.

It was a rough area, and the parking lots behind the stores were circled with eight-foot chain link security fencing. We arranged the drop, and I, along with a dozen or so other agents, positioned ourselves in cars a distance away from the drop point. Closer were two agents in the Rolls-Royce, our nickname for the battered old Ford Econoline van stocked with radios and electronic equipment that served as our surveillance vehicle.

At the appointed time, the merchant dropped the bag in the doorway specified by the bad guys. A few minutes later, a kid about eighteen walked past the doorway, stopped, looked around, and grabbed it. The two agents in the van jumped out and started chasing him. He headed into the parking lot, and in a move that would have done credit to Redskins quarterback Sonny Jurgensen, he threw the bag over the chain link fence to a buddy, who caught it and headed off into the night. The agents in the Rolls-Royce nabbed the first guy, and the rest of us arrived in cars moments later. First, we checked out the alley, touching the hoods of cars to see if any were warm. One was, and when we ran its registration, we learned it was owned by a guy with a criminal record who lived a few blocks away. We staked out his house, and about a half hour later nabbed him as he was walking down the street on his way home. Nice. Case closed.

Later that night, I heard that when some other agents went back to the scene, they saw the van kind of bouncing, and heard noises coming from it, like muffled shouts. And then it dawned on them. The two FBI agents inside were shoving the kid around.

In that arrest, we all had the same goal—IDing the kid who got away. But at the same time some of us were out in the alley doing good, basic investigative work, these guys were in the van, taking a shortcut. If stopping a crime calls for the use of physical force, I'm okay with that. But two grown men bouncing around a teenager whose hands are cuffed behind him? That made my guts churn.

Some of the other guys were as outraged as I was. We were all in the FBI together, and in the FBI you didn't do that kind of thing. If a guy swung at you, yes, he'd lose his teeth. But using physical force on a teenager who's helpless? That was bullshit. The problem was figuring out what to do about it. My first option was to go to the supervisor, but that wasn't going to cut it. I was going to have to keep on working with these guys, and one day my life might depend on them. So I went to Plan B: I was going to have to confront them.

One guy was a real asshole, and there wasn't any point in trying to turn him around. The other was a pretty good guy, actually. As it happened, a couple of nights later, he and I were the last two guys in the gym before closing. He was coming out of the showers just as I was going in, and it seemed like the perfect opportunity. Two human beings in their nakedness.

So I went up to him and said, "You know, I'd like to talk to you about something. The other night on that extortion case, you guys were in the Rolls and you got that kid. And what I'm hearing is that when you had him, you beat him up. You worked him over pretty good."

It was obvious he was trying to cover himself, putting his towel over his privates, looking down and shifting his weight from foot to foot.

"Did you do that?" I said.

"Yeah, but we didn't hurt him," he said finally, "and it wasn't my idea. It was the other guy. He started it . . ."

I looked at him, full in the face for a moment. And then, straight into his eyes, I said, "You used to be ten feet tall to me."

You cannot let people get away with things like what these guys did. You have to police your own. If you don't, it's like a cancer that only gets worse. The only solution is for good people to take action themselves, because in a tight-knit group, there is nothing stronger than peer pressure. What I said to him devastated that guy. He had tears in his eyes. And when I turned and walked away from him, as if to say, "I'm writing you off," it cut him to the heart.

Two days later, he came to me, trying to reestablish contact. He said he needed to apologize. "You don't have to tell me you're sorry," I said. "There's someone else you need to apologize to." And then I tried to explain to him what it feels like to be cuffed and helpless, to be completely at the mercy of someone who, maybe just for a few minutes, is stronger than you and has an unfair advantage.

"Can you even begin to imagine what that feels like?" I said.

I've often thought that everyone in law enforcement ought to have their ass beat at least once in life, because it teaches such a valuable lesson. It lets you know, clear and simple, what it really feels like to be a victim. It was something I'd learned some years earlier outside a gas station in Detroit on New Year's Eve. At the time, I vowed that if I couldn't find the guys who hurt me, then someday, when I happened on two strong guys working over another who was weaker, I'd step in and do my best to make it a fair fight. I was glad I had the chance to make good on that promise. I just wished it hadn't been within the FBI.

In all, probably the most frustrating part of the job was coming up against things you couldn't solve. In 1972 roughly a dozen young girls, aged eight to seventeen, were found murdered in the D.C. area. One victim was stabbed repeatedly, and then dumped outside an emergency room, just close enough to see it as she bled out and died. Another, a little girl about ten years old, was standing outside a grocery store when she disappeared. The store owner walked outside, found a bag of groceries lying on the sidewalk, took the stuff inside, and restocked his shelves, as if she had never existed at all. Still another victim, a little girl snatched off the street, was found wearing a brand-new pair of patent leather shoes. It turned out she was no stranger to the prostitution game. Twelve years old, and she had paid for those shoes herself.

That string of homicides, known as the Freeway Phantom Murders, was never solved to our real satisfaction, and many of the agents who worked the case are still bothered by that. At the time, our best guess was that the killings were the work of a roving team of predators, rather than a single serial killer. In the end, all we knew for sure was that for too long a stretch of time it was open season on young girls in Washington, D.C., and we couldn't do a damn thing about it.

As a member of the C-4 squad, my main job was tracking down fugitives and wanted men, and I saw a lot of young victims who'd been caught in the crossfire. Not a hail of bullets, necessarily, but they were victims nonetheless. I can't count the number of kids I saw in those inner-city smack houses, in the same rooms with heroin, guns, and some pretty mean people, or how many times I literally stepped over frightened children whose only mistake was being born to parents who didn't want them in the first place.

They were just innocent little kids. Squalling babies and bewildered, dirty-faced toddlers. In the years since, I stayed haunted by the thought that maybe it would have been better, not just for them, but for society as a whole, if rather than chasing the bad guys, we had stopped to scoop up those little kids, and done everything in our power to save them instead.

CHAPTER FIVE

THE BEHAVIORAL SCIENCE UNIT

I LOOKED OUT INTO THE AUDITORIUM at a sea of two hundred men in blue, most with blank faces. Actually, the blank ones I was grateful for. It was the openly hostile ones I was worried about. When they first arrived at the FBI Academy for training, all I had to do was read their body language. "Yeah, you think you know so much about the street?" some seemed to say, leaning back in their chairs, arms folded defiantly across their chests. "Well, let's see how much you know. You go right ahead and teach me something."

I first came to Quantico in 1973 after being tapped as the senior counselor for the ninety-fifth session of the FBI National Academy program, a tough, twelve-week residential training course for upper-level law enforcement officers from around the U.S. and the world. The program was something J. Edgar Hoover conceived as a kind of two-way street—a place that could teach local police the latest in crime-fighting techniques, and help the Bureau establish relationships with law enforcement in the field.

I'd cut a bit of a swath as a new agent, making a lot of cases, going to school nights, and showing some ability to be able to work with almost anyone. But getting assigned to the Academy was still quite a leap. I was responsible for fifty of the two hundred fifty men in the incoming class, all ranked sergeant or above, most in their early forties or older, with an average of about fifteen years' professional experience. At the time, I was thirty-four years old.

It was a lot to handle. The guys in the program were away from home for three months, under tremendous pressure, largely sequestered from the rest of the world, and couldn't just go home at the end of the day to unwind. Any personal problems they might have had coming in—a roving eye, a drinking problem, a wife back home with a roving eye—tended to get worse rather than better. Acting as their guidance counselor wasn't easy, but it did give me the chance to put some of my psychology training to work, and showed me as the kind of guy who was good at managing other people.

During my time on the fugitive squad in the Washington field office, I'd been taking a lot of in-service training courses, always trying to sharpen and broaden my skills. I was also still in school, working toward my graduate degree, and I was taking classes in psychology and the social sciences that I thought would help with my work. What was the best way to handle a violent felon? Was there any way we in law enforcement could help cool off some of the racial tension in our communities? What kind of people were the likeliest to turn to a life of crime? In retrospect, that interest probably doesn't sound very remarkable. Suffice to say that at the time, I was something of a rarity. Of the five-hundred-man Washington field office, I was one of maybe a handful doing graduate work in criminology.

By that point in my career, I was coming to the conclusion that what separates a good investigator from a great one is what he does after an arrest. An average investigator will shut the book, case closed. But the great one will keep pushing. For me, if I captured a fugitive who'd been on the lam for five years, I'd go back to him afterward and try to develop a rapport. Where had he lived while he was on the run? I would ask. Had he gone back to his family, or steered clear of them? How had he supported himself? Had he found honest work, and if so, what kind? The answers to those simple questions were beginning to give me an insight into who these fugitives were, how they operated, what their chances for recidivism were. In effect, I was out on a limb, conducting my own little research project in the area most fascinating to me—the aberrant criminal mind.

A few months after my three-month stint as a counselor, my performance was apparently judged satisfactory, because my bosses decided to recommend me as a full-time behavioral sciences faculty member at the FBI Academy. In the early 1970s, there were a number of good schools of criminal justice around the country, places like American University in Washington, D.C., and the John Jay College of Criminal Justice in New York City. But they were strictly academic institutions; they really didn't offer much in terms of practical application for members of law enforcement.

When the FBI Academy, a twenty-one-building complex on the Marine base at Quantico in rural Virginia, opened in 1972, all that changed. The Academy's main job was training new and in-service agents from the Bureau's fifty-nine regional field offices. But it was also accredited through the University of Virginia, which meant that it was the first institution in the country to combine the study of criminology with the practical training of police officers.

As an instructor, I had a tall order. It was my job to find a way to make behavioral science theory relevant for the men in my classes. It was pretty obvious to me that the most sophisticated knowledge in the world wouldn't do anybody any good if we couldn't find a way to make it useful to local law enforcement. That was where my experience gave me an edge. As a former street cop and police chief myself, I realized something most academics didn't: In the heart of every dedicated investigator is something that never stops gnawing at him—his unsolved cases, the troubling, haunting, open-ended ones you can never let go.

I tried to draw on that when I was lecturing about a specific mental aberration, or the characteristics of a bizarre crime scene. When I was successful, I could see something remarkable happening. Out there in the audience, the body language of these hardened, skeptical police officers would begin to change. Slowly, they'd uncross their arms and lean forward in their chairs. And then, all of a sudden a hand would shoot up, and one of them would utter the magic phrase: "You know, *I* had a case like that once . . ."

When I arrived in Quantico, one of its most respected instructors was Howard "Bud" Teten, six-foot-four, a former Marine, and the pioneer who is generally regarded as the father of modern criminal profiling. Back in the early 1960s, Teten, then a police officer and crime scene specialist in San Leandro, California, got the groundbreaking idea that by exhaustively studying one particular aspect of a crime—the actual crime scene itself—

investigators could gain a wealth of information about the perpetrator.

The general theory of modus operandi had of course been around since long before Sherlock Holmes, but Teten, a dignified, cerebral man, advanced the concept by a giant step. Teten had consulted with Dr. James Brussel, a Greenwich Village psychiatrist who, in the mid-1950s, played a key role in the so-called Mad Bomber case. At the time, New York City was rocked by some twenty explosions over a seventeen-year period, at such landmarks as Penn Station and Radio City Music Hall. At wit's end, police called on Brussel to see if he could help them come up with a suspect. Brussel studied photos of the bomb scenes, as well as the taunting letters the bomber sent to local newspapers, and eventually came up with a detailed analysis.

The perpetrator, he surmised, was an obsessive-compulsive paranoid personality and most likely a native of Eastern Europe, where, at the time, bombs were almost an accepted form of political protest. Like most of his countrymen, he was probably Roman Catholic. And, since the largest population of first- and second-generation Europeans in the U.S. was clustered in southern Connecticut, it wasn't unlikely that the bomber lived there, too. Since he was of a nationality that kept strong family ties, and was likely unable to form romantic attachments, Brussel's guess was that he roomed with a brother or sister.

At the end of his written assessment, Brussel advised the police to look for a foreign-born, heavyset man, Roman Catholic, forty-five to fifty years old. Since the bomber was meticulous and probably somewhat feminine in appearance and character, Brussel suggested he'd likely dress in "the neatest, primmest, and most protective male attire possible"—a double-breasted suit, which he probably wore buttoned.

As a result of their own investigation, police had come to the conclusion that the bomber might be a disgruntled current or former employee of a utility company. They compared employment lists with the analysis done by Brussel, and discovered a match in one George Metesky, who'd worked for Con Ed a decade or so before.

When police went to Waterbury, Connecticut, to pick up Metesky on a cold January night in 1957, they were stunned to find the living incarnation of Brussel's profile—a heavyset, single, fifty-three-year-old, foreign-born Roman Catholic. In fact, the only detail Brussel got wrong was that Metesky lived not with a single sibling, but with his two maiden sisters. The pièce de résistance came when the arresting officers told Metesky to get dressed for a trip to the station, and he emerged from his bedroom wearing his favorite suit—blue, double-breasted, and neatly buttoned.

Instead of studying a person and trying to predict his behavior, Brussel studied evidence of behavior and then predicted the characteristics of the individual—a revolutionary concept that effectively turned normal investigative technique on its ear. And Teten, who met several times with Brussel to compare notes, realized the full significance of that development.

Teten formed a team with Pat Mullany, a former New York agent and Christian Brother who had a psychology degree, and began teaching his ideas in 1970 at the FBI Academy—how to look at unsolved violent crimes, especially homicides, to pull out and interpret the behavioral characteristics of the perpetrator. Some things might seem obvious, that a killer who carried his victim from the scene of the murder most likely had upper body strength, for example. But other lessons were more subtle. By carefully studying the body at a murder scene, it is possible to tell whether a victim has been redressed. Creases in clothing result both from ironing and from wear patterns. Are there wrinkles in the shirt at the elbows, and at the point where the hip joins the body trunk, or have they been shifted? Are there horizontal creases across the back, between the shoulder blades, or are they off to the side? When most people dress, they put their belt buckle in front, right in the middle. Is it still that way?

That kind of information could be enormously revealing in helping determine whether or not a body had been moved or violated after death. And even one small puzzle piece might be crucial in determining a perpetrator's motives and actions, which could in turn make it easier to identify and catch him. It also underscores why it is absolutely critical that a dead body not be disturbed in any way until investigators sign off on it at the scene.

I began working with Teten, exchanging ideas, soaking up whatever I could, and drawing on his insights to refine my own. Despite his enormous contributions, he was facing an uphill battle. For starters, in Hoover's day, the so-called soft sciences hadn't been given much attention or respect within the Bureau, and Teten had to be careful about being too public with his radical new ideas. In addition, the early 1970s were the days of antiwar protesters and street demonstrations, and there was a lot of animosity between social science types and everyday police officers. Psychologists and sociologists were fond of critiquing the police for being fascists, and a lot of law enforcement types thought psychologists were anti-establishment pot-smokers.

The men who signed up for Teten's course, which he called Applied Criminology (there were no female agents in the FBI until after Hoover's death in 1972, and in the years immediately following, women made up only about one percent of the new agents-in-training), generally weren't administrators or management types. Instead, they were street cops—detectives, sergeants, and shift commanders from places like Dubuque. And they were clear about their priorities. They didn't give a damn about the Oedipus complex. They wanted to know what words they could use to disarm a huge guy with a broken bottle who was coming at them from the wrong end of a dark alley. As we instructors began to prove ourselves to this tough crowd, gradually the walls came down. We realized that National Academy students, all front-line law enforcement, had in their heads a tremendous raw body of unstudied information about killers and their crimes. For their part, they began to understand that the Academy's body of knowledge in human behavior and criminal investigation might very well be useful to them.

As a counselor I got to know Jack Pfaff, then the unit chief of a small group of special agent-instructors who were part of the main training division and taught courses in psychology, sociology, criminology, and political science. The name of the group, logically enough, was the Behavioral Science Unit. One day, Jack came to me with an offer. "Roger, would you be interested in coming to the Unit?" The idea was irresistible. Given my background in law enforcement and psychology, as well as my interest in the aberrant criminal mind, I felt as if I was entering a brave new world. At the age of thirty-six, I officially became an instructor in the fledgling BSU.

Pfaff was the kind of guy who had no problem whatsoever delegating responsibility. Before long, in fact, he gave me, in addition to my teaching load, the job of handling the Unit's entire budget process. It was a pretty thankless task, with one redeeming feature. Besides giving me a crash course in navigating FBI bureaucracy, it also taught me everything there was to know about the running of the Unit, from the inside out. The experience proved to be particularly valuable in 1979, when Pfaff's successor, Larry Monroe, was promoted, and the job of Unit chief opened up. One of the profilers in the Unit, John Minderman, who'd been a friend since our days together on the SWAT team, gave me a sit-down. "You're the best candidate for the job, Rog," he said. "You know the programs, the operation, everybody in the Unit. And you're a 'big picture' guy. With all of that and your background in behavioral science, you're the logical guy to step in and take over." I listened to him, took his advice, and decided to throw my hat in the ring. Three months later, after a round of interviews, and Larry Monroe's wholehearted recommendation, I was appointed chief of the Behavioral Science Unit.

Even though Monroe had supported me, one of our perspectives about the job couldn't have been more different. The way he saw it, the FBI's role was to train local law enforcement but not take the lead in actual crime investigation. The FBI's forensic science unit didn't go out and dust for fingerprints, he said, and the photography unit didn't photograph crime scenes. So why should the BSU involve itself in investigations? "What's that got to do with training?" he'd say. "We're not in the business of handling cases."

That was where we parted philosophically. I felt that getting involved in cases was one of the things that truly justified our existence. Aside from my academic study of psychology, after all, I was still at heart a working law enforcement officer. Our goal at the Unit, I felt, was to broaden our base of knowledge, expand our expertise, and share whatever we could to help stop the overwhelming wave of violent crime threatening to engulf the country. I hoped I could bring something to the Unit. At the time, I had no idea I would help chart its course to the forefront of modern crime fighting.

"Ten times deeper than dead people."

That was our address. Nearly a decade after it began in 1972, the Behavioral Science Unit was relegated to a subbasement sixty feet below the Academy gun vault, in what was once a bomb shelter for high U.S. government officials in the event of a nuclear war. It was the slowest elevator in the whole Academy, and it deposited you in front of a huge door, like a bank vault's, with locking mechanisms and a metal wheel that creaked when turned.

The idea had apparently been that in the event of a nuclear attack, the rooms could be sealed off, and when we first arrived, there were still little hand-lettered cardboard signs designating cots for, among others, the heads of the FBI, Drug Enforcement Administration, and Bureau of Alcohol, Tobacco and Firearms, along with a few dusty boxes of munitions and survival rations. We used to say that if anyone dropped by, it wasn't to use the phone or ask for directions. It meant they really wanted to see you. The official story from management was that the Unit was growing, and this was the only available space for it. I used to say the Bureau's administration put us down there because they were afraid of us.

By this stage in my career, I knew a lot about high-incidence crimes—con games, simple robberies, street muggings, and the like. I could walk onto the scene of a burglary, for instance, and just by looking at the place, determine how it was tossed, and the approximate experience level of the perpetrator. Some of that I could tell from looking at how a chest of drawers was rifled—from the top down, or from the bottom up. Think about it: A novice will first open the top drawer, which means he has to take the time to close it before opening the next one. But a more experienced burglar will know to open the bottom drawer first and work his way up from there. That way, he doesn't have to waste time closing drawers. It's a quicker, more efficient method. Armed with knowledge like that, I could walk onto a burglary scene, take a look around, and after just a few minutes say, "This wasn't done by kids. This was somebody who knows what he's doing."

But the unsolved crimes coming over the transom of the Behavioral Science Unit—bizarre homicides, serial rapes, child murders, even cannibalism and disembowelment—were not like anything I, or most members of law enforcement, had ever seen. In terms of manpower, more than half of the eighteen thousand state and local law enforcement agencies around the country had fewer than ten officers on staff. Furthermore, because of the growing mobility in our society, a string of related crimes was often not committed within the same county or even state, and therefore wouldn't be seen by the same officers. A small-town cop could go his whole life and never see one of these crimes, and if he did it was the case of a lifetime.

But if we saw a report from Lake Sammamish, Washington, about a woman who had both hands chopped off, or a prostitute with messages carved in her abdomen, and then heard about a similar report from Apalachicola, Florida, the alarm bells sounded. We at the Behavioral Science Unit could do something local officials couldn't: spot common elements in the crimes and begin to connect the dots.

The way to become proficient is by working a lot of cases, and that's exactly what the BSU was beginning to do—linking seemingly unrelated crimes together and extracting meaningful information about the perpetrators. If an offender took his victim from a crowded area, we learned it was usually safe to assume he had good verbal skills and at least a measure of self-esteem. That's really the only way, short of brute force, that a child molester could get a little boy away from his mother in a shopping center. He might say, "You know, your mom could be quite a while in the store. Do you want to go and look at some video games with me?"

Similarly, we realized that if a rapist begins his assault on a woman by jumping her from behind and hitting her with his fist, you can tell a lot of things about him—that he is more primitive, less intelligent, and has little self-esteem. Brute force, rather than charm or seduction, is the major weapon he has. If a rapist of this type launches a brutal blitz, knocking the victim out completely, it may mean he actually fears direct contact with her. Rendering her unconscious not only puts him in complete control, but also eliminates having to confront her.

Some of those conclusions, in this day and age, might seem pedestrian. However, at the time they were pretty revolutionary. They marked the first time analytical observations about these very violent acts were being formalized on this scale. And that now, for the first time, a small, local police department without the resources or investigative expertise to handle a particularly baffling crime had a place to turn: the Behavioral Science Unit of the FBI. As a result of the training they'd received, National Academy graduates from around the country were returning to their departments and saying, "You know, guys, there's this thing they taught us about called profiling. You know those three unsolved cases that we've got? Why don't we see if they'll look at them for us?"

At the same time, the Unit was beginning to get the reputation as a potential resource within the Bureau, and our own parent agency began turning to us for help in emergency situations.

But as we all knew, behavioral science was not necessarily precise, and there was always the possibility we could be wrong. In fact, at the top of our profiles, a piece of boilerplate appeared, this from a faded early analysis we provided in the Atlanta Child Murders case: "The information provided is based upon reviewing, analyzing, and researching criminal cases similar to the case submitted by the requesting agency. The final analysis is based upon probabilities noting, however, that no two criminal acts or criminal personalities are exactly alike and therefore the offender at times may not always fit the profile in every category."

It was our own disclaimer, a way of making it clear that profiling wasn't infallible. But as the guy at the helm of the Unit, I didn't want us to be wrong, period. Especially in those early days when it really counted.

———

By the beginning of the 1970s, the term "hostage situation" usually meant one thing for law enforcement: assemble a tactical team and make your plans for containment or assault. There was no such thing as a hostage negotiation specialist. In fact, we were so naive in those days that we didn't know enough not to answer a demand for food by sending in coffee and donuts during a bank standoff—just the kind of sugar and caffeine jolt a jittery hostage-taker with a hair-trigger finger shouldn't have.

But at the Unit, we began to look at managing hostage/barricade situations and terrorism in a more enlightened way. For us, the goal wasn't going in with firepower. Our definition of success was to avoid bloodshed and get everyone out alive, including the hostage-taker. In 1976, the BSU spun off a unit that would come to be known as the Special Operations and Research Unit,

SOARS, which specialized in this new concept. And on a sweltering August night in 1979, we had the chance to try it.

Eight years earlier, on November 24, 1971, a man in a dark suit and sunglasses boarded the 2:50 p.m. Northwest Orient flight from Portland to Seattle and, in midflight, passed a note to a stewardess. He was carrying a bomb, he said, and he wanted two hundred thousand dollars, four parachutes, and "no funny stuff." After landing in Seattle, the passengers and flight attendants were allowed to disembark, and the FBI handed over the parachutes and money in used twenty-dollar bills. The man, who called himself Dan Cooper, then told the pilot to fly slowly at ten thousand feet in the direction of Nevada. Not long after takeoff, somewhere over southwest Washington, he gathered up the ransom, lowered the plane's back stairs, and parachuted into the night.

D. B. Cooper, as he was mistakenly referred to by a law enforcement officer, was never found, but he became an overnight celebrity in absentia, and "para-jacking" became an epidemic in American skies. Of thirty-one hijackings in the U.S. the following year, nineteen were Cooper-style extortion attempts, and fifteen demanded parachutes. Things got so bad that, as a protective measure, Boeing even installed a special latch on its 727s to prevent the tail stairs from being lowered in flight.

Against that backdrop, I got a call at the office one night from the executive assistant director of the FBI, informing me that there'd been a commercial airline hijacking at Sea-Tac (Seattle Tacoma International Airport). A 727 with fifty-five innocent people was on the tarmac, and it soon became apparent that its young hijacker thought that he was going to be the next D. B. Cooper. His demands included a hundred thousand dollars, a parachute, and use of the jet and its pilots, or, he said, he would blow up the plane and everyone onboard.

Headquarters wanted some "profilers" to head over to the FBI command center in Washington, D.C., to appraise the subject and help plan the negotiation strategy. When Jim Horn, Jim Reese, and I got to the FBI special ops center in the J. Edgar Hoover Building, we found ourselves in stellar company. This was a dangerous, high-stakes situation, and about twenty key players—including the executive assistant FBI director, bomb experts, and several FBI agents, some of whom were former pilots—had gathered in the operations room. On the ground in Seattle, another old buddy, Doug Cannon, who was a supervisor there at the time, had assembled state and local police, the FBI SWAT team, and his own squad of negotiators.

We had radios, computers, and open phone lines to Seattle, the Federal Aviation Administration, the National Weather Service, the Department of Transportation, and the Air Force all set up for us, and the FBI director was standing by to run interference with other agencies. We made sure that if we needed to say something to the hijacker, we had sufficient clout to get the president of the airline on the line. We also had to factor in what might happen to international flights and communications if a communication intended for the hijacker was overheard by other pilots, or if something we broadcast later proved to be erroneous. We knew we might not be able to take it back. All in all, it was a pretty tense time.

As emissaries from the BSU, we were onstage. While everyone else was laying the tactical groundwork, it was our assignment to do a personality assessment of the hijacker, plan a strategy, and guide the hostage negotiator about what might or might not work. At first word of the incident, agents in the

Seattle division had begun scrambling to try to ID this guy and, little by little, were able to find out who he was. Immediately, they ran background checks of available records, and sent agents to his neighborhood to interview anyone who might know him. At the same time, we made suggestions on what kind of questions to ask—to find out whether he was an inadequate personality, for instance, or had a history of instability. The more we knew about this cipher, the better we could predict his behavior in different scenarios.

Early on, it became apparent that the hijacker, identified as seventeen-year-old Glen Kurt Tripp, clearly had emotional problems. He wasn't particularly rational, and he wasn't very smart. He seemed too disordered and unsophisticated to be capable of devising a bomb and orchestrating its detonation. In short, we determined that he was bluffing. He had no bomb. The trick now was to get him out of the plane without anyone getting hurt. Mulling over the situation, we came up with what seemed like a workable plan: we'd concoct a story to convince him that because of the placement of the plane door, it wasn't possible for anyone to parachute out of it. The chute and lines would catch on the tail, we'd tell him, and he'd be ensnared and likely killed before he ever hit the ground.

Working with pilots and navigators who fed information to a hostage negotiator on the ground, we presented a bewildering array of stats on wind velocity, airflow, and the plane's flight trajectory. Tripp bought it. Within four hours, we negotiated him down from a hundred thousand dollars, a parachute, and a plane— to no money, a bag of McDonald's hamburgers, and a taxicab. When he deplaned and came down the gangplank, he saw a cab and driver waiting for him. What he didn't see was the SWAT team positioned under the aircraft. They swooped in, grabbed

Tripp, put the briefcase carrying the "bomb" on the tarmac, and spirited him away.

Afterward, we all exhaled for the first time in hours. "It's four a.m.," I said to Reese and Horn. "Let's get the hell out of here."

One of the guys in the command center looked up and said, "But that briefcase is still sitting on the tarmac. Aren't you going to stick around to see if it's a bomb?"

"Maybe *you* guys have to stick around to see if there's a bomb," I said, with bravado, "but *we* don't have to. We're going home."

My guys and I went outside, and as soon as we all got into the car, I said, "Quick. Turn on the radio, would you?"

"What for?" asked Reese.

"Because," I said, "I want to see if we were right."

We were. Though there was no bomb, Tripp was arrested for the hijacking, and later served time in a mental institution for his crime. But in January of 1983, after being released, he tried the same dangerous stunt again, this time in Portland, on the same flight number. Only this time, as Tripp held passengers in the cabin, two SWAT-trained FBI agents climbed up and quietly entered the cockpit through the co-pilot's window. Crew members opened the locked cockpit door, and the agents told Tripp, who was brandishing what he said was a bomb, to freeze. Instead, the young man reached into his pocket as if to detonate it, and the lead agent fired one round into his chest. Tripp was declared dead at the scene.

It wasn't an outcome anyone wanted, and I certainly would have been more cautious the second time around. But within the sad news was a kind of validation. We'd obviously been correct in our psychological assessment that Tripp was too disordered to plant and detonate a bomb. Because after his second, and fatal, hijacking attempt, Tripp's alleged "explosive device" was X-rayed after being removed by the Portland bomb squad, and it turned out to contain nothing more than a wad of crumpled-up paper.

That wasn't the only time we had the chance to show the FBI just what its own behavioral science team could do. In the summer of 1983, a series of suspicious fires broke out in the city of West Hartford, Connecticut. The first two were set at synagogues, the third at a rabbi's home, and the fourth, in the predawn hours of Yom Kippur, at the home of a Jewish state representative. Despite working double shifts and adding extra patrols, local police hadn't come up with any leads. The situation was potentially volatile because of rising fear within the close-knit Jewish community that these were anti-Semitic hate crimes. Since the case was a possible civil rights violation, the FBI was brought in. Lon Lacey, the special agent in charge (SAC) of Hartford, called me, outlined the case, and asked if the Unit might be able to help. "We've done some work on fire setting," I said. "I think we can."

I'd heard about the work of a bright young Ph.D. from Cleveland, Dave Icove, who was making some pioneering inroads in the field of arson investigation. Dave could plug stats about a particular arson into a computerized system, plot the geographical results on a map, and use it as a tool to help predict where follow-up fires were likeliest to occur, and where the fire setter would live or work. After mulling over the Connecticut case, I called and asked him to pack up his computer and go to West Hartford, where he teamed up with one of our best new profilers, a guy by the name of Blaine MacIlwaine.

My game plan was to have Icove set up his grid, have Mac construct a profile of the fire setter, and then put the two together to start canvassing the area. They got to work, studying every angle of the case, even flying overhead for an aerial view of the neighborhood. At first, the only thing they knew for sure was that the arsonist disappeared into thin air after every fire. But as they looked into the case, they found some interesting things.

In the first fire, set at the Young Israel Synagogue, the most severe damage was to the reading table and the ark, both significant religious symbols. In the second synagogue, the offender burned the Torahs from right to left, in the same direction in which they are read in Hebrew. And in the most bizarre twist of all, when they examined phone records from the first synagogue, they found eighty-five phone calls placed from it to a series of bars and strip joints in Dallas, Texas.

Mac's written analysis determined that the fires were not the work of anti-Semites or the Klan, but instead of a "mission-oriented" inadequate personality who in his daily life was having trouble with authority figures. Because the fire setter was able to make eighty-five phone calls to strip clubs from the first synagogue and remain undetected, chances were that he was comfortable and familiar with the place. He did not have successful sexual relationships with women, was engaging in sexual sublimation, and was probably still living at home with his parents, or perhaps a dominant female figure, such as his mother. Since he'd moved through the community without causing suspicion, he was likely from the area. And his physical appearance would reflect his low self-esteem. Since he saw himself as weak, inconsequential, and almost invisible, he was probably thin and small, rather than overweight, and might well have a physical problem, like a speech impediment or bad acne. The bottom line, said Mac, was that we weren't looking for a neo-Nazi. Our most likely suspect was a troubled young Jewish kid.

Needless to say, the profile caused a bit of an uproar in some quarters. But I knew Mac was competent, and we stuck with his program. In the meantime, Dave constructed his maps showing the locations of all the fires, and drew a small circle indicating where he thought we'd locate the perp. Then investigators started canvassing the area. At the second door they knocked on, when they provided a description of the suspect, the man turned to his wife and said, "That sounds like our son."

On December 14, 1983, seventeen-year-old Barry Dov Schuss surrendered voluntarily to police. He ultimately received a fourteen-year prison term, which was suspended on the condition he receive in-patient treatment at a private psychiatric hospital. He was thin, slight, emotionally troubled, and had a history of psychiatric problems. And he was Jewish. In fact, about the only detail that diverged from Mac's profile was the lack of a physical disability—unless you counted the boy's thick, Coke-bottle eyeglasses.

"Rog, you're not gonna believe how well this thing worked," Dave Icove said when he called to give me the details. "What should I do?"

Easy, I said, breathing a huge sigh of relief. "Act like it happens all the time."

By that time, I was completely immersed in the job, not just staying on top of cases and running the Unit, but also waging a campaign to make sure it gained the recognition it deserved. Sometimes I felt like a lone voice in the wilderness, but I used whatever ammunition I could to make sure the higher-ups realized the value of what we were doing. One piece of early evidence came in 1981, when we asked Howard Teten, then chief of the research and development unit, to try to come up with some hard numbers that would demonstrate the value of profiling. His team went back to state and local law enforcement agencies who had come to us for help in a total of one hundred ninety-two serious cases, and asked if the psychological profiles we provided had been useful.

These cases were all old dogs in the first place, crimes where all means of logical investigation had already been tried, and had failed. If they were easy, they would've been solved long ago, but now, in terms of solvability potential, they were the worst of the worst. It would've been remarkable if even one in a hundred were solved. As it was, the survey showed that suspects had now been identified in eighty-eight, or nearly half, of those one hundred ninety-two cases, and in sixty-eight, psychological profiling was what had refocused the investigation. Even more incredible was that in fifteen cases, profiling had identified a suspect outright.

Whether or not profiling had led directly to an arrest, the respondents called it valuable in nearly all of the cases, because it spurred thorough, complete investigations. "All users overwhelmingly agreed that the service should be continued," the report said. In short, even in those early days, we were getting feedback, straight from the horse's mouth, that profiling was a useful tool for law enforcement.

Before long, so many requests for help were streaming into the Unit that I sometimes felt we were on a treadmill, struggling to keep up with the growing caseload. Still, I found the work exhilarating, even if the deadlines were a little challenging. Sometimes, as on the evening of August 17, 1982, it seemed as if we were playing mental speed chess with perpetrators, and the stakes were people's lives.

That night at around 6:00 p.m. just as we were all getting ready to go home for the day, I got a phone call from the Springfield, Illinois, field office telling us that a couple—Dr. Hector Ze-vallos and his wife, Rosalie, also an M.D.—had been kidnapped from their home in nearby Edwardsville. A short time later, after an anonymous tip, a ransom note was found by FBI agents taped under the sink of a public restroom in a city park, along with a forty-four-page manifesto called "The Epistle."

The Springfield SAC made it clear this was no leisurely as-signment. There was the very real possibility that two people might be killed within hours, and we needed to move as quickly as possible. "Fax us the document," I said. "We'll see what we can do."

I did a quick spin around the office to see who was still around—Roy Hazelwood, Ken Lanning, and Dick Ault—and I called them in. We all sat down around a conference table, and I dealt pages of the document out like a deck of cards. Then we all started speed-reading.

"Okay, so what do we have here?" I said, and started going around the table.

"Male, undoubtedly white. Late thirties, early forties." "Col-lege education or above." "Extensive religious training, possible former seminarian. Protestant, not Catholic."

"Professional, born in the U.S., middle-American upbringing, married with children, recent marital stress." "If he has military service, he's a veteran of ground forces, either Army or Marine Corps, possibly an officer."

"It mentions that Zevallos works at an abortion clinic, so there's the religious angle. The perp's mission-oriented."

"On page six, evidence he's had some recent problems with the court. He's bitter. He's made some comments about the judicial system. Maybe not criminal, but civil court."

I was furiously writing everything down. And so it went, for the next ninety minutes.

The kidnapper, I believed, exhibited some characteristics of chronic paranoia, but was also capable of logical and clear thought processes. He wasn't "insane" as such, but could rationalize killing because he viewed himself as an instrument of God. He'd manifested a marked change in behavior within the past three years—from conservative and reserved, to obsessed with abortion, bordering on the delusional. He was a member of a civic group such as Kiwanis, Rotary, or Civitan, was patriotic, a compulsive letter writer in the past. May have lost a job, been laid off from a government job, been bounced from the military, or had other negative experiences with "the establishment." He was a neat to meticulous dresser. Lived in a comfortable, single-family home. Drove a conservative, four-door family-type vehicle, either sedan or station wagon, well maintained, four or more years old.

By the time we finished, it was just getting dark out. The whole process had taken a couple of hours, tops.

"That it?" I said.

A moment of silence. From around the table, a collective, "Yeah."

"Okay, I'm going to call 'em." I did, and when Springfield answered, I asked if they had a stenographer. They did, and I dictated the results over the phone.

As it turned out, the Zevalloses operated an abortion clinic, and had been kidnapped by one Don Benny Anderson, an Oxford, Wisconsin, father of seven, who called himself the leader of a group called the Army of God. Along with two accomplices, Anderson held the couple for eight days in an abandoned ammunition bunker, and vowed to kill both unless they pledged to stop performing abortions. They did, and both were released.

The following year, we got a letter from the Springfield office with a follow-up report to tell us how accurate our profile was. It had led them to identify the perpetrator, someone they'd completely overlooked—a guy who was actually in their custody on another, unrelated charge.

Consistent with our analysis, Anderson had been involved in a string of assaults against abortion clinics, including attempted bombings. His wife told investigators her husband's behavior had changed dramatically two years before, when he was convicted of illegal efforts in attempting to have a tenant evicted from a home he was foreclosing. Ever since, he'd considered the government to be "screwed up," and had claimed to be receiving direct revelation from God that he was to perform a mission.

In fact, wrote the SAC, the only characteristic we predicted that definitely wasn't present was that Anderson was not a military veteran. In addition, the letter said, "It should be noted that the profile analysis points out that the writer of the epistle would own a family-type vehicle, a 4-door station wagon, a functional kind of vehicle, and that it would be four years old or older." Anderson had used one particular vehicle in his travels to abortion clinics in Illinois and Texas, it said: "a 1976 Ford LTD, 4-door sedan, dark blue over silver gray in color."

That wasn't the sum total of the BSU's contribution, though. Five years before, Tom Strentz, another member of the Unit who'd taught one of the original criminal psych courses with Con Hassel at the Academy, did most of the original research on something known as the Stockholm Syndrome, a term they coined to describe a psychological phenomenon that occurred in the wake of a 1973 bank robbery in Sweden, in which the victims began to identify with their captors.

Special agent Carl "Dutch" Schultz, who was an outstanding hostage negotiator in the St. Louis field office, interviewed the Zevalloses after their release, and learned they hadn't had an easy time of it during their ordeal. The kidnappers, for example, put headphones on them and played deafening music to disorient them. Schultz realized that Hector Zevallos was trying to provide as much information as he could to help investigators, but his wife, Rosalie, seemed far more reluctant to talk. When he learned Hector had been blindfolded for the entire time—while his wife's blindfold was periodically removed at the kidnappers' discretion—it occurred to him she might be a victim of the syndrome.

Schultz decided to explain the phenomenon to Rosalie, and gently, he introduced the idea to her. "What do you call that again?" she said. "I've never heard of it."

Drawing on the BSU's analysis and insights, he explained how the syndrome is an automatic and often unconscious emotional response to the trauma of being victimized, and that it can actually be a good thing, because it enhances a victim's chances of survival. The more Schultz talked, the more interested Rosalie became. And it didn't take long for her to understand not only the concept but also to realize that she herself had fallen victim to the phenomenon. Suddenly, it was as if a light bulb flashed on. At first, she'd been reticent. Now, she looked at Schultz and said, "What do you want to know?" The testimony she provided contributed to Anderson's eventual conviction for the kidnapping, and was the first salvo fired at the so-called Army of God, a dangerous radical group later implicated in a string of deadly bombings and assaults.

Despite our inroads, the Unit was still taking a lot of criticism from other unit chiefs who either didn't understand what we were doing, or didn't realize its importance. Sometimes it meant playing the tough guy at meetings with management. Whenever they turned negative, I'd jump right in with a little Detroit attitude. I'd say, "My phone's always ringing with requests for help in major investigations. How many times does your phone ring over there in management with calls like that, huh? How many times?" That would shut 'em up.

In 1980, the year after I took over the Unit, the first publication about our work appeared when Dick Ault and Jim Reese co-authored an article in the *FBI Law Enforcement Bulletin* entitled "Profiling: A Psychological Assessment of Crime." The fact that FBI brass gave permission to publish it at all represented the first internal acknowledgment of the significance of the work that we were doing. Then, in 1981, John Hinckley tried to assassinate President Ronald Reagan.

By that time, Bob Ressler had begun delving into the mind of the assassin, interviewing Sirhan Sirhan, Arthur Bremer, Squeaky Fromme, and Sara Jane Moore as part of his research. One of the things we were learning was that in foreign countries, assassinations were often politically motivated. But in the U.S. they were more frequently carried out by aberrant types, mentally disturbed persons, or inadequate personalities who saw assassination of a high-visibility public figure as a way to gain the fame and acknowledgment they so craved.

Hinckley was already in custody, but the Bureau needed some guidance on what kinds of materials to look for when agents searched his motel room and home in Colorado, and Ressler was summoned to the case. Investigators especially wanted anything providing a record of Hinckley's strange obsessions, premeditations, or attempts to make contact with the president. It was a critical time, since, as we knew, agents on the scene might well overlook material that could shed light on Hinckley's fantasies, or reveal key evidence crucial for a successful prosecution. There was tremendous pressure to make sure that affidavits and search warrants were prepared thoroughly.

After hearing what the FBI already knew about Hinckley, Ressler quickly dismissed the idea that he was a paid assassin or part of a conspiracy. Hinckley, he said, would prove to be an introvert, a loner, and, as someone who was likely unable to establish satisfactory romantic relationships, was likely consumed by fantasy. Ressler told the agents to seize any materials that might contain them: diaries, books, magazines, scrapbooks, even a tape recorder and audiotapes. He also suggested there might be photographs related to Hinckley's fantasies. In all, Ressler came up with a dozen items in his list of probable finds, all of which were incorporated into the search warrant.

Remarkably, nearly everything he specified was later found among Hinckley's possessions. There were tapes of his conversation with Jodie Foster, an annotated script of *Taxi Driver*—a film about an assassin in which Foster had a role—and a postcard with a picture of the Reagans that Hinckley had addressed to Foster, along with the notation, "One day you and I will occupy the White House and the peasants will drool with envy." There was also a photograph of Hinckley taken shortly before his attempt on the president's life, posing in front of the building where Abraham Lincoln was assassinated—Ford's Theatre in Washington, D.C., as well as a snapshot showing him in front of the White House. It wouldn't be much of a stretch to argue that the photographs were tangible indicators of Hinckley's personal plan to make sure that he'd have a place in the history books—the would-be assassin's Holy Grail.

———————————

Over time, I realized that in order for the Unit to stay afloat, we were going to have to standardize operating procedures, and so we did. Whenever a request for help came in, one agent would be assigned the case, and it was his job to become thoroughly familiar with every aspect of it. Except in extraordinary cases, profilers rarely visited the crime scene themselves. Instead, they would begin reading hundreds, if not thousands, of pages of interview transcripts, as well as investigative, autopsy, forensic, and toxicology reports, and would also view any photographs, maps, or aerial views of the crime scene. We were called into crimes, after all, only after local police had come to a dead end. Our goal was to see an unsolved case with a completely fresh eye, to disregard any pre-existing theories, and be as coolly analytical as possible. We weren't trying to learn what the local detectives thought. We were trying to think the way the criminal thinks.

The analytical techniques we were developing fanned out into a whole range of crimes and subspecialties. The BSU's elite corps of mindhunters, as they came to be known, were all pretty proficient at homicides, but as the workload increased, the profilers began to diversify, too. Beginning as early as the mid-1970s, Con Hassel and Tom Strentz specialized in the psychology of hostage takers; John Minderman, Jim Reese, and Jim Horn were turning their attention to stress management, helping treat agents who were experiencing post-traumatic stress after terrible experiences in kidnappings, shootings, and murders. Dick Ault was looking into the characteristics of traitors and spies, Ken Lanning delved into child abuse and crimes against children, and Roy Hazelwood turned his attention to rapists, the sexually oriented killer, and crimes of sexual predation.

It was fascinating to see how the work they chose dovetailed with their personalities. When Dick Ault decided to focus on the study of spies, for example, I can't say it surprised me. The most cerebral agents I ever knew tended to be the ones working espionage, and in terms of sheer intellectual brainpower, they were among the most impressive. An ordinary homicide almost always leaves some sort of evidence—a body, the clues at a crime scene. But in the tradecraft of the spy, the whole idea is either to hide evidence altogether, or else to plant false clues to throw the investigator off the track. It's as if the profiler is working in a world of smoke and mirrors, where secrecy is paramount, and things aren't necessarily what they seem. It takes a certain kind of mind to be able to see through those distortions to the eventual end-game, and that's the kind of incisive mind Dick had. He also had a temper, and was sometimes a little too outspoken. But hands down, he was the single best clinical psychologist I had in the Unit—meticulous, precise, and cerebral.

Ken Lanning was equally impressive, but in a different way. Somewhere in him was the ability to compartmentalize his work, to keep aspects of it separate from his personal life. I believe that's why he was so gifted at doing the work he chose, which was the study of the monsters who prey on children. Ken saw some of the darkest crimes imaginable, perpetrated against the most helpless of all victims, and some of us wondered how he could handle those kinds of cases, especially since he had kids of his own. I can't explain precisely why he was able to do it, but I think that in Ken's case, the urge to fight evil was just somehow stronger than the impulse to turn away.

Roy Hazelwood was an introspective type, a true perfectionist, and absolutely the best profiler when it came to crimes of sexual predation. After arriving in 1978, he took over the sex crimes course, officially called "Interpersonal Violence," and transformed it from what I used to call a "porn show for cops" into one of the most sophisticated and valuable investigative courses at the Academy. Later on, his research, based on prison interviews with forty-one notorious serial rapists, revolutionized the process of rape investigation.

In later 1980, Roy'd been invited by the Atlanta police department to consult on the city's investigation into a case beginning to make national headlines, the murders of a string of young black children in some of the city's poorest neighborhoods. By June of that year, eight boys and two girls were dead, and if that wasn't bad enough, existing racial tensions in the city were being ignited by rumors that the killings were a white-led, racist plot.

After he arrived, Roy began studying the case, and became convinced almost immediately that the deaths of at least some of the victims were the work of the same person. Roy also visited many of the black neighborhoods where the crimes took place, and was struck by how much attention that he, as a white man, attracted, just by his presence. "People stopped talking to each other and stared at us," he would later write. "It was like one of those old E. F. Hutton ads on television." It was enough to bring Roy to the conclusion that, in order to have moved freely and unnoticed in those areas, the killer had to have been black.

It took guts to come to a conclusion that flew in the face of prevailing thought, but Roy, like every one of the profilers, was perfectly capable of making the tough calls. In fact, it sometimes seemed as if a strong ego was a requisite for the job. That attribute was probably nowhere more evident than in John Douglas and Bob Ressler, who began to specialize in the horrific cases that would eventually be most associated in the public mind with the Behavioral Science Unit—the handiwork of the serial killer.

Of all the profilers, Ressler was the most tenacious. When he was tracking a case, he was like a hound dog on a scent. If you were a killer, you wouldn't want him on your trail, because he would pursue you until the end. He also jealously guarded his territory. He didn't want anyone else horning in on his work, to the point that, as Unit chief, I sometimes had to say, "Hey, Bob, let some of the other guys have a piece of the action."

Douglas, on the other hand, was more laissez-faire, and also probably the best all-around profiler in the BSU. John, who joined the Unit in 1977, and became head of a unit subgroup called the Profiling and Consultation Program, could generally get more out of a study of the life of the killer's victim—what we called "victimology"—than other agents could from an entire case. Douglas had remarkable intuitive powers, but he wasn't as territorial as Ressler. If anyone was around when he found something interesting, he was likely to say, "Hey, take a look at this," or, "We talked to so-and-so and this is what he told us." Douglas was an open, honest guy, maybe a little too open sometimes. At one point, he got into trouble by talking to the media too much, and I had to defend him to the boss.

In his book *Mindhunter*, Douglas wrote: "Profiling is like writing. You can give a computer all the rules of grammar and syntax and style, but it still can't write the book." I certainly can't argue with that. Most of the really good profilers had strong egos. I remember once asking a friend who was a nurse what single quality is necessary to be a good cancer surgeon. Without batting an eye, she said, "Megalomania." It was a joke—partly. The point is that someone who has to make high-pressure judgments about life and death isn't very likely to be successful if he's indecisive, prone to excessive self-examination, or inclined to constantly second-guess himself. Self-assuredness is, if not a job requirement, then at least not too surprising a quality in the type of personality drawn to such work.

I think there's an analogy with top-notch profilers. You have to be smart, prepared, and ready to go with your instincts. When I found someone with all of those qualities, along with the rare gift for reading the criminal mind the way my team did, then I was willing to excuse a little bravado, especially if they were getting results. And they were.

Not long after Roy made the Unit's first trip to Atlanta on the child murders case, he called Douglas, and the two worked together to construct a profile of the unknown subject, or "unsub." According to their analysis, the killer was an African-American male in his mid- to late twenties, responsible for most, but not all, of what would eventually reach thirty homicides, was intelligent, from a middle-class or higher socioeconomic background, and was single, sexually inadequate, and attractive to children. He also craved attention so much that he might well have insinuated himself into the investigation. Lastly, because he longed for the trappings of power, we might find him driving an old police car, or else a model resembling one.

Police began looking for just that kind of guy, and when Wayne Williams, a single black freelance photographer and musician, came under suspicion after being spotted not far from one of the crime scenes, he matched virtually every one of those traits, right down to the last detail, including his age. At the time he was apprehended in June of 1981, Williams, who was eventually convicted in two of the murders, was twenty-three years old. Roy and Douglas had nailed that, too.

In the late 1970s, while teaching what we called "road schools"—intensive versions of Academy courses that Quantico instructors taught to local police departments and training groups around the country—Ressler got an idea. There were a lot of criminals in prison, some on death row, who'd committed heinous crimes, and had never really been asked about how and why they committed them. Many of these offenders were no longer of any interest to the justice system, and there was nothing for them to gain by cooperating with us, in terms of a lighter sentence, points toward parole, or any information that might aid in an appeal. That was when he and Douglas began to kick around the idea of going straight to the source. "Why don't we go into the prisons ourselves," they thought, "and ask these killers if they ever returned to the scene of the crime, or if they were in the area when the body was found, and if so, why?"

As a result, over the next five years, members of the Unit would interview more than fifty violent offenders in American prisons and penitentiaries, including thirty-six sexually motivated serial killers. Not just the superstars like Charles Manson and David Berkowitz and Richard Speck, but also the lesser-knowns: Richard Marquette, who murdered and dismembered a woman in Portland, Oregon, and then, after being paroled from prison after serving twelve years, killed and dissected two more women before being captured; or Jerome Brudos, who had a bizarre shoe fetish, and cut off the feet and breasts of four women after dressing them in his own collection of female clothing.

The first wave of prison interviews was conducted by Ressler and Douglas, and in 1979, Ressler was officially put in charge of the effort, called the Criminality Personality Research Project.

After the first twenty or so, everyone participated—John Campbell, Jim Horn, Jim Reese, Ault, Hazelwood, and Ken Lanning, the expert in crimes against children. Every interview was different, and each profiler brought something to the process. Ressler and Douglas, for example, never hesitated to be confrontational, even combative in interviews, getting right into the faces of the killers, if that was what it took to break through their BS. Roy, on the other hand, tended to be more clinical in his approach, and made a point of being completely neutral and nonjudgmental, even when interviewing the most brutal sexual sadists. It was a technique that worked for him, talking with offenders about their crimes on an equal footing, in the most matter-of-fact way.

As head of the Unit, part of my job was managing these independent, sometimes headstrong, and very different personalities, and it wasn't always easy. I sometimes felt like the coach of a team with eleven quarterbacks who were all trying to call the plays and threatening to head off in different directions. I remember many a meeting when the crossfire got loud, and I had to intervene with an "All right, that's *ENOUGH!*"

But I also realized that sometimes what was required was the velvet glove. My office had two doors, and I made a point of keeping both of them open, more as a statement of principle than anything else. I wanted to let everyone on the Unit know I was always available to them, and I was happy to help steer, guide, and offer insights where I could.

One afternoon in 1985, we were having a meeting when the name Ted Bundy came up. Bundy, then on death row in the state prison in Starke, Florida, was the most calculating and cunning of all the serial killers, and a suspect in the murders of at least thirty-six young women. Obviously, we wanted to talk with him, but Bob Ressler had tried and gotten nowhere. At this meeting, when a new profiler named Bill Hagmaier spoke up and volunteered to make an approach to Bundy, the other agents shut him down. "What makes you think he's going to talk to you?" they said. "We've been at this a lot longer than you have, and he's not going to talk to anyone." The reaction was part genuine cynicism, and part hazing. Bill backed down and didn't say anything more about it.

A little while later, I ran into him in the hall and asked if he had a minute. I'd thought about the idea of having him try to talk to Bundy, and it wasn't that far fetched to me. In a way, Bill was an innocent among the other members of the team—sincere, earnest, and, I suppose, still a little new to how the game was played. It seemed to me that such an interrogator might actually stand a better shot of getting through to the notorious Bundy than one of the more experienced types. Maybe a killer who fancied himself a great intellect would be more inclined to talk to a young man who, at least on first impression, came across as just a bit pliable and naive. At the very worst, Bundy might try to toy with him. But what was the harm in a cat-and-mouse game? If Hag was eventually shot down, he could survive a little wounded pride. And there was potentially so much to gain. As far as I was concerned, it was a no-lose situation.

"You know, Bill, if you feel you've got a shot at getting this interview, then I think you ought to follow through," I said. "No one else has been able to get to Bundy, and maybe you're the guy. At least that's the way I feel about it. And I just wanted you to know that if you decide to go ahead, I'm behind you a hundred percent."

According to Bill, my encouragement was what tipped the scales. He decided to go ahead and write a letter to Bundy, and on January 14, 1986, Bundy responded from the Florida State Prison in Starke.

"Dear Mr. Hagmaier," he wrote. "No problem. You're certainly welcome if you want to drop by. I would certainly be interested in talking with you about the research being done by the BSU. . . . P.S. If you do come to see me, please make sure to take extra care that it is not announced to the entire wing that the FBI is here to see me. . . . I don't need the rumors that such a bit of news would spawn."

Over the next three years, Hagmaier would have a number of personal meetings with Bundy, and carry on a correspondence that resulted in a thick black loose-leaf binder filled with dozens of Bundy's handwritten letters. It was obvious that this sociopath had his own agenda. In claiming to provide information about what may have been as many as a hundred murders, and holding out the promise that he could be useful to police in their investigation of the then unsolved Green River Killings, he was proving yet again how manipulative he could be. At one point, his attorney called me and said the FBI should continue studying him because he could shed such tremendous light on the mind of the serial killer. He wanted us to stop the execution. I told him it was too late. We'd completed our research.

In the end, of course, Bundy didn't help catch the Green River Killer. He was only feigning to offer help as a means of forestalling his own execution. But that doesn't mean he didn't help us nonetheless. One of the other profilers once accused Bill of having his objectivity clouded by getting too close to Bundy. I didn't see it that way. In January 1989, Bill spent four harrowing days at Starke, talking with the killer just before his execution. That was when, in what amounted to a deathbed confession, Bundy admitted to murdering at least thirty women and girls.

Beyond that, as I saw it, everything that Bill got from Bundy added to our overall proficiency in dealing with serial killers. It provided a chilling look into the darkest recesses of their minds. In the broadest sense, like all the interviews, it helped flesh out a picture of the true enormity we were up against.

Bundy talked about forcing his helpless victims to re-create his favorite pornographic poses, and about how he cut the heads and hands off at least a dozen corpses with a hacksaw, to impede identification. He talked about how, in one dual murder, he kept one victim alive so she could see her friend being killed. He talked about clubbing his victims with a crowbar, handcuffing them, and then chatting with them when they regained consciousness, just for sport. The one thing he never expressed was remorse. Not a word of it. Ever.

Hagmaier later said the one thing that Bundy didn't understand was why ordinary people simply couldn't grasp the fact that the reason he killed was because he wanted to kill. But in all of the conversations and correspondence with Bundy, the words that are still clearest in my mind were the ones he used to describe his own feelings at the precise moment of taking another human life.

"You feel the last bit of breath leaving their body," he said, lost in a reverie. "You're looking into their eyes. A person in that situation is *God*."

CHAPTER SIX

THE VALLEY OF DEATH

SHE HAD BEEN PLAYING *out in front of the house, eating a Popsicle, when she disappeared. No one saw who took her, but even the most naive knew why. A little girl, blond, blue eyes. Loved and perfect and without guile. It would have been easy, for anyone who had the intent. A sudden stop, an opened car door, a quick sweep of the arm. A pillow or blanket, perhaps, to stifle the cries. She would not have fought. She would not have known to. She was three years old.*

Her parents, working-class, searched, cried, panicked, called the police. Did not sleep, refused food, went through the motions. Three days gone by, without a trace of her. The detectives knew what that meant, as did the savvier reporters and even the novice foot patrolmen, who had not experienced this kind of thing before. They did not say or acknowledge it, but they all understood. The unwritten expiration date had passed.

As the witness, an amateur naturalist, remembered it, dawn broke damp and cold that August morning in the mountains, foretelling winter. These were gentle people, the two of them, a man and woman, hiking through the remote, rock-strewn foothills of Colorado. Birdwatchers who had ventured out in hopes of spotting something rare this time. They had glimpsed a flash of red on the wing, through the conifers, and found a deep blue feather lying, as if discarded, on the trail. Nothing more. And then they heard it. Thin, high-pitched, faint at first. They stopped, straining to listen, poised like animals trying not to break the stillness.

Then it came again, undeniably, a sound like keening. They edged closer, following its lead, trying to place the sound. A young fox, possibly, or a feral kitten. Then, through the trees, they made out what looked like a shack, a weathered outhouse standing in the vicinity of the sound. They listened again, motionless, and heard it.

"Mommy."

As he would later tell it, they at first thought it was a terrible joke. Hunters in the woods hiding a tape recorder, for a prank. But even in that initial moment, against all reason, he knew what it was.

"Where are you?" he called.

The voice came back, small and insistent. "I'm here."

The sound came from below ground. He drew out a flashlight, wedged himself into the privy and pointed it down, into the darkness. There in the pit, twelve feet down and barely visible amid the filth and excrement, he could just make out the sight of it—two blue eyes.

"What are you doing there?" he asked the voice.

"I live here," it said.

From the mountains outside Denver came news of the miracle. When found, wearing just panties, she had survived for three frigid nights in the stench and cold. Her abductor had done what everyone feared, but not all of it. When he was finished, he did not kill her, did not have the mercy to end her life as one would an injured dog's. Instead, in a perfectly articulated gesture of contempt, he had committed one final act of disdain. After defiling her for his own pleasure, he had discarded her, defecated her, as one detective put it, into a residual pool of human waste.

So young, she had of course not understood it all. When the nice policeman asked her, gently, how it had been, she explained: "There were monsters in there. But I fell asleep." A child's fantasy, of course, because, as everyone knows, there are no such things as monsters. Just the woods, and an earthen pit, and the man who put her there.

It would be easy enough to wallow in the horror of it, but some chose not to focus on that. What they remembered was what came later, when the investigators peered down into the hole, and saw what she had done. From the dirt walls grew branches and tree roots, gnarled like an old woman's fingers. Somehow, with small hands, she had broken them off and collected them. At least, that was what the investigators surmised. Because at the edge of the pit, just above the foul morass, was a small platform, built of sticks and twigs. A nest.

For three days, the little girl perched there, calling out to be saved. And on the morning of her rescue, when a strong man's arm reached down to her in the dark, she clung to it tightly, and was pulled up into the light.

It sometimes seemed as if there was no end to the evil crossing our threshold. That particular case, which happened in 1983, was especially haunting. But there were others. Just when you think you've seen the worst thing one human being can do to another, something even worse comes along. A rape? Bad enough— forcible vaginal penetration with a penis. But what about someone who uses his penis to penetrate a wound in a living or dead victim? I saw that, too. And, just when I thought that was the lowest thing one human being could do to another, I learned about the practices of an Edmund Kemper or a Jeffrey Dahmer, who decapitated their victims, and then had sex with the heads of the deceased.

If asked, nearly every seasoned member of law enforcement can name his "once-in-a-lifetime case," a particularly vicious or complex crime that leaves an indelible mark on his psyche. The members of the Behavioral Science Unit could each name fifty or sixty. Every case we handled was one-of-a-kind. What it meant in practical terms was that members of the Unit were gaining a unique perspective on the darkest crimes man commits. Not only did they become intimately familiar with the details of those acts, but they also saw more of them than perhaps any other investigative body, anywhere.

In 1979, fifty requests for profiles were received by the Investigative Support Program alone—the BSU offshoot headed by John Douglas that provided aid on unsolved homicides. The next year, the number of requests doubled, and in succeeding years it would grow at an even faster rate. The Behavioral Science Unit was becoming a court of last resort, brought in to consult on the most serious crimes, but only after all other avenues of investigation had failed. The Unit became a repository of unusual, bizarre, and particularly violent crimes—a type most local jurisdictions had never seen.

The work itself was terribly isolating, and in some ways, we became a world unto ourselves, joined by shared experience, a common sense of purpose, and even a language of our own. The last became clear one day on the elevator in the Academy library. A sweet young college girl, an intern, was on the elevator when one of our agents talking about a case with a colleague casually referred to it as "a stick job," which was our shorthand for a crime in which a foreign object had been inserted into the victim's vagina. That caused a bit of a dustup with the library staff, and I had to remind everyone they needed to be really careful about talking shop when civilians were around.

Still, even with everything we knew about homicide at the time, there remained a whole list of unanswered questions about the nature of these crimes. Some were age-old: "Does the killer return to the scene of the crime?" "Is the killer in the crowd when the body is found?" We were interested in taking those questions a step further, in becoming more sophisticated about our approach. How does a killer select a particular victim, and why? How does he control that victim, or—as in the case of Richard Speck, who murdered eight student nurses in Chicago in 1966— more than one victim at the same time? We of course had hunches, but quantifiable, hard, and fast answers simply didn't exist.

The more I thought about it, the more it seemed to me that trying to study criminals without analyzing their crimes was like claiming to understand van Gogh's genius without ever having seen his paintings. Just the idea of it was absurd. Anyone who studies an artist wants to know the inspiration for his work, wants an answer to the question of how he creates magnificence where others—even those more intelligent or technically proficient—can't. It's no different with serial killers. Their legacy, their "greatest work of art," is the string of crime scenes they leave behind. Crime is significant human behavior, and homicide is the single most significant act of crime. How, I asked, could anyone truly understand the criminal without looking at his most significant act?

There are always messages at crime scenes, intentional or not.

The victim will leave clues about what happened in the struggle to survive; the killer will leave traces of his personality—rage, anger, degree of impulsivity. If you read those clues, you can extrapolate to make assumptions about the killer's nonhomicidal behavior. If he's impulsive at the crime scene, he'll be impulsive in real life. If he's enraged at his victim, he'll show flashes of anger in daily life.

That was why it was so crucial to go into prisons and interview the killers themselves. For the first time, we were dealing with them on their home turf, stepping through the looking glass, to see whether or not what we learned from them matched up with the conclusions we'd come to after observing the scenes of their crimes.

In the late 1970s, Ressler and Douglas conducted the very first inmate interview, with Edmund Kemper, a six-foot-nine, three-hundred-pound necrophile with an IQ of 140 who was serving seven life sentences at the California State Prison at Vacaville. Kemper had killed six young women in the vicinity of the University of California at Santa Cruz, but not before he'd already murdered his own grandparents. His final victim was his own mother, whom he decapitated. With his high intelligence and cool, rational manner, Kemper was the antithesis of a wild-eyed perpetrator. He was intelligent, aware, deliberate, well spoken and apparently without any remorse.

At home late at night, as I listened to the tapes, I was struck by how Kemper's terrible crimes hadn't just exploded out of nowhere. They seemed to have started tentatively at first, and then escalated over time. Early on, before he began actually murdering coeds, he seemed genuinely curious to see whether or not hitchhiking girls would even get into his car with him.

A few did. At first, he just talked with them, drove them where they wanted to go, and let them out. But after a time, that changed. He had a gun, and when he got two girls in the car, he put one in the trunk, drove to some woods, and murdered the other. The second one was still conscious. She would have heard her friend being killed, and known the same thing was going to happen to her. The horror was terrible, but what struck me was the escalation in his killing. He had started out tentatively, and then it had grown. It seemed to me that these killers didn't necessarily emerge full-blown. They, like any novice, had to work up to things. Sometimes they killed out of curiosity, sometimes as a means of gaining expertise.

Later in the tapes, Kemper talked about how, after decapitating several of his victims, he had conversations with the heads, had sex with them, and then sometimes perched them on the backs of chairs. Once, he said, one of the heads fell. A full-grown human head can weigh fifteen or twenty pounds, and when it hit the floor, it must have sounded like a bowling ball. Hearing the noise, the downstairs tenant apparently yelled up about keeping the noise down. Kemper leaned out his window and shouted, "I'm sorry. I lost my head for a minute." The memory of it made him laugh. To him, it was an inside joke, highly entertaining, like so much cocktail party chatter.

Until we at the Behavioral Science Unit came along, the only professionals who interviewed incarcerated killers tended to be forensic psychiatrists and psychologists, whose main interest was in determining whether they were sane enough to stand trial. Unlike them, we weren't mulling over the idea of rehabilitating anyone. Our goal was to identify perpetrators, apprehend them, successfully prosecute them, and then incarcerate them for as long as we could.

It took a while to get our footing for the interview process, and answers to our questions didn't always come easily. Psychopaths are accomplished liars and con men, masters of deceit. It's a talent they've been getting by on for years. That's why exhaustive advance preparation was so absolutely critical. Every agent who conducted one of these interviews had to be completely conversant in the details of the killer's crimes. If a killer stabbed his victim twenty-seven times, and now claims there were fourteen stab wounds, the agent could say, "I think the victim was stabbed more than that. In fact, I think she was stabbed twenty-seven times."

At that point the killer thinks, "Wow, this guy knows it better than I do." In some cases, the killer himself might not remember specific details of a murder, and if a good investigator can volunteer that the victim's body was dragged five hundred and twenty-five feet, that kind of specificity is impressive to the criminal. It works to keep the interview honest.

As the interviews progressed, I supported my team, asked questions, tried to fill gaps in the profilers' questions. I helped refine the probes, encouraged them to cover territory that might not have occurred to them, or suggested alternate lines of questioning. Always, my main interest was in taking a proactive approach: What could we learn to make us better able to help prevent these terrible crimes?

How close did the victim live to the killer? That could be important in determining how we organize a search. Was the killer in the crowd when the victim's body was found? If so, then standard police procedure should include having a photographer scanning onlookers at the scene. Did the killer pay close attention to media coverage of the crime, and for what reason—to avoid capture, or to relive the excitement of the crime? If we knew more about how he followed the coverage, then we'd be better able to determine if feeding specific information to the media could help in a capture.

One of the avenues I was most interested in was determining whether the killer used murder as a means of relieving stress. Many of these serial killers were virtual time bombs, able to control their urges—sometimes for long periods of time—before succumbing to a sudden, explosive homicidal outburst. David Berkowitz, the so-called Son of Sam killer, for example, told us how the pressure would build in him, and that it was relieved only by committing another murder.

For the same reason, we began to pay special attention to the anniversary dates of the victims' deaths. That's when the killer's juices would be flowing again as he remembered his crime, began fantasizing about it, and maybe even revisited the murder scene. I also suggested the profilers begin to ask whether killers ever attended the funerals of their victims, or visited their gravesites. As it turned out, many of them had, and it didn't take long for that kind of information, once it was disseminated to local law enforcement, to become part of their arsenals.

In 1982, for example, twenty-five-year-old hairdresser Susan Marie Schaaf was found in her apartment in Chicago, raped and brutally murdered. Local police had few leads, and when they contacted us, one of the things we suggested was staking out Schaaf's gravesite on the first anniversary of her death, on the chance the killer might show up, out of anger or remorse.

Three officers were stationed at the cemetery, watching the grave for twenty hours through their binoculars. Finally, thirty-two-year-old Glen Simkunas drove into the cemetery, parked his car, and walked to Schaaf's grave. Until that point, he hadn't been part of the investigation. But when the officers approached him, the first thing he said was, "I knew you guys would be here. What took you so long?" It was our prediction of a possible gravesite visit that led to his apprehension as Schaaf's killer.

While we realized that many aspects of crime once considered inconsequential were actually extremely significant, we also learned that some things given great credence—the propensity of some killers to leave "messages" at the scene, for instance—were so much urban myth. As far as I was concerned, the phrase "Stop Me Before I Kill Again" scribbled in lipstick on a mirror, or an anonymous letter from the killer begging to be caught, were little more than ruses. In my experience, if a killer wants to be arrested, he'll pick up the phone and tell you where he is.

Beyond that, I was intrigued with a more fundamental question. Why did these criminals consent to be interviewed in the first place? For some, it was boredom. I'm sure a man like Kemper, a killer with a near-genius IQ, didn't find the prison routine intellectually challenging, and would have found visitors of Douglas's and Ressler's caliber, at the very least, stimulating. The profilers were businesslike, speaking as equals, and quick to demonstrate their own expertise. It was a way of convincing these killers they were on equal footing. In other instances, the killers succumbed to flattery. Some had tremendous egos, and responded to approaches like, "You're one of the most prolific killers currently incarcerated in the U.S., one of the best there is. You're obviously very good at what you did. We'd like to know how you did it, and how you got away with it."

As the profilers charged ahead with their work, I always made a point of trying to step back a bit, to get some distance on the process, to make sure we weren't missing the full significance of the raw data they were collecting. If someone is going to spend the rest of his life in prison, for instance, I wanted to know how he comes to grips with it. How does he make sense of it? It occurred to me he might welcome the chance to sit with someone who understands his crime, perhaps better than he himself does.

Some of these compulsive killers, I believe, realized we had sought them out because we truly wanted to learn from them, and they appreciated our sincerity. Many had no real answer for why they'd done the horrible things they did, and for them, cooperating with the profilers might be a way to gain, for the first time, some meaningful insight into their own behavior. Sometimes they talked to us, I felt, because they were searching, too.

By 1980, we began to see that most homicidal crime scenes fell into one of two categories. The first was a scene of wild violence and physical trauma committed by a perpetrator who seemed driven by forces beyond his control. This kind of killer, typified by Richard Trenton Chase, the so-called Vampire Killer, had full-blown mental illness. Too disordered even to drive, for example, he probably would walk to and from a crime scene. His victim hadn't been stalked, but was a hapless individual who, sadly, just happened to be in the wrong place at the wrong time. This killer lacks the mental acuity to plan his actions, and he has few social skills to entice his prey. He is impulsive, unprepared, reactive. He may mutilate or disfigure his victims in bizarre ways. In the most generic terms, he is driven by his madness. It's as if the crime scene reflects the confusion in his own chaotic mind.

Then there was another, very different, type of homicide. In contrast to the disorganized killer, these predators systematically stalk their victims, plan their actions, and carry out their crimes methodically, carefully disposing evidence linking them to the scene. They wash or burn away evidence and don't leave fingerprints. They transport, hide, or destroy the bodies of their victims, perhaps relocating the corpse, to avoid leaving clues to their own identity. Sometimes, they leave evidence of elaborate, almost scripted violence, as if acting out a complex and precise fantasy. They may even stage their crime scenes in a deliberate effort to pull investigators off the track. This criminal type, known as the organized killer, is often what most people think of as the classic psychopath.

The prison writings of Gerard John Schaefer, a former police officer and convicted Florida serial killer, give a glimpse into the mind of the organized killer, showing just how calculating and deliberate he can be. In one excerpt, Schaefer, a sexual sadist, writes what amounts to a set of instructions for anyone thinking about following in his footsteps:

> *The execution site must be carefully arranged for a speedy execution, once the victim has arrived. There will be 2 sawhorses with a 2x4 between them. A noose is attached to the overhanging limb of a tree. Another rope to pull away the 2x4, preferably by car.*
>
> *A grave must be prepared in advance away from the place of execution. The victim could be one of the many women who flock to Miami and Ft. Lauderdale for the winter months. Even two victims would not be difficult to dispose of, since women are less wary when traveling in pairs. In any case it may be more preferable to bind and gag the victims before transporting them to the place of execution.*
>
> *Then again, depending on what torture or defilement is planned for them, other items may be useful.*

She may be revived before death if desirable and subjected to further indecencies. After death has occurred, the corpse should be violated if not violated already. The body should then possibly be mutilated and carried to the grave and buried. All identity papers should be destroyed and the place of execution dismantled.

The identification of those two distinct types of killers—the organized versus the disorganized—was one of the most profound contributions the profilers of the Behavioral Science Unit made. We took the crimes once described as "senseless killings," "random homicides," or "pattern killings" and gave investigators a new analytical framework, in effect a set of fresh investigative eyes.

For the most part, the disorganized killers weren't of much use to us during interviews. Most had low intelligence, or were psychologically disturbed, or simply had too little self-awareness to offer any insights into their own behavior.

Organized killers, on the other hand, were a treasure trove. Totally lucid and frighteningly deliberate, they had precise, almost cinematic memories of their crimes. In fact, once they made the decision to cooperate with us, they were intelligent, articulate, and often seemed to delight in the retelling of their horrible escapades. It was as if they took pride in their work.

Not every killer fit neatly into one of those two categories, of course. The mutant team of Henry Lee Lucas, a big ugly guy with one eye staring off in the wrong direction, and his partner, Ottis Elwood Toole, a gap-toothed sociopath, were thought to have been involved in as many as several hundred random murders throughout the U.S. But they were such liars that authorities couldn't sort their stories out, or even reach a certain tally of their victims. They showed no conscience, little self-awareness, and no remorse. There was no existing terminology to describe that particular criminal pathology. We just called them the "recreational killers."

The organized killer, the true psychopath, is the most dangerous and intractable of all human predators. The evil in him exists alongside rationality and total self-assurance. We learned that he is less likely than other criminals to use alcohol or mind-altering drugs. The reason? He wants to be present and fully aware during the commission of his crime. He enjoys what he does. He has chosen evil, and now interprets the world as his own private playground for exploitation.

He is totally narcissistic, and concerned exclusively with fulfilling his own needs. His dominant personality traits are fantasy, control, and domination. The actualization of his fantasies is the central motivating factor in his life. He prowls for his victims, in much the same way any cunning animal does. His mentality is typified by men like Keith Hunter Jesperson, an Oregon long-haul trucker suspected in one hundred sixty-six killings, who scrawled a string of taunting confessions like this one on roadstop restroom walls: "I killed Tanya Bennett . . . I beat her to death, raped her and loved it. Yes I'm sick, but I enjoy myself too."

Not surprisingly, it wasn't easy to get these manipulative, egomaniacal personalities to warm up to the interview process. Ted Bundy, a classic example of the organized personality, had snared his victims by being articulate and charming, and he talked to us in great detail about his techniques. Yet he refused to admit to several killings police believed him responsible for. We'll never know why. It was as if some of his crimes were so heinous, even by inmate standards, he didn't want to risk anyone finding out about them. He may not have wanted to risk losing status. And maybe he was just holding on to the dream of someday being freed.

In a case like that, our best hope was to create a hypothetical, using third-person questions to devise a "what if" scenario to draw the killer out.

"Well, if the killer had taken her to a remote site, would she have walked, or would he have carried her?" the interviewer might say.

If the subject answers, "I think he would have parked the car, taken her out of the trunk, and, because it was so great a distance, decided it would be easier to have her walk than to have to carry her," and the information matches up with the fact that the victim's bare footprints were found in the dirt at the crime scene, then you know you're getting somewhere. The killer is telling you things only he could know.

With techniques like those, we began to accumulate answers to many of the questions long wondered about. Do these killers return to the scene of the crime? In many cases, yes. Sometimes, if the killer is inexperienced and has never killed before, and especially if he was known to the victim, he may return to make sure she's dead. That's especially common in strangulation cases. At the beginning of his career, the serial killer, like anyone embarking on a new trade, really doesn't know what it takes to successfully strangle another human being. Is she really dead, or just unconscious and likely to come to? He's new to the game. He's still mastering his craft.

Killers also return to the scene for other reasons. For some, it is the urge to relive the pleasure of the crime, which is so powerful it outweighs even the fear of being apprehended. David

Berkowitz went back to the scene of his crimes to masturbate, or get out of his car and reenact a shooting. In fact, it was only after police realized that they had issued a parking ticket to him in the vicinity of one of the crime scenes that he was finally apprehended.

Other killers go so far as to actually try to insert themselves into the crime investigation itself. Edmund Kemper chose to drink in a bar where police officers were known to hang out, and actually talked to one about his work on a case of the unsolved murders of college girls—the very murders Kemper was responsible for. That was his way of participating in the excitement of the chase. And Wayne Williams, convicted in the Atlanta Child Murders, volunteered his services to the Atlanta police department to take photographs of the crime scenes.

It occurred to me that these killers are like moths drawn to a flame. It isn't enough for them to commit the crime and get away with it. They're lured back to the scene of the crime because it gives them exhilaration. They reminded me of the graying guy with a paunch who goes back to the turf of his college stadium to relive the day he scored the game-winning touchdown. The killer, too, has a kind of nostalgia. He wants to imagine the triumph again, to hear the cheering in his head.

As we accumulated data, we began to get a more sophisticated understanding of certain facets of the crimes we saw. We knew that some sexually oriented serial killers will insert an object into the vagina of the victim, a broomstick or tree branch, for instance. But after talking with them, we found that sadism or sheer brutality isn't always the reason. Sometimes the motive is curiosity, or exploration, which will be apparent at autopsy. The amount of damage to the victim internally will be much less in that case; far more if the goal was to punish or degrade.

We came to recognize the significance of other artifacts of these crimes—the trophy, and the souvenir. A trophy represents a conquest, a sign of victory. A killer might take a piece of jewelry from his victim, but won't necessarily keep it. He might give it to his girlfriend. A souvenir is something quite different. It, too, might be a piece of jewelry, a driver's license from a wallet, a picture. But it could also be a pair of panties, or a button from the victim's coat. The souvenir exists as a means to regenerate the excitement of the crime. It is a talisman the killer can look at, fondle, or employ sexually to rekindle his fantasies.

One serial killer told us about the great pleasure he'd taken in murdering a child. In order to extend the satisfaction of the crime, he took to writing letters to the dead boy's parents, detailing just exactly what he had done to him. It was his sadistic way of reenacting the crime, of re-creating the pleasure of the kill by reliving the fantasy.

What was the true nature of these monsters? Was it really possible for human beings to exist in the world without even the vestige of a conscience? I wondered. My experiences were telling me, "yes."

In 1980, during one of the first lengthy interviews that we ever conducted with a pedophile, a self-described "chicken hawk," he discussed, in great detail, how he assessed a child's potential for victimization. He watched to see how adventurous they were, how they walked with their mother, how far away from her they were willing to venture.

This was an adult who spent his days sitting in the mall, sizing up children. He was like a child psychologist, studying the traits of children for his own evil purposes. On the tape, he recounts in great detail how he lured young boys, stationing himself in places like the video arcade in a shopping mall, spending days and weeks surveying children. He would focus on a lone, quiet little boy who seemed isolated and vulnerable, or one who appeared confident and outgoing, and finally settle on his victim. His one point of pride was in claiming never to have snatched his young victims against their will. The challenge for him was in enticing the child to come with him voluntarily, in spotting a little boy who was shopping with his mother, and finding a way to get him physically away from her. The part he loved best, as he put it, was the seduction.

We asked him what parents might do to protect their children from someone like him. "I'll tell you something," he said. "I'm willing to spend more time with your kid than you are. I don't have to get 'em today. Today, I can just make contact with 'em. I have from now on. I can do it at my time, and my pace. I've got all the time in the world."

As head of the Unit, I worked at maintaining my objectivity, and tried hard not to let moral judgments interfere with professional assessments. But it was sometimes difficult not to step back in disbelief at the evil human beings were capable of. I knew most good people really had no comprehension of it, or the tremendous risk it posed. How could they? They hadn't seen the things I had. Sometimes, in my darker moments, it seemed to me that good human beings were little more than unsuspecting prey.

The videotape shows two men in suits, sitting at a table in a paneled room, flanking a mustachioed man in a white T-shirt. The agents were Ken Lanning and Roy Hazelwood, and the man in the middle, Jon Barry Simonis, is six-feet-two-inches tall, one hundred seventy-five pounds, and thirty-three years old. This tape is a record of a meeting that took place in the summer of 1984 at the Louisiana State maximum security prison at Angola, the very first research interview conducted with a serial rapist by the Behavioral Science Unit.

By his own count, Simonis, known as the Ski Mask Rapist, committed forty robberies and as many as seventy-five batteries and sexual assaults in a crime wave that began on November 1, 1978, moved through twelve states, and ended with his arrest in November 1981. At the time of this interview he'd been incarcerated for two and a half years, and was serving twenty-one life sentences, plus 2,386 and a half years, without possibility of parole.

Simonis was the archetype of the roving serial sexual predator. He was reasonably articulate, physically unremarkable, and appeared intelligent, rational, well-spoken, and cooperative. Tests put his intelligence quotient at 128, well within the "gifted" range. He estimated that in one ten-month period alone he'd driven eighty thousand miles. His oldest victim was fifty years old, the youngest, thirteen.

In response to Lanning's and Hazelwood's questions, Simonis matter-of-factly described his modus operandi. Typically, he said, after entering a home, he bound his victims, and then sexually assaulted them, often in front of their husbands, male family members, or boyfriends. He was fastidious in his preparations, cutting telephone lines so his victims couldn't call police, slicing their car tires beforehand to prevent them from traveling, assessing the distance between his targets and the homes of neighbors. "My face was covered," he said. "I wore gloves. I also wore baggy clothes, like coveralls, to kind of conceal my build." He packed pre-cut lengths of rope or handcuffs to bind the victims with, duct tape in case he decided to blindfold or muzzle them, and a pistol that, at least at first, he might just threaten them with.

Initially, Simonis's motive was robbery. He would find a woman at a shopping center, accost her in the parking lot, and put a screwdriver to her throat. He would rob her, but not physically abuse her. As his spree progressed, he became more selective in his victims. He would drive through a neighborhood, pick what looked like an affluent household, or, at a shopping mall, focus on a woman driving an expensive car, wearing a gold watch, large diamonds, or flashy jewelry. Did a woman's physical appearance matter? "Attractive ones would have an appealing effect on me. It wasn't always the motive for following them, but it was a major one. I figured that if a woman was attractive and her husband was well off, he'd do things to keep her happy. Buy her expensive jewelry and other nice things."

Simonis went on to describe other methods for procuring victims. At one time, he worked in a hospital as a cardiovascular specialist, and "I had access to all the medical records. I knew where the patients lived, what their husbands did, whether he worked in or out of town, who was home during the day, and who wasn't. Also, if they were having surgery, I'd have access to their keys, which they usually left in their nightstands by their beds. I'd go down and have a copy made, and return the original back to the key ring, and copy down their address and later on use that to get into their house."

Over the course of his criminal career, Simonis's violent impulses increased dramatically. He began to physically assault his victims, demanding anal sex, forcing women to fellate him, and punching them, often in the breasts. One night he broke into a home and assaulted the thirteen-year-old baby-sitter, forcing her to perform oral sex. She tried to frighten him off by telling him, "You know, a police officer lives here."

"No shit," Simonis responded. "What time are they going to get home?"

She told him it would be at least a couple of hours. Fine, he said, "Then I'll wait."

Not long afterward, the detective and his wife returned home. They'd been out celebrating their fifteenth wedding anniversary. When they came in, Simonis overtook them both, handcuffed them, and raped the wife in front of her husband. At one point, the husband asked, "Are you all right?" and she said, "Yes, he's being a gentleman."

At that point, Simonis became enraged, and began beating and burning the woman's breasts so furiously that she later required a double mastectomy. When Roy asked him why he'd done that to his victim, Simonis said, "Who the fuck was she to tell me that I'm being a gentleman? I was no gentleman, and I proved it."

Was Simonis himself aware of the escalation in his violence? "Oh yes. It started out very mild and progressed very heavily." But ultimately, ordinary sexual gratification wasn't his goal. What was important was "degradation to the women, making them feel completely dominated. My intention was to inflict fear in them." At one point, Roy and Ken asked Simonis directly if he was a sexual sadist. "Absolutely," he said. "I enjoy their suffering."

Later, after the video camera was turned off, Simonis told Hazelwood it was probably a good thing he'd finally been apprehended. The reason, he said, was that rape was becoming boring for him. More and more often now, his fantasies were of sadistic murder.

Of all the things Simonis told us in that milestone interview, there was one exchange that best illustrated the single-minded ruthlessness of these perpetrators, and of the vulnerability of the rest of us. At one point, Simonis was asked if there was anything an ordinary woman could do to keep from becoming one of his victims. "Barry, is there anything a woman could do to protect herself from someone like you?" Ken asked. "Are there any preventions she could take to lessen the chance of becoming one of your victims?"

For a moment, Simonis thought about the question, and then shook his head. "Not really, no," he said, matter-of-factly. "If I really want a woman, there's nothing she can do to stop me."

As our resident expert in crimes of sexual predation, Roy Hazelwood would eventually identify four main types of rapists, from the power-reassurance (sometimes referred to as the "gentleman rapist," who acts from the fantasy of a consensual relationship with his victim), to the power-assertive (the macho, gold-chain-wearing, self-confident type), to the anger-retaliatory type, who strikes in fury to get even with women for real or imagined transgressions. But the last subtype represented the bottom rung. These sexual sadists were men who punished innocent women because they perceived them as both evil and possessing power over men. Since the suffering of victims was what sexually excited them, this type was formally designated the anger-excitation rapist. But Roy had another name for them. He called them "the great white sharks."

We learned it wasn't uncommon for these predators to keep diaries, journals, audiotapes, and videotapes of a victim's torture. In the early 1980s, Charles Ng and Leonard Lake, a team in California responsible for twenty-five homicides, abducted young girls, imprisoned them in a cinder block bunker, and left documentary evidence of their blood-splashed torture sessions. Roy Norris and Lawrence Bittaker, who murdered five young women in California in 1979, stabbed two of their victims through the ears with an ice pick, and tape-recorded their torture of the victims with coat hangers, hammers, and pliers. To this day, Bittaker, still on death row in California, signs his answers to prison fan mail with the nickname, "Pliers."

In 1983, when the Secret Service apprehended James Mitchell "Mike" DeBardeleben, who was wanted for counterfeiting, they found two oversized foot lockers filled with women's blood-stained undergarments, handcuffs, and bondage paraphernalia, and hundreds of sexually explicit photographs. DeBardeleben also kept tape recordings of his torture sessions with a number of victims, and they were terrible to hear—a woman crying and screaming repeatedly, pleading with him not to hurt her. Those tapes were graphic testimony from beyond the grave of a human being going to her death while begging for mercy, and from a sadist who inflicted pain because it was pleasurable for him.

DeBardeleben, suspected in an untold number of killings and rapes over an eighteen-year spree, once wrote of what he called his "central impulse . . . to have complete mastery over another person, to make him or her a helpless object of our will, to become the absolute ruler over her, to become her god, to do with her as one pleases, to humiliate her, to enslave her as a means to this end. And the most radical aim is to make her suffer. Since there is no greater power over another person than that of inflicting pain on her. To force her to undergo suffering without her being able to defend herself."

In 1980, the author Thomas Harris had come to us for help in researching his novel *Red Dragon*, and years later, we had a similar visit from the director and cast of the film *The Silence of the Lambs*. When the actor Scott Glenn, who played the movie's Unit chief, said he wanted to know about the true nature of evil, John Douglas took him into an office and played him one of those tapes. A while later, Glenn emerged, clearly shaken, and with tears in his eyes. I knew how he felt. I had heard the tapes myself.

It is difficult to find words to describe the pitiful cries of a woman in such terror and pain, and know there's nothing you can do, because it's too late to help her. Even now, the memory of those tapes still comes into my mind, as if from nowhere. They began with an innocent victim begging for her life, and ended, hours later, as she pleaded for death.

The killers themselves told us the reason they kept tapes like those was because their victims had died too easily. They could learn from their recordings, they said, by listening to them over and over again, in hopes of finding a way to better prolong the next victim's agony. For a long time I felt that no one outside our profession could ever conceive such cruelty even existed. Then I came across something written by the poet Lisel Mueller, called "Small Poem of the Hounds and Hares":

> *After the kill, there is the feast.*
> *And toward the end, when the dancing subsides*
> *and the young have sneaked off somewhere,*
> *the hounds, drunk on the blood of the hares,*
> *begin to talk of how soft*
> *were their pelts, how graceful their leaps,*
> *how lovely their scared, gentle eyes.*

In order to do the work we did, it was necessary for a certain emotional blunting to take place, not unlike what EMS techs and hospital emergency room physicians experience. It's a self-defense mechanism. Still, what health care workers see is often the result of accidental injury, or violence by, say, knife or handgun. What we saw was something else entirely.

Howard Teten, the godfather of profiling, said he himself experienced what Freud termed isolation of affect. "The years of profiling have taken their toll," Teten said in an interview for a book titled *Into the Minds of Madmen*. "I have few friends, and there are even fewer people that I really trust. Knowing what humans are really capable of doing to each other makes you aware that civility is a luxury which can be discarded at will. This knowledge robs you of your feelings and makes you far more wary of your fellow man." Teten wasn't alone. In his book *Mindhunter*, John Douglas also wrote about the emotional distancing that he experienced, even with his own little girls. Sometimes, he wrote, he "found it difficult to get involved in the minor, but important, scrapes and hurts of childhood. When I would come home and [my wife] Pam would tell me that one of the girls had fallen off her bike and needed stitches, I'd flash to the autopsy of some child her age and think of all the stitches it had taken the medical examiner to close her wounds for burial."

Sometimes, no matter how hard the profilers tried to avoid it, the evil got through even the best-laid defense mechanisms. In 1980, Jim Reese, a former platoon leader in Vietnam who eventually became assistant unit chief of the BSU, and Dick Ault went to Jacksonville to teach an advanced criminology school. While in Florida, they arranged to interview Arthur Frederick Goode III, a convicted child abductor and killer who was awaiting execution at Florida State Prison in Starke, Florida. Goode was on death row for the rape and strangulation of nine-year-old Jason Verdow in 1976. His pattern was to kidnap little boys, force them to engage in sexual behaviors, and then murder them. In a final coup de grâce, he spent his time in prison writing taunting letters to the parents of those dead children, describing in great detail just exactly how he had molested and murdered them.

Ault and Reese interviewed Goode for six hours about his homicidal behaviors, and got cold, remorseless responses to even their most sensitive questions. Then, just as they were leaving, Goode, with a big grin on his face, turned to them and asked, "Do you have any little boys at home?" It was too much for Reese, who had a child of his own about the same age. He balled up his fist and slammed it into the door with a force that stunned even Goode. Technically, that was unprofessional behavior, and it couldn't be condoned. But there wasn't anyone in the Unit who couldn't relate.

Another agent in the Unit was profiling a case in which all of the children in a family had been shotgunned in the face while sleeping in their beds. In preparing a profile of the suspect, he had to spend long hours staring at the remains of those children. He later said that one night, when he walked into his young daughter's room to tuck her in, she was lying in bed with her back to him. He found himself having to walk around her bed to see the front of her, and reassure himself that she was, in fact, all right. In law enforcement, this is referred to as "vicarious victimization." It was the result of work-related stress.

Profiler Jim Horn, a former Marine officer, recalls that he once worked three cases in a row involving the murders of blond-haired, blue-eyed little boys who looked not so very different from his own blond, blue-eyed son at home. He and Bill Hagmaier carpooled together for a time, and they talked about how they simply had to quit taking cases home to work on them. "When you're home at midnight with a case spread all over the dining table, the inevitable creakings of the house take on a whole new dimension," Horn says. "If you're working on a case where a family has been totally slaughtered by some maniac, you're not going to ignore those sounds. The hair goes up on the back of your neck, and you're alert, hyper-vigilant. So we learned to stop taking those cases home at night."

Even for Roy Hazelwood, who seemed to have a knack for keeping an even keel, one case penetrated the armor. Hazelwood interviewed wives and girlfriends of this sexual sadist. It got to him. I knew why. It was because he was from the same generation I was, and we were both raised to believe women and children are to be protected, and men are the ones who should do it. Outdated chivalry or not, it was a feeling running deep in both of us, and Roy's reaction to the victim interviews, after all of the horrible things he'd been able to brush off, only underscored that.

Once, in tracking a sexual predator, Roy had to study the crime scene photos of a little eight-year-old girl who'd been sexually assaulted and murdered. That was horrible in and of itself, but this was even worse. The killer had reached up inside the little girl, pulled her intestines out, and used them to strangle her.

We all knew that serial killers were a minuscule percentage of the population, maybe thirty of them wandering the U.S. at any one time, out of more than two hundred and fifty million people. But the damage they caused was way out of proportion, and we were seeing it on a daily basis, in concentrated form. It would have been completely unrealistic to expect any human being to remain unaffected by that amount of evil. It could distort your perception of the world after a while. And one of the most important aspects of my job, as I saw it, was to make sure the men and women in my Unit didn't become overwhelmed by it.

The profilers all handled the stress differently. Once, when Roy was working on the Golden Gate Trail Murders, in which a string of hikers, both men and women, were being killed, the pressure really got to him. He was working a tremendous caseload at the time, and had just completed and turned in his profile of the killer when word came that two more bodies had been found. It was the only time I ever saw Roy show even a hint of caving in. It was the pressure of the self-imposed burden, the terrible knowledge all profilers had, that their job performance might mean the difference between life and death. And then it happened—another victim. Even then, all he did was come to me and say, "Roger, I want to take two weeks leave." Roy went home and painted his house. Then he came back and said, "Okay, let's get on with it."

After *The Silence of the Lambs* was published, a rush of eager, starry-eyed kids who all wanted to be the next Clarice Starling came knocking at our door. I turned many of them away with the warning that they could be hurt, really damaged, by the work.

Even some of the more seasoned profilers eventually came to the conclusion they just weren't cut out for working the more horrible homicides, and if they wanted out, I always respected that decision. Dick Ault, for one, eventually decided he preferred work in the field of counterespionage. I'd been invited to speak at a CIA adjudicator's conference at Langley. Dick and I went together to the conference, to tell about our research on serial killers, rapists, and child molesters. I talked about how we were gaining a lot of insight into their minds, personalities, and fantasies, and suggested the CIA do something similar with convicted traitors and spies. Dick took the lead and ran with that idea, putting together what eventually came to be known as the Slammer Project. In the course of it, he's conducted a series of interviews with incarcerated masters of spy tradecraft, and has probably debriefed more of them than anyone else in the world.

Jim Horn and Jim Reese made the decision that work with serial killers wasn't for them. Both had great insight and sensitivity, so they went into the area of stress management, which provides support for other members of law enforcement who've undergone terrible trauma in the line of duty—seen partners or innocent people shot right in front of them, taken statements from the young victims of pedophiles, carried out the bodies of dead children from horrendous crime scenes, or experienced life-threatening situations themselves. Our work with serial killers might have gotten more ink in the media, but the stress management program was one of the most valuable the BSU ever created. I know, because I took the phone calls asking us for assistance, and there were more requests for that kind of help than any other.

As for me, I always thought of myself as being pretty well defended. I had stability in my family life, and balance. The hardest thing for me was being in a shopping mall, watching as a little kid wandered away from an inattentive parent. It was all I could do to restrain myself from going over like a crazy person and warning them not to let their kids out of their sight.

If there was one area that fascinated me about homicidal sexual predators, it was how key fantasy was to their development and the evolution of their crimes. In time, we began to understand the mechanism. A little boy begins to have fantasies of violence. He might kill small animals or a family pet. Then, as he approaches adolescence, he begins to become sexualized. The pleasure that he finds in violent fantasies becomes entangled with pleasurable sexual fantasies. He may masturbate a dozen times a day, or more, while he fantasizes about violence. If violent tendencies become intertwined with the sexual urge at an early age, in later years it is impossible to untangle them. Once sexuality is destroyed as a means of expressing love, that capacity is, in all likelihood, gone forever.

And over time, the fantasy grows into action. Especially in crimes of sexual predation, the presence of fantasy is key. A rapist breaks into a home, approaches the bedroom, sees the victim in bed. Stands there, considering it. The longer he stays, the greater the risk of being seen, caught, or surprised. But he will risk it all the same. Because it's worth it to him. Enjoying the anticipation is worth heightening the risk. He stands by the side of the bed, looking at her. He may softly stroke her hair, muse about precisely how he will wake her. Imagines the look in her eyes. This is all part of the ritual, which is what these crimes are really about.

Still, though the fantasy is always perfect, the crime never is. Too many things can go wrong. She becomes terrified, screams, defecates in fear. So each commission of a crime marks an enlargement of the fantasy, and a further perfection of it. How can he do it better next time?

I'd seen graphic proof of just how strong those fantasies could be. Even in prison, predators continued to cling to them. Deprived of the ability to act out their crimes, they did the next best thing. They nurtured them, talked about them with cell mates, replayed them, over and over, in their heads. James Odom, a convicted serial rapist, once recalled how he first met the man who would become his partner, James Lawson, Jr., when both were incarcerated at a state mental institution in California. The two

154

spent hours making elaborate plans to rape, mutilate, and eviscerate women. "We'd fantasize so much that at times I didn't know what was real," Odom said.

Another killer, Danny Rolling, convicted of murdering five students in Gainesville, Florida, went so far as to write a kind of handbook describing how to stalk and murder a victim. It contained drawings, remarkably realistic depictions of slashed breasts, torture, and bizarre types of physical restraints, and other violent offenders passed them around to each other as entertainment, like so many cartoons.

———————

One thing that never ceased to amaze me was the way so many of these killers appeared "normal" to the outside world. The classic example was Ted Bundy, who at the beginning of his criminal career was handsome, engaging, and articulate. But the more I studied these predators, the more evidence I saw of something I termed "leakage."

If a person believes strongly enough in a set of ideas or a particular value system, manifestations of it will leak out of them, no matter how hard they try to conceal it. The same is true of serial killers. Whether it is immediately apparent or not, they are nurturing fantasies, which, if not acted upon, can seep out in things like substance abuse, alcoholism, fanatical religious beliefs, or irrational anger. We can't look inside people to find out who is having violent fantasies, but we can see evidence of it in their expressions, their eye contact, the way they talk, and in the material they seek out to fuel their inner life.

Sometimes leakage escalates dramatically. Bundy, who was at first cool and deliberate, began to deteriorate over time. When police start to zero in on a killer, he's feeling a new kind of pressure. The endgame is approaching, and on some level he knows it. When Bundy's murder spree first began, he was clear-eyed and incredibly creative and cunning. He wore a phony cast on his arm so he'd appear helpless to his victims. Then he'd say he couldn't lift his surfboard onto his car. Could they please give him a hand? They would, and that was how he captured them.

By the last of his crimes, the bloody murder of young women in a Florida sorority house, he was no longer in control. Completely consumed by what he himself termed "the malignancy," he'd become a wild-eyed maniac whose last murders were committed in a violent frenzy. His whole modus operandi had changed. He had lost all the social skills once used to lure his victims. He was disintegrating, and seeing this kind of progression was like seeing the breakdown of the soul itself. It was as if, at some point, an outside force has taken root in these killers, come to inhabit their psyches, and left them with only vestiges of normal human emotion and response.

I witnessed the same thing in the case of Christopher Wilder, whose double life was exposed in 1984 after he murdered at least eight young women in a sudden killing spree that stretched across the country. Before that deadly outburst, the Australia-born sometime race car driver was an affluent sportsman, builder, and bon vivant, described by neighbors as unfailingly polite, and known as an animal lover and good tipper in the Florida town where he was a fixture at bars and the beach. Posing as a modeling agent, he used his good looks, custom Porsche, and dockside speedboat to seduce a string of women.

What wasn't so well known was that in 1976 Wilder had been charged with the sexual assault of a sixteen-year-old girl, three years later had tried to rape a seventeen-year-old, and in 1982 was charged with indecent assault against two fifteen-year-old girls, whom he blindfolded and forced to pose for nude pictures.

Then, in the spring of 1984, Wilder's twenty-three-year-old girlfriend, citing their sixteen-year age difference, said firmly that she'd never marry him, and something apparently snapped. In a six-week rampage stretching from Florida to California to New England, Wilder tortured, sexually assaulted and killed as many as eight young women, and perhaps more, using a 110-volt electric prod on some, trying to seal shut the eyes of another with glue.

In all, we had some five hundred FBI agents on his trail, which ended in a New Hampshire gas station when a state police detective recognized and tried to question him, and Wilder lunged for his glove compartment. By the time he was killed by a bullet to the chest, Wilder had completely unraveled. He no longer bore any resemblance to the suave ladies' man who had, for so long, been at least partly able to contain the depth of his violent tendencies.

I termed this phenomenon "psychopathic panic," and defined it as a trait manifested in a killer who is losing his ability to function in the calculating and methodical manner that characterized his behavior in the past. Facing certain pressures, these killers at first begin to deteriorate, and eventually self-destruct.

If anything was clear to me from these observations, it was that, at a certain point, once evil has taken hold in a person, it becomes too powerful to reverse. For these killers, regrettably, rehabilitation is simply no longer an option. The same was true of certain sexual predators, especially the serial sexual sadist. Once the most basic of all human urges, the sexual urge, merges completely with violence, the link can never be broken. The damage is irreversible.

It's a difficult conclusion to accept, in human terms, but I had to. The notion of rehabilitating some of the killers we saw was simply inconceivable. But if I accepted that idea, then where did it leave me as a human being? How was I supposed to deal with the knowledge that such evil exists, and can't be reversed?

I began to focus on the question of how and why these dangerous fantasies began, and what allowed them to take such hold. The more we learned about the specifics of the criminal mind, the more I became interested in what had spawned it in the first place. Here we were, immersed in the terrible aftermath of evil. But what mechanism had caused it? How is the serial killer made?

There were no easy answers. Some said the emergence of serial killers was a function of a violent American culture, or a byproduct of the modern age. But I'd read about the life of Gilles de Rais, a contemporary of Joan of Arc, who in the early fifteenth century had sadistically murdered some eight hundred children. And I knew there certainly weren't any violent video games when Jack the Ripper disemboweled at least a half dozen women in London in 1888.

Even before I began in the Behavioral Science Unit, researchers had already coined the term "homicidal triad" to describe a cluster of behaviors in children—bedwetting, fire setting, and cruelty to animals—that seemed to be a predictor of future homicidal behavior. Later, Jonathan H. Pincus, a noted neurologist and frequent lecturer at the FBI Academy, studied one hundred fifty murderers and found a common thread in all of them: childhood physical abuse, neurological damage, and some form of psychiatric illness. Pincus theorized that childhood abuse creates anger and the urge toward violence, while physical brain damage and psychiatric disorder inhibit the normal human capacity to stop that impulse.

I couldn't help but think back to my work as a juvenile officer, and the terrible things those kids had suffered. They may have been psychologically damaged by their experience, some quite severely. But it hadn't made them serial killers, not one. Still, the question nagged at me. I once read the psychiatric report on the sociopath Ottis Elwood Toole, who before his death in 1996 was best known as the leading suspect in the 1981 kidnapping and murder of Adam Walsh. Toole was the youngest of nine children of an alcoholic and a mother who suffered from mental illness. As a boy, he ran away from his abusive home many times, and was insulted by other kids, who called him a "retard." His formal schooling, which consisted of special ed classes, ended in the seventh grade. He'd suffered seizures ever since being hit in the head with a rock as a boy.

Toole had begun setting fires as a kid, and went on to untold other violent acts, including complicity in a string of murders with his partner, Henry Lee Lucas. But of all the details in his clinical history, what most struck me was how whenever Toole, an itinerant drifter, returned to his hometown of Jacksonville, he would visit his dead mother's grave, lying down in the dirt beside it, he said, because the earth there was warm and sometimes he could feel her move.

In adolescence, the very first serial killer we studied, Edmund Kemper, was already clearly troubled. He was isolated, aggressive, and had tortured animals and buried the family cat alive. The crimes he went on to commit were ghastly, inexcusable. Still, I couldn't help but wonder if he'd have gone on to murder his grandparents, six coeds, and decapitate his own mother if things had gone a little differently for him in boyhood. If, say, someone had intervened when he was being locked in the basement for days on end, staring for hours into the flames of the furnace, which is where, as he later told us, he saw the Devil's face for the first time.

As Unit chief, I didn't ordinarily conduct the prison interviews personally, but in November 1985, when I had the chance to go with Roy Hazelwood on one of his serial rapist interviews, I took it. We drove up to Baltimore, to the Maryland Penitentiary, built in 1811, an urban prison that still stood in the heart of the city. At the front gate, we surrendered our sidearms, and moved into the processing section. Each time we heard the clank of the steel bar door closing behind us, we knew we'd penetrated into the interior a little farther. We were given the office of the prison therapist, because it afforded some privacy. It was outfitted with a table and four chairs, not very comfortable, and nothing more. The guard escorted us in, and once the prisoner was brought in, they left.

Unlike many of the earlier subjects, this one wasn't arrogant. He was subdued, actually, even defeated. He told us he'd finally allowed himself to be apprehended because he "didn't care anymore," and was cooperating with us "because I would like to do anything I can to help change the society's outlook in regards to rape and child molestation." He added, with what seemed like sincerity, that he didn't believe he'd be around much longer. "I'm not going to live the rest of my life in here," he said.

He was a serial rapist, twenty-six years old, a native of North Carolina, an electrician by trade, serving life plus fifty years for rape, assault and battery, kidnapping, and what had been described in the official charge as "unnatural and perverted sex acts." Standard procedure for these interviews ordinarily called for interviewing the subject about his first rape, a middle one, and the last. Since many of these offenders had forty or more cases on their records, we couldn't talk about them all. What we were most interested in was the progression of violence, which we called "increase," that marked the overall trajectory of the criminal career. Did he, for example, start out by screaming at his victims, then begin beating them, and finally end up torturing and killing them?

He was most forthcoming. In fact, we were surprised at how much information we began to get from him, about his background and personal history. In the end, we talked with him for hours, and garnered enough material to fill out the standard fifty-seven-page questionnaire. He had a lot to tell. His father, also a serial rapist, had been physically and emotionally abusive. As far as the offender knew, his father had never killed anyone. But from the time he was ten years old, the father had taken the son along for the hunt, using him as a lure when he went into bars and convinced drunken women to leave with him. After they got into the car, he'd drive to remote locations, beat and rape them in the back seat, and force the young boy to watch. When he was a little older, the father made him take part as well.

These interviews were always conducted with the utmost professionalism. They were devoid of emotion or sympathy, of anything beyond clinical objectivity, even when the discussion turned to the most heinous aspects of a crime. It was important to remain detached, no matter what was being discussed, to let the offenders know that no matter what ground they chose to cover, we could walk right alongside them. They couldn't repulse us. We were beyond shock.

Outwardly, I maintained detachment. But as I listened to this man's story unfold, I couldn't help but ponder what brought him to a life of such violence. His own father had raped him routinely for more than six years, beginning in early childhood, and had exposed him to a kind of horror before he was twelve that most people never witness in a lifetime. This was not one, isolated event. It was a pattern that repeated itself for nearly half of his life.

What kind of chance did that little boy have in the real world? What kind of therapy would have fixed all of that? As I was turning those thoughts over in my mind, I realized there was something that I needed to know. I spent a few minutes formulating the question, and then asked it.

"Tell me, William," I said evenly. "Do you have any memories of your father ever showing you affection?"

It was the first time in nearly seven hours of interviewing that I saw any emotion in him. He was silent for a while, and then his face clouded over. Yes, he said. It was when he was twelve years old. His father was having anal sex with him, and "he would kiss me on the back of the neck while he was doing it."

CHAPTER SEVEN

THE ACADEMY GROUP

BY 1988, NEARLY A DECADE after I'd taken over the helm, the Behavioral Science Unit was making its mark in the world. We had helped integrate the study of the human mind into the techniques of modern law enforcement, and over time, the Unit's work was having a cascading effect. As Unit chief, I oversaw the training of special agents whose job it was to spot evidence of aberrant behavior at crime scenes and then put local police departments in touch with the BSU. Now these so-called profile coordinators were institutionalized as fixtures in all fifty-nine field offices of the FBI.

At the same time, we spearheaded a move to bring in outstanding young detectives from around the country for a year of training and actual casework with our veteran profilers. Eventually, some fifty detective profilers from that elite Fellowship Program fanned out and started behavioral science units not only in the U.S., but around the world. Then, in 1988, I hit a milestone of sorts myself. After twenty years of service with the Bureau, I was eligible for retirement.

At age fifty, I certainly wasn't ready for a rocking chair. In fact, a number of my colleagues were at the same juncture in life I was—ready to get out of the Bureau, but not really sure about what was going to replace it. Collectively, we had a lot of talent and expertise, were all proud of putting the Behavioral Science Unit on the map, and none of us wanted to just disband and hang up our badges and guns.

I started looking around the private sector—investigation, industrial and business security—and saw no counterpart to the kind of service the Unit was providing for law enforcement. I realized that if I'd done this work for the FBI, I could do it for myself, and I could probably get some of my top colleagues to join me. I talked the idea over with two of my closest friends, Bert Brown, who had been the White House psychiatrist during the Kennedy administration, and also former director of the National Institute of Mental Health; and Con Hassel, who retired after heading the Bureau's anti-terrorism operation and went on to work for the CIA.

The date of my official retirement was April 1, 1989, which seemed fitting. I figured that if I really couldn't stand retirement, I'd just show up back at the Unit and say I'd only been fooling. At my retirement party, a lot of good people said some very nice things about me. One of them was my son, Steve, then twenty-five, who stood up and said, "Growing up, a lot of kids I knew had celebrities or sports figures as their heroes. But my hero was always at home."

And although I've received a number of awards over the course of my career, few meant more than the one presented to me that night by Barry Colvert, who showed me the ropes during my first week's training all those years before in the Washington field office. For twenty-one years after we lifted that curved linoleum cutter off a fugitive in a basement locker room of the Shoreham Hotel, Barry had kept it in his desk drawer as a letter opener. But I recognized it immediately when he handed it to me, fastened to a plaque engraved with the words, "First Arrest."

———

At first, I wondered if The Academy Group, Inc., as we called it, would be able to make a go of it. But within a few months, it was obvious the new venture was going to float. People started hearing about us, casework started coming in, and I soon realized there was going to be a need for our services for as long as there were bad guys in the world. Our first case, which Tom Strentz and I handled without even getting on an airplane, involved the successful return of a U.S. corporate executive who was kidnapped by guerrillas in Guatemala. We went on to handle other such cases, sometimes in conjunction with the State Department, always in utmost secrecy, since—as corporations well knew—having a story like that splashed across the headlines would be very bad for business.

Far more difficult for me was the first major domestic case AGI accepted. My colleague Don Bassett and I were approached, confidentially, by the mayor of a major U.S. city, who wanted us to look into allegations of serious sexual harassment and domestic abuse against his city's police chief. The charges turned out to be true, and I spent an uncomfortable two days testifying in an open hearing, under the watchful eye of the city's police commission.

Not long after The Academy Group was up and running, I received a call from an old friend of mine, Jim Murphy, a fifteen-year FBI veteran and former assistant special agent in charge in the New York office. Now he was the head of a private detective agency called Sutton Associates, located on Long Island. In July of that year, he'd gotten a call from the attorney for Rushton Skakel, a wealthy heir to his family's mining fortune whose sister, Ethel, was the widow of Bobby Kennedy.

On the night before Halloween in 1975, a bunch of rich kids, including Skakel's two sons, Michael and Tommy, were hanging out at the Skakel home in Belle Haven, a wealthy gated community in Connecticut. Also in the party was their next-door neighbor, Martha Moxley, a pretty fifteen-year-old. That night, Martha didn't come home, and at noon the next day, her body was found under a tree not far from her house. She'd been bludgeoned with a golf club, and stabbed once through the neck with its broken shaft.

It was a vicious, high-profile crime, but it was never solved, and in time, it faded from the headlines. Then, in 1991, another Kennedy, William Kennedy Smith, was charged in the rape of a young woman in Florida. He was acquitted, but during his trial, a rumor surfaced that Smith had been at the Skakel home on the night Martha Moxley was murdered. It wasn't true, but it was enough to revive press interest in the Skakels.

Connecticut authorities announced they were reopening the case, and by the following year, Rush Skakel, an alcoholic and widower heading a wildly dysfunctional household, was at the end of his rope. Tommy Skakel, seventeen at the time of the crime, was the last person known to have seen Martha alive, and speculation had long placed him as the prime suspect in the killing. Rush firmly believed his kids were innocent, and decided it was time to put an end to all the speculation once and for all.

Through his attorney he contacted Sutton, and Jim Murphy agreed to take on the case.

Forensic behavioral profiling was in its infancy at the time Martha Moxley was murdered. But it had come a long way since then, and Murphy thought the case might well profit from it. He called me, and hired the AGI to provide what analytical help we could.

Many key pieces of information simply weren't available to us, but we did a lot with what we had. Because the police wouldn't release the autopsy photographs, for instance, Ken Baker, a colleague at AGI, and Willis Krebs, Murphy's chief investigator, both went to Cincinnati to track down the original medical examiner, who reconstructed its details from memory.

In all, there were fifteen wounds on the body, many of which could have proved fatal. This was overkill, not a stranger killing. Also, there were no defensive wounds found on Martha, no evidence she'd raised her hands to ward off the attack. It indicated that, at least until the blows began to fall, she felt she had nothing to fear. In short, we concluded, she knew her attacker.

The wound from the broken golf club shaft was what we call a "through-and-through." It had pierced one side of the victim's neck, and fully exited the other side. It even drew some of her long blond hair through the wound as well. Some might think that indicates the fury of the attack, but in this case, it didn't. When found, the body had been moved after death, dragged across the lawn, which would have dislodged the club. For that reason, we concluded that the stabbing with the club took place at the body's final resting place, after it had been moved.

Why would the perpetrator do such a thing? It's actually common among first-time killers. Since they've never murdered anyone before, they're not always sure the victim is really dead.

Furthermore, if the assailant was known to the victim, he'd have even more reason to want to make sure she'd never reveal his identity. In short, that final wound indicated this was an unsophisticated first-time killer, and that the victim knew him.

After analyzing the available material and constructing a profile of the offender, we compared it with a list of possible suspects, and eventually came to focus on three main potential suspects—Tommy, his younger brother, Michael, fifteen at the time of the crime, and Ken Littleton, the family's live-in tutor. The profile didn't fit Ken Littleton. It did fit Tommy, who had for a long time been the prime suspect. But it also drew in Michael Skakel, and in some ways pointed to him quite strongly. "In general," we wrote, "it seems as though Michael has been overlooked to some degree."

Next, we studied the considerable psychological data collected on the two Skakel boys, including professional assessments and the results of Sutton's own interviews with the two brothers. Tommy was indeed a likely candidate. But so, too, we thought, was Michael. Both boys had clearly demonstrated emotional problems, but as I saw it, Michael was the only one with a motive. Martha liked Tommy, had been flirting and spending time with him. Michael liked her, too. But she hadn't liked him back. Michael was the brother Martha had spurned.

In October 1993, we handed in our fifty-page analysis, which in turn became part of the Sutton Report. At a certain point, Jim Murphy realized that, even though Rush Skakel had gone into this truly believing his two boys were innocent, it was now time to tell him that might not be the case. Needless to say, he wasn't going to be happy about it.

We arranged a meeting with Skakel's attorney, Tom Sheridan, and Sutton Associates. They flew down to D.C. and met at a private conference room in the commuter jet terminal at National Airport, about thirty miles from our suburban Virginia office. Ken Baker and I were there, and we invited Roy Hazelwood, who was also now on board at AGI, just for the sake of getting as many eyes as possible on a case.

When Sheridan arrived, we went into a private conference room where drinks and sandwiches had been set out, and gave him the word. He nearly exploded. "You're wrong. That's not what happened. We have good reason to believe Martha Moxley was the victim of a serial killer," he said.

We were ready for it, and every time he said something like that, we hit him with the truth. "No, she was *not* the victim of a serial killer. And here's why . . ."

"No, it was not a stranger killing, and here's why . . ."

We explained about the golf club stabbing, the type of assault, the lack of defensive wounds. Things kept going back and forth, and it didn't really stop. Sheridan was angry when we gave him the word, and he left angry. Needless to say, that was the end of our efforts on the Moxley case. Not long afterward, Sheridan told Murphy he would be paid his six-figure consulting fee, but his services were no longer needed.

That seemed to be the end of it. This was not a police investigation, after all. We weren't working a current homicide investigation as members of law enforcement. We'd been subcontracted by Sutton, and Sutton was contracted by Rush Skakel, a private individual.

If there's one major difference between working as a government investigator and one in the private sector, this case illustrated it. Murphy and Willis Krebs were both good investigators, and they did their job. But both men were also bound by attorney-client privilege from talking about what they had unearthed. As potentially explosive as the information was, they were simply not morally or legally free to divulge it to anyone but the Skakel camp. Everything was confidential, and we kept it that way. We honored our side of the contract. Murphy honored his.

That's why I almost fell out of my chair one night when I looked up to see the title page of the AGI Moxley report on the nightly news. I went right up to the screen to make sure, and watched again at eleven because I still couldn't believe it. I wasn't mistaken. It was our report.

As it turned out, one of Murphy's employees had stolen the report and given it to author Dominick Dunne, who at the time had already written a fictionalized book about the Moxley case. Dunne in turn gave it to Mark Fuhrman, a former detective best known for his involvement in the O. J. Simpson case, who used it as the basis for *his* best-seller, *Murder in Greenwich*.

I don't have a problem when reporters uncover material legitimately, but I found it outrageous that both Dunne and Fuhrman simply ran with material that didn't belong to them in the first place. I didn't have a problem about not being acknowledged for our work. That happens all the time in the consulting business. What bothered me was that our analysis had never been intended as the final word on Michael Skakel as a possible suspect.

Parts of the Sutton Report were clearly marked "purposefully prejudicial analysis," because that's what they were. An attempt to shake up the case, play devil's advocate, suggest some new theories. It was intended as a tool, something to spur on the investigation. Not to summarize it in a single bottom line.

But that's how it was portrayed in the press, and because of that, it played a role in the resurgence of the case against Michael

Skakel, and his ultimate conviction. But the Sutton Report represents only a small fraction of the full Moxley case file, much of which is still in the hands of Skakel family attorneys, protected by attorney-client privilege. Was Michael Skakel guilty of the murder? I certainly leaned in that direction. Jim Murphy and Willis Krebs are not convinced. They lean more toward Tommy. Profiling, as I've said many times, is not infallible. But what I do know is that we at the AGI tried to get at the truth in the Martha Moxley murder. We didn't make it all the way. But we damn well got it into the right house.

Not long after our work on the Moxley case came to a close, I got the phone call from the law firm of Harris and Harris, in Bucks Country, Pennsylvania, asking for our help on the cold case Terri Brooks homicide, which involved the murder of a young employee of a fast food restaurant. After viewing the horrific crime scene photographs, both Ken Baker and I had had the same initial reaction—that the brutality of the crime, involving four distinct modes of death, meant that in all likelihood the killer had known his victim. And it was that element—the presence of personal animus—that might allow Terri's heartbroken parents to at least collect some financial damages for what they, and their daughter, had suffered.

Ken and I began the way we always do, by reviewing everything we could get our hands on. This time, we were lucky. Unlike the Moxley case, the local PD was relatively cooperative. Even though we didn't even have professional law enforcement status, they gave us access to whatever we needed—evidence reports, photographs, interview files, the autopsy report.

We read documents, talked to the medical examiner, looked at aerial photographs of the restaurant taken years before. Ken and I even went to Pennsylvania to make an on-site visit at the restaurant itself, because, by standing in the very place where Terri was murdered, we hoped to get an even better understanding of what had taken place on that terrible February morning in 1984.

The initial police investigation at the crime scene had shown no evidence of forced entry. We narrowed it down to three possibilities: Either the killer forced Terri back inside as she was leaving, or she knew him and had let him in, or else he was someone who hid on the premises until all the other employees had left. Assuming the latter, we walked through the entire restaurant, looking for hiding places.

Could he have been in the men's room? No, that was one of the places she would've routinely checked. There was also a storage attic, and we went up into it to see if someone could have hidden there. It may have been physically possible, but that didn't square with the timetable. The restaurant had closed before midnight, and Terri was killed after 2:00 a.m. If someone had been hiding there, why did he wait for up to three hours before revealing himself?

In reality, it was far likelier that she had let him in, which meant only one thing. Terri was a smart girl, and at that hour, she wouldn't have let a total stranger into the closed restaurant. What made a lot more sense was that she probably knew and trusted the person who would soon kill her.

After our preliminary inquiry, the law firm that had hired us called together a meeting of the major players in the investigation, eight people, including the forensic pathologist who had conducted the autopsy, a private investigator who had been involved in the case, a forensic psychologist, and three attorneys.

We were there as forensic behavioral scientists, the new kids on the block.

We all met in a conference room at the law firm, and decided that, going around the table, each of us would give his or her impressions and conclusions. Everyone concurred with the feeling that the Terri Brooks murder had been the result of an armed robbery gone bad, and offered reasons to support that conclusion. Someone, for instance, pointed out there were highways and wooded areas in close proximity to the Roy Rogers, which would have provided an easy staging area, and a point of egress. Another noted that armed robberies had been fairly common in the area at the time. All of them said they couldn't see any evidence of personal animus, which was at the heart of the civil case.

As the most recent additions to the investigation, we went last. I cleared my throat and said, "I'm afraid we disagree with your conclusions. We don't think it was an armed robbery. We believe the killer knew the victim. And we believe this case can be solved."

There was dead silence. Everyone stared at us. Finally, someone said, "What are you guys—hired guns? You're saying that because you're being paid to?"

"It's possible the *initial* motive was robbery, and we'll certainly entertain that notion," I said. "But we believe personal animus clearly existed. In fact, our first inclination is that this killer had a close, personal relationship with the victim. As we see it, there's simply too much emotion evident in the crime scene. There are four modes of death present, and that indicates overkill. Whoever killed Terri really wanted to make sure the job got done."

There was a lot of back and forth, and everyone disagreed with us. But we held our ground. Many years before, I'd read a book called *My Life in Court* by one of this country's great civil trial attorneys, Louis Nizer. Nizer said his methodology in any given case was to look at all the facts, gather absolutely as much information as was available, digest it all, and then apply what he called the law of probability. In other words, the operative question should not be "What *might* have happened?" or "What possibly *could* have happened?" Instead, it should be "In all likelihood, what *probably* happened?"

That's what we did. We asked the question: "Who was the most probable suspect?" And the answer was: someone who knew her. Our presentation must have made sense, because the attorney from the law firm of Harris and Harris, Greg Sturn, gave us the official green light to proceed with our investigation.

The next step in the process was the most difficult. It always is. But it's an essential, necessary part of the examination of almost any homicide. We had to know everything we could about the victim, because that's the most logical starting point in the solution of a crime. So Ken, Greg Sturn, and I made a trip to Warminster, Pennsylvania, to visit Terri's parents. It was eveningtime, just beginning to get dark, and we pulled up to the house, a modest two-story in a working-class neighborhood, and rang the bell. From within came the faint sound of a musical chime. Betty Brooks appeared at the door and invited us in. We walked through a small foyer into the living room, and sat down.

George Brooks was a gentle giant, very kind, very loving with his children. We talked mostly about the kind of daughter Terri had been, what activities she was involved in, how she had played intramural sports in college. What he told us dovetailed with what we had intuited from the crime scene photos. Terri Brooks was not the kind of person who would have surrendered without a fight.

It's never pleasant to look at crime scene photos, and it hadn't been easy to see what had been done to Terri by her killer. But that's never as difficult as then suddenly seeing pictures of the victim, alive. The photographs of Terri in that living room showed a vibrant young woman, just ready to really head out into the world. Something significant was missing from her father's life. He was still suffering. You could see it in the pictures of Terri in the house. You could see it in his face.

At that point, what did we have? We believed that whoever had killed Terri was someone who knew her, so Ken and I began by looking at anyone who fit that bill—friends, employees, even her fiancé. In all, there were four or five potentials, right off the bat. We decided to start interviewing them.

We prioritized the list, and chose to begin with her fiancé, Alfred Scott Keefe. The attorneys from Harris and Harris knew where he was living, that he was still working at a fast food restaurant in the area, and they said they'd arrange an interview. But on the day that Ken and I made another trip down to Bucks County after making arrangements to interview him, Keefe pulled a no-show. The lawyers were a little flustered, and very apologetic. "Don't worry about it," I said. "We're former federal agents. If he doesn't come to us, we'll find his ass."

Ken and I located Keefe's apartment complex a couple of hours later. At 6:30 p.m., we rang the downstairs bell, and in response, he opened the door and stuck his head over a second-floor railing. "What's this about?" he hollered.

We identified ourselves, told him that we had a few questions for him, and they were about Terri. Then, Keefe said something that I will never forget.

He looked down at us and said, "I don't care to get involved."

I don't care to get involved?

Keefe was living with another woman by this time, so I suggested that he step outside the apartment, and come downstairs for a minute. We coaxed him to a door at the bottom of the stairs. When I got my first good look at him, I realized that he looked just like his photograph, a weaselly-looking guy, about five-foot-eleven, thin, with a mustache—the kind of guy you'd expect to see still working at a fast food restaurant at age twenty-nine, which he was. Then he said the words again: "I don't care to get involved."

"What the hell do you mean you don't want to become involved?" I said. "Terri was your fiancée. You were going to be married to her. You *are* involved."

That was how it started.

Ken and I took turns. It was a friendly interview, nothing confrontational. Maybe a little healthy tension, just to keep things rolling, but that's all. "All we want is background information," I said.

You don't want to tip your hand. You just collect as much information from the subject as possible. We talked to him on the landing for about twenty minutes. He kept edging back toward the door. He was anxious for it to be over. How long had he and Terri known each other? Did they go to school together? Was she the kind of person who would fight in an assault situation?

We asked if Terri was right-handed, and he said, no, she was a lefty. We asked if she smoked, and he said no. Then we had asked him how he had found out that Terri had been killed. He said when he woke up in the morning, he drove past her house on the way to work, as he always did, but this time noticed her car wasn't there. He knocked on the Brookses' door, and said, "Is Terri home? I don't see her car." Then they went up and checked her bedroom and saw she hadn't come home.

We knew the last three answers were lies. Terri was right-handed. She smoked. And when we drove to the place where Keefe had lived at the time, and then to where he had been working at the time, Terri's house wasn't on the route between the two. In fact, it was a pretty fair distance away.

It's always interesting when a person lies about relatively insignificant things. You have to ask yourself, "Why is he lying about something like that?" To some people, truth is a mutable concept. Truth is so unimportant to them, they'll say anything, just to get rid of you, or for no real reason at all. The question then becomes, "Okay, if he lies about the small stuff for no good reason, what else is he lying about, maybe *for* a good reason?"

At the end of the interview, Ken and I walked back to the car. We looked at each other and, again, were of one mind. "This guy's our primary," we said. "He's good for this homicide."

As far as we were concerned, it was going to involve a lot of legwork, but there was little doubt. We called up the law firm and spoke to attorney Greg Sturn.

"Greg, we know you're not paying us to solve this thing, but this is solvable," I said. "We believe Keefe killed Terri."

We filed our report, a fairly thick profile, with the law firm. In it we said that, in our expert opinion, there had indeed been personal animus between Terri Brooks and her killer, and that we could testify to that, with confidence, in a court proceeding. And then we went a step further.

We said that, while we knew our report was proprietary information, we believed the case was solvable, and the prime suspect was Terri's former fiancé, Alfred Scott Keefe. And although we had gone beyond what we were technically contracted to do, we stated that we hoped the law firm would forward our report to local law enforcement.

And they did. Terri's family eventually received a substantial financial settlement, and afterward, our report remained the private property of Harris and Harris. But at some point, they sent it over to the police department, because of the bearing that it had on a possible solution of the case.

At one point, we had gotten a call from the Falls Township police, who said they were interested in coming down to discuss the case. We said we'd help them out, and a few days later a couple of detectives arrived at AGI's offices in Manassas. We told them about our theory. They went through the motions, took a few notes. But as it turned out, what they were really interested in was taking a tour of the FBI Academy. So we did the gracious thing. We took them over to Quantico, and they walked around, bought some souvenirs, and then went home. They didn't have much to say about Terri's case, and we never heard from them again, either.

Terri Brooks was a lovely young woman who had promise, and ambition, and a family who loved her very much. The idea that her murder remained unsolved after all those years continued to nag at me. So did an image that never really left my mind. It was the memory of the final expression on her face, the indelible image I saw in the crime scene photos: lifeless eyes, half-open, with a look of resignation and unutterable sadness in them. "It's over now. I can't fight anymore. I have given up," they seemed to say.

By this time, I was beginning to realize that while working in the private sector had its advantages over working for the government, in at least one way it was a lot tougher. In law enforcement, the game plan was straightforward. You got a case, you worked it to the best of your ability, and if luck was with you and you did your job well, you scored an indictment and maybe a conviction.

But in the private sector, the people paying your salary could, at any moment, simply say, "Thank you very much. Here's your check. We don't need you anymore."

That's what had happened with our Martha Moxley investigation. It wouldn't be long before it happened again. And at least for the time being, it was what also seemed to be happening with the Terri Brooks homicide, since I could never have imagined the remarkable turn of events in that case that were still to come.

In the spring of 1992, I received a call from an attorney in Tampa by the name of Lyndi Gordon. Her law firm, Salem, Saxon & Nielsen, had been retained by the De Soto County, Florida, prosecutor's office to reexamine the prosecution and conviction of a man named James Joseph Richardson. Once she began to refresh my memory, I realized that I did have a vague recollection of the case. Three years before, there'd been a spate of articles in the press about Richardson, a fifty-three-year-old fruit picker who'd spent twenty-two years in prison, four of them on death row. In 1968, Richardson had been tried and convicted of a particularly heinous murder in the small town of Arcadia, Florida. His crime, according to the state, was using lethal insecticide to poison and kill his seven young children.

A few years after Richardson was sentenced, a Washington, D.C., attorney named Mark Lane, best known as a JFK assassination conspiracy theorist, stumbled across the case and became convinced Richardson was innocent. In time, he mounted a "Free James Richardson" campaign, and enlisted support from Hollywood celebrities and the Congressional Black Caucus, among others. A year later, in 1989, Florida's governor, Bob Martinez, announced the state would reexamine Richardson's case. And within months of that announcement, Richardson walked out of prison a free man.

That day, according to press accounts, Richardson had wanted all his supporters from around the country to know how grateful he was that they'd gone to the trouble of helping set him free. But he apparently wasn't without vengeance toward his accusers. Prosecutors had "treated me like I was some kind of dog," he said. "And I want them to know how it feels."

Now, three years after his release, Richardson had filed a $35 million lawsuit against the state of Florida, alleging he had been wrongfully prosecuted and convicted, and naming the former prosecutor, Frank Schaub, and former sheriff, Frank Cline, as principals. That was the reason for Lyndi Gordon's call; the law firm of Salem, Saxon & Nielsen had been retained to reexamine the Richardson case, in an effort to clear the state's name.

We decided to take on the case, and a few weeks later, my colleague Ken Baker and I began our reinvestigation.

About an hour outside town, past long ribbons of fetid drainage canals and miles of nameless commercial orange groves, I finally spotted our destination, right where they said it would be. I wheeled the air-conditioned rental car into an empty asphalt parking lot, and opened the door into a wall of central Florida's sweltering white summer heat. With one hand I reached for the last of the clean cotton handkerchiefs I'd packed into my suitcase nearly a week before. With the other, I fished in my suit jacket for the scrap of paper with a map of burial plots that had been sketched for me in smeared ballpoint by one of the paralegals back in the Tampa law office.

As Ken and I headed out into these so-called memorial gardens, it was obvious we had been directed to a poorer section of the cemetery. It shared a name, just as improbably, with the small town it sat on the outskirts of—Arcadia. But these were no Elysian Fields.

From the looks of things, some of Arcadia's former citizenry— whites, mostly—had done pretty well for themselves, headquartered now in marble, two-tiered mausoleums, some partly shaded by scraggly cypress draped with Spanish moss, others adorned with precast simulated stone-carved angels. But the gravesite we were looking for was farther on, toward the chain link fence that bordered the cemetery's perimeter, beyond where mowed lawn had given way to scrub grass, which was now mostly giving way to sand.

It took only five minutes' walk in the broiling sun to find them, the simple granite markers, not standing upright, but lying flat against the earth. Other headstones nearby had wilted carnations in jelly jars beside them, or a few gaudy plastic bouquets. But these didn't have even that much. They were unadorned, these markers, all seven of them, lying in a cluster. Children's headstones, all by themselves.

They were together now in death, as close as they had been in life. Ken and I stood over them and realized that, even after reading thousands of pages of police reports and court transcripts and grim autopsy summaries, what we were seeing now conveyed the true enormity of what had happened—the finality of it—in a way nothing else could.

"Good Lord," Ken said, in his soft tidewater Virginia drawl. Characteristically, I suppose, I didn't say anything at all.

The entire event was now reduced to seven pieces of cut stone, arranged in descending order: eight-year-old Betty Jean next to Alice, who was seven, followed by Susie, age six. Next to her were Doreen, five, Vanessa, four, Diane, three, and the last, James Jr., who died just two and a half years after his life began. There were no epitaphs along with those names, no "Beloved Child" or "In the Arms of Jesus." Just the dates of entry and exit from this world. The birthdays, of course, were all different. But the markers all shared one thing— the date of death, "October 25, 1967," twenty-five years before.

Ken and I had seen as much as we had needed to, and there was no point in staying any longer. But before I turned to walk back to the car, I couldn't help but notice how, over the two and a half decades that those small granite tablets had aged in the sub-tropical heat, a funereal black mold had settled deep into their hairline cracks and engravings. The sight of it is what I remember most clearly about that airless afternoon in 1992. And also the way, as I raised my handkerchief to wipe my forehead, that a small black snake sunning itself on the headstones suddenly roused itself and slithered off into the tall weeds.

———

This was going to be difficult work—the examination of a multiple murder that had taken place nearly a quarter century before. But the facts of the case were compelling, and after mulling over the offer for a few days with my colleagues, we decided to take it on. By consensus, we picked Ken Baker, a former Secret Service agent and a highly respected expert in the field of violent crime, to go along with me to Florida. Ken had another relevant credential, too. He had a particularly vivid memory of the Richardson murders because, during the 1960s, as it happened, he'd been a deputy sheriff in the next county over from Arcadia.

There was no point in asking Sharon to come down to Florida with me, as much as I would have liked to have her along. By this time, our three kids were all grown and out of the house, but she still liked to stay close to her children and grandchildren in case they needed her for anything. I would miss unwinding with her over dinner at the end of a long day. But it didn't seem fair to ask her to come with me, since I'd be hunkered down in a Tampa law office for weeks' worth of ten-hour days.

A few weeks later, Ken and I found ourselves seated at the mahogany conference table in the offices of Salem, Saxon & Nielsen, waiting as a paralegal carried in box after box of the records left by the Richardson case, thousands of pages in all.

For now, I would begin with the written material: yellowed interview transcripts, dog-eared court filings, crumbling newspaper accounts. The earnest young paralegal carried in the last of the boxes. "That's it for now, Dr. Depue. Can I bring you all a coffee or anything?"

"That'd be great," I said, sitting down to a mountain of cardboard boxes that gave off the unmistakably musty smell of damp decay.

Twenty-five years ago in the quiet town of Arcadia, at a two-story, cinder block and stucco flat-roofed apartment building known to locals as the old Barnes Hotel, the morning of Tuesday, October 25, 1967, began as it usually did. Just after 6:30 a.m., James Joseph Richardson, thirty-two, and his wife, Annie Mae, twenty-nine, woke the oldest of seven children, Betty Jean, as they dressed for work at the Ryles County Line Grove some four-teen miles away, where they would spend a backbreaking day picking oranges for twenty-five cents a crate.

While Richardson washed up, Annie Mae packed a lunch of fried chicken for herself and her husband, and made the children's breakfast grits. Because little Doreen was in the habit of getting into the cornmeal and lima beans and spilling them all over the floor, food was kept in two padlocked refrigerators in the kitchen. From one, Annie Mae took out leftovers from the family's dinner the night before—a pot of beans, rice, and hogshead gravy—and put it out on the stove for the children's lunch. It would be Betty Jean's job to wake the other children: Alice, Susie, Doreen, Vanessa, Diane, and James Jr.

As she and her husband were leaving the apartment, Annie Mae gave her set of refrigerator keys to Richardson, who put them with his own set of keys on a string around his neck. Then the couple checked in with Bessie Reese, forty-six, a next-door neighbor who today, as she often did, would look after the Richardson children while their parents were at work. James reminded Bessie not to let the kids dawdle at lunch. "They waste time over their food, and you have to help them finish it," he said. When the three older children left for school a few blocks away Bessie settled on her porch to keep an eye on the four youngest.

Just before eleven, Betty Jean and her sisters came home for lunch, and she heated up the meal for the brood. She could manage almost all of it by herself, but when she needed help cutting up the rice cake into seven servings, Bessie helped her. A half hour later, after the kids had finished eating, Betty Jean cleaned up, took the four youngest children next door to Bessie's and, with her two sisters, headed back to school. It was not long afterward, according to the official records, that something horrible began to happen.

In a first grade classroom, teacher Myrtice Jackson saw seven-year-old Alice sweating profusely. "She grabbed ahold of her desk and her mouth came open. She was retching and her head was going back. I asked what was wrong. She never said anything. Never made any noise." The little girl was obviously in pain, "drawing up" as Jackson put it. "I thought she was having an epileptic fit, and I sent for help." Then another teacher, Ruby Faison, came into the room and saw Alice in seizure. The two decided to take Alice to the principal's office. But first, said Faison, "We pried her hands from the desk. Her eyes weren't focusing. I said to myself, 'It must be poison.'"

Within minutes, teachers were racing Alice and her sisters to Arcadia General Hospital. In another car, Ruby Faison asked a still conscious Betty Jean what she and the other children had eaten for lunch. "We had rice, gravy, and beans," she said. A few minutes later, Betty Jean said, "I'm all right, there is nothing wrong with me." Principal Lewis Anderson replied, "Sure you are."

Meanwhile, back at the Richardson apartment, Bessie Reese saw that the four younger children had also become violently ill. She called the school, only to learn the older children were already on their way to the hospital. Just before noon, several teachers raced to Reese's, and found one of the children lying on the front porch. Doreen and Diane were standing behind a broom, crying. Bessie was holding little James in her arms. They, too, were rushed to the hospital.

At Arcadia General, Betty Jean was placed on a canvas cot, her baby brother James at her feet. A nurse checked the baby's pulse with a stethoscope and said, "This one is gone."

When Dr. Elmer J. Schmierer arrived on the scene, he was directed to Vanessa, who was being given artificial respiration by nurses, who were frantically trying to clear her mucus-filled airways with wooden tongue depressors. "I listened to her heart and found no heartbeat or breath at the time," Schmierer remembered. "I pronounced her dead."

Summoned to another room, Schmierer found that Alice, too, had died. Then he was directed to Doreen and Susie, who shared a stretcher, and Betty Jean, who was now on a cot by herself. Another local physician, Dr. Calvin Martin, later said their most striking symptom was a pronounced "twitching, like a bag of worms contracting by themselves without any coherent action."

By then, Schmierer was in the tiled X-ray room, attending Doreen. "The child was rolling around on the X-ray table moaning and groaning, and I again noticed there was an odor of fecal material in the air," he said. Asked if she appeared to be in pain, he replied simply, "Yes."

Parathion was first developed in the waning months of World War II by German chemists, who were studying its potential as a chemical weapon. Instead, it was developed for peacetime application as an agricultural pesticide, and eventually became a staple in the Florida citrus industry. But it was also notoriously lethal. Just three drops of parathion oil placed on unbroken skin could kill a man within minutes.

Now, on this afternoon in Arcadia, Schmierer and the other ER doctors quickly suspected parathion as the likeliest cause of the day's terrible events. By 1:00 p.m., six of the seven Richardson children were dead. Only three-year-old Diane was still alive, desperately fighting for her life. Months later, Dr. Calvin Martin would be asked in what order the children died. "They were so close together," he said, "it was hard to tell."

As I paged through the hundreds of documents, crime scene photographs, and police reports that revealed the events of that day, I had to keep fighting off the mental images of my own children when they were so young, and thought back to the inevitable childhood accidents that had taken us to the emergency room. I remembered how four-year-old Renee screamed when her finger was accidentally slammed in the car door, the look of cold terror in Sharon's eyes when we found Arleen, then ten, semiconscious after falling from a backyard gym set.

But nothing in my experience was even remotely in the same league as the horror that was unfolding in those documents on the table in front of me. Death by poisoning, as I well knew, is a terrible way to die. I stayed focused on my research, and continued taking the careful notes that would help me construct a clear timeline of the events that occurred that long-ago day in Arcadia.

At 12:20 p.m., Lieutenant Joe Minoughan of the Arcadia police department was the first law enforcement officer to reach the Richardson home. When he arrived, he found both floors of the duplex filthy and littered, with both refrigerators still padlocked. A quick search of the house showed no obvious sign of poison, but as he later said, "I smelled that poison. I smelled it twenty-five feet from the house. Did you ever put a penny in your mouth? Well, that's what it smelled like"—the unmistakably metallic smell of "cooked" parathion.

Meanwhile, James and Annie Mae Richardson were notified at work that they were needed at the hospital. By the time they arrived at Arcadia General, a local minister, the Reverend L. T. Fagan, and a county judge, Gordon Hayes, were also present, along with police and the teachers. Fagan, well aware of the

Richardsons' dire financial straits, asked James if he happened to have any insurance coverage to help cover burial costs. His response was stunning. Richardson, a poor, uneducated man who barely had enough money to pay rent, reported that he did indeed have insurance. In fact, he said, he had taken out a double indemnity life insurance policy on his children just the night before.

At 4:00 p.m., Richardson was officially read his rights and questioned by state attorney Frank Schaub and his assistant, James Foy. When they, too, inquired about insurance, Richardson stammered. "I thought I had some. I had intended to take out some insurance last night, but—I'm going to tell you the truth." Then he said, "I ain't got a nickel."

In the course of their interview, the attorneys asked if Richardson had ever lost any other children. This response, too, was shocking. "I had three die in Jacksonville," he said. Two of those children had been born dead, he said, and the third, a three-year-old boy named Sampson, "died when my mother had charge of it, that one." The cause, he said vaguely, was "something about diarrhea."

Next, Annie Mae was questioned, and she filled in some of the details of a complicated domestic history. The three oldest of the children who died that day were actually Annie Mae's from a previous marriage—to Richardson's brother; the three youngest were her biological children with James; and seven-year-old Alice—Richardson's child from one of his two prior marriages—had only been living with them for a few weeks.

Annie Mae was also clear on the issue of whether her husband had taken out insurance on the children the night before.

"Do you have any insurance on the children?" Foy asked her.

"Yeah," Annie Mae said. "My husband, he doing insurance last night."

"He took out some insurance last night?"

"Yes."

"Do you know who all he insured?"

"He told me he insured all of us, the children and us."

"Who told you that?"

"My husband."

At 6:10 p.m. that evening, with her last remaining child, three-year-old Diane, still fighting for her life in the intensive care unit, a distraught Annie Mae was injected with a sedative and left the hospital to go home. Richardson, who never asked to see the children, seemed remarkably unaffected by the deaths. "He seemed very cool during the whole ordeal," Reverend Fagan told investigators. "He didn't seem too much concerned about the whole situation."

That evening, with their apartment secured as a crime scene, Annie Mae stayed at their friend Bessie's, and James slept at the home of a nearby friend, who was in the hospital at the time. Meanwhile, the local sheriff, Frank Cline, continued his investigation at the crime scene. Lab tests conducted that day showed parathion contamination of several items removed from the locked refrigerators—a box of soap powder, talcum, and flour. Now Cline continued to collect evidence—several items of clothing, work gloves, and two pick sacks of the type used by workers in the orange groves. At 1:00 a.m. he called it a night, but not before searching the area around the house, including a small shed in the front yard, about fifty feet from the Richardsons' door.

Early the next morning, police were called back to the scene when neighbors reported something strange inside that small storage shed—a partially empty two-pound bag of parathion. When police arrived, they saw that, unlike anything else in the shed, which had been thoroughly searched the night before, the bag of parathion was wet with dew. It had obviously not been in its present location long. Someone had recently moved it there.

Just before dawn that morning, on October 26, the last of the Richardson children, three-year-old Diane, died at Arcadia General Hospital. Later that morning, it fell to Sheriff Cline to give Richardson the sad news. According to Cline, Richardson's only response was "Yeah?" And when Cline suggested Richardson tell his wife, who was on the porch just twenty-five feet away, Richardson instead continued to follow Cline around as he examined the house.

Out of Richardson's earshot, another investigator had a question for Annie Mae: "What would you say if I told you that you and your husband killed the children?"

"You would be wrong about me," she said.

Then another fact jumped out at me from the record. In an interview, Annie Mae told police that she was the one who always did the family's laundry. Yet on the day after the murders, Richardson's first act after being allowed back into his house was to gather up his clothing—including the pants and shirt he wore on the day of the murders—and carry them to a neighbor's house to wash them himself. Why, I wondered. Could it have been because he knew that, if tested, they would surely show trace evidence of parathion?

By the day after the deaths, local police, the Florida attorney general's office, and the state agriculture and health departments were all in on the case, and began to learn even more about Richardson's personal history. In 1965, *following* his marriage to Annie Mae, he had fathered a daughter with one of his two ex-wives. More recently, his other former wife had filed a complaint for desertion and nonsupport. And seven months before the children's deaths, Annie Mae herself had also sworn out a warrant against him for nonsupport. Richardson, it seemed, had been facing a number of mounting financial pressures, most apparently related to the care and feeding of his children.

They also learned more about the earlier deaths of two children from his previous marriages. In 1959, Richardson, who had done time at a juvenile correctional facility as a boy, fathered a little girl by his first wife, Priscilla Bing. During an interview with Arcadia police, he recalled the little girl, but said he didn't know anything about her death, since he had left the area when she was seven months old. "I don't remember, 'cause I wasn't there really," he said.

In fact, police learned, records listed the baby's cause of death as "undetermined," stated that she had died at the age of seven months—and that at the time, Richardson was living nearby.

Investigators also questioned Richardson's mother, who had been caring for another of Richardson's children, three-year-old Sampson, at the time of his death. Richardson stated that he hadn't been living with the baby at the time, and didn't know what had caused Sampson's death. Again, official records disputed Richardson's version.

In fact, on the night Sampson became ill, Richardson was the one who took him to the hospital and signed his death certificate. The baby, records showed, had suffered from vomiting and convulsions—symptoms, as investigators noted, that were not inconsistent with poisoning.

On Sunday, October 28, 1968, a funeral for the seven Richardson children was held at Arcadia's local high school gymnasium—the only building in town large enough to hold the crowd of one thousand mourners. Seven small white caskets formed a crescent, and in the front row, before a raft of news cameras, Richardson, in apparent grief, wept and collapsed.

Three days later, he failed a polygraph, and was arrested and charged with the murder of the oldest child, Betty Jean Bryant. The reasoning, said prosecutors, was if he were acquitted, they could still try him for each of the other children's deaths.

The trial began seven months later with an opening statement by prosecutor Frank Schaub, who charged the defendant had been motivated by a desire "to collect life insurance policies on the children's lives." Richardson, said Schaub, was a cold-blooded killer who "was looking for a way out from under the children, and he had become disenchanted with Annie Mae."

For its part, the defense focused mostly on testimony from character witnesses like Bernice Hartley, a longtime family friend. Asked about Richardson's relationship with his children, she said, "They run like rats running to meet their daddy. They would be on his legs and shoulders dragging him in the house." The defendant's sister, Martha Tinsley, also recalled that "The children would be all over him. When they got tired of doing that, they went to singing . . . mostly Christian songs . . . like 'Let God Abide.' " Annie Mae testified she and her husband had begun putting clothes and toys for the children in layaway "because we had so many that we couldn't buy." Her husband, she said, "devoted all his time with the children when he was home and we got off of work. He would sit up and play with them and sometimes go outdoors and run around and all like that."

On May 31, 1968, after just eighty-four minutes of deliberation, the jury found Richardson guilty of the premeditated murder of Betty Jean Bryant, and he was sentenced to death in the electric chair. Five years later, the U.S. Supreme Court struck down the death penalty, overturning 131 pending death sentences, including Richardson's. He was then resentenced to twenty-five years in prison. Which by all accounts is where he might have remained, if it weren't for the sad ramblings of an addled old woman on her deathbed in a nursing home.

In late 1986, former neighbor Bessie Reese, by now suffering from Alzheimer's disease in an Arcadia senior care facility, began to talk about her role in the notorious Richardson case. Overhearing her, a staffer named Brenda Frazier became curious, and decided to ask her outright: "Did you kill those kids, Bessie?"

"Yeah, I did that," Bessie replied.

At that, Frazier asked Bessie why she had killed the children. But Bessie never really did answer. "She'd just start crying, going off to herself singing church songs and praying," Frazier later said. "Like she was asking for forgiveness."

Anyone who had even a cursory knowledge of the case would have understood what that meant. As early as the day after the murders, Bessie had volunteered to Sheriff Frank Cline that she felt responsible for their deaths. "If I hadn't a fed those kids," she told him, "they wouldn't a died."

In fact, in the wake of the Arcadia murders, Bessie had come under suspicion for a time. The reason was that, years before, she had been convicted of shooting and killing her former husband in what she said was an act of self-defense. In addition, her husband at the time had just left her for a cousin of James Richardson. In my opinion, both of those facts certainly warranted investigation. But as the record showed, they *had* been investigated, thoroughly. At the time of the murders, police questioned

Bessie at length, conducted a polygraph (which she passed), considered all the evidence—and ultimately cleared her.

Still, Bessie's so-called confession in a nursing home was enough to rekindle Mark Lane's interest in the case. He wrote a seven-page letter to Florida governor, Bob Martinez, claiming Richardson's conviction provided clear evidence of "the total collapse of the judicial system in Florida due to racism."

Lane began beating the drums, threatening to take the story to the national media, and promising that the Congressional Black Caucus would organize a national boycott of Florida products and cripple the state's economy. Within weeks, the chairman of the Black Caucus, Congressman Mervyn M. Dymally, called the Richardson case a "terrible miscarriage of justice [which] was not the result of error, but rather deliberate efforts to convict an innocent man."

On February 1, 1989, in response to public pressure, Martinez signed an executive order directing the Florida Department of Law Enforcement to reinvestigate the Richardson case, and assigned it to state attorney Janet Reno, the future U.S. attorney general. Her staff reviewed the then twenty-two-year-old murder case, and eight weeks later issued a thirty-five-page *nolle prosse* memorandum (Latin for "not willing to pursue"), which asserted that Richardson "was probably wrongfully accused."

Based on Reno's recommendation, on April 25, 1989, Judge Clifton M. Kelly vacated Richardson's conviction, on the grounds that Richardson had not received a fair trial. By then fifty-three, Richardson was released from prison, and immediately launched his suit for $35 million in damages for his ordeal, and filed for divorce from Annie Mae. That December, he appeared in *People* magazine, smiling broadly, with his arms around a beaming thirty-seven-year-old woman, whom he would identify only as Lizzie. The two had met while he was in prison and intended to marry, said Richardson proudly, because she was now pregnant with his child.

In reviewing these yellowing case documents, sifting through a small mountain of material, and conducting interviews with witnesses who were still alive, it became clear to me that, as thorough as the initial investigation was—and I felt that local law enforcement had done the best it could with limited resources and the techniques available at the time—there was one thing that *hadn't* been done. No one had ever gone back and conducted a careful analysis of the statements made by James and Annie Mae Richardson.

In sum, what we at The Academy Group discovered was that Janet Reno's review of the case had a major flaw: It didn't examine the statements and behavior of James and Annie Mae Richardson with the same scrutiny that it did other witnesses. In fact, sworn statements were never even taken from Richardson or Annie Mae, despite obvious perjuries during questioning and at trial. And the Reno report failed to take into account the fact that Richardson had failed a polygraph exam. Rather than drawing the most plausible conclusions from the evidence, Reno's review strained to prove alternative possibilities that, ultimately, did not make sense—even using Bessie Reese, who was no longer alive to defend herself, as a convenient scapegoat.

And as old as the case file was, much of the information it contained was still as valid as it was on the day of the murders. All that was needed was for someone to put the pieces together.

At the time of the murders, James Richardson had been charged with nonsupport of his children and family at least three times. He also knew through personal experience that if he left them he could be arrested for desertion. Unable even to make a $6.50 per week grocery payment, he was sliding ever more heavily into debt and had few hopes of getting out of it. How, then, could he possibly afford the continuing care of seven children, three of whom were not his? Seven children who, with double indemnity coverage, would be worth a total of seven thousand dollars dead?

The only plausible scenario for the murders, I believe, is that sometime between 4:00 and 4:30 a.m. on the morning of October 25, Richardson retrieved the parathion that he had obtained through his work from a hiding place (most likely at a neighbor's, to which he had a key) and brought it into his family's apartment. He put on a work glove, sprinkled the poison into the pot of beans and gravy, then unlocked both refrigerators and sprinkled it in the lard. Castoff poison from the glove contaminated articles near these items, leaving trace amounts in soap powder and a can of talc. Richardson then returned the parathion bag back to its original hiding place.

That noontime, his seven children ate the poisoned hogshead gravy, as Richardson had planned. When Betty Jean, the oldest, rinsed the plates, trace amounts of parathion were transferred from the heavily laced pot of hogshead to a frying pan and grits pot—which explained trace findings in those items.

Finally, early the next morning, as the last of his children lay dying in the hospital, Richardson removed the poison from its temporary hiding place and moved it to a location that, as he well knew, had already been searched by the police—the small shed within sight of Bessie Reese's front porch.

Taking into account the state of the investigative arts in 1967, we concluded that the police had in fact conducted a competent investigation, and that both Prosecutor Schaub and Sheriff Cline had done their jobs properly and well. And that led to a further finding. We weren't claiming to be infallible, but in our expert opinion, which is what we had been hired to provide, there was only one person who had both motive and opportunity to commit the Arcadia murders. And that person was James Joseph Richardson.

Richardson's trial might not have been perfect. No trial ever is, and legal technicalities can always be dredged up to try to cast doubt on either side. It may be that the people who worked on Richardson's behalf were truly convinced of his innocence, and believed he was an honest man wrongfully accused and tried by a racist system.

But as I saw it, good intentions were no excuse for the ultimate outcome. The people who worked so hard to exonerate Richardson blamed his conviction on a racist system, and they may well have been sincere. But that claim completely discounts the fact that the state's prosecution effort was conducted on behalf of seven poor, black—and innocent—children. What about their fate? Who besides the sheriff and prosecutors fought to protect their civil rights? Who wrote books, threatened boycotts, and lobbied lawmakers in an effort to secure justice for those children? My own feeling is that a reflexive response to past racism does not translate to justice if it results in the acquittal of a guilty man who murdered his own seven children.

Given the evidence in this case, I believe, a grand jury would indict Richardson today, and a jury would probably convict him. I have studied human behavior for more than three decades, in its worst and most aberrant forms. And as an expert in the field of forensic behavioral science, I believe that the reason James Joseph Richardson did what he did is crystal clear. He killed his children in the hope of collecting seven thousand dollars in insurance money. He put poison in their food because they were a hindrance. He murdered his seven children because they were an impediment to him.

In June 1992, I submitted our findings to Salem, Saxon & Nielsen. AGI's conclusion became part of an exhaustive review the firm officially presented, four months later, to the state of Florida. It termed the overturning of Richardson's conviction "a terrible miscarriage of justice," called for a reexamination of the case, and expressed a belief that his exoneration could easily be overturned. The real miscarriage of justice, as far as I'm concerned, took place when Richardson walked out the door of Raiford prison a free man.

I also noted that, in my opinion, there had never been a proper investigation into the death of three-year-old Sampson Richardson back in 1963. At first, police reports called it a possible homicide. Just two weeks later, the case was closed as "natural death caused by probable dehydration and electrolyte imbalance associated with prolonged vomiting." Even though those symptoms are not inconsistent with poisoning, there never was an official exhumation of Sampson's body. In fact, there is no evidence that anyone cared enough about the death of one poor, black baby in the Deep South at the time to make a serious effort to find out what had really killed him.

What I do know is that parathion, like some poisons, remains permanently in the body's hair and nails after death. If it was once present, it still would be today. And it would take only a fairly simple examination at autopsy to find it. Such an effort would not be a pointless exercise. Legally, as we pointed out, the order vacating Richardson's conviction is not the same thing as an acquittal. It doesn't prevent a reprosecution of Richardson, or a reinstatement of his conviction.

After his legal exoneration, Richardson lived what was, by all accounts, an unremarkable life. He was never arrested for another crime, was never charged with anything so much as a parking ticket. Instead, in prison he learned to read and write, and after his release became an instant celebrity. HBO and Michael Douglas's production company both optioned his life story, and comedian Dick Gregory offered him a one-hundred-thousand-dollar-a-year job at a nutrition clinic.

But the job didn't pan out, and Richardson suffered a series of setbacks. He went through the twenty thousand dollars he earned for selling his story and suffered two heart attacks, which he attributed to the lingering effects of prison food and poor medical care. He received one hundred fifty thousand dollars in an out-of-court settlement with De Soto County, but a big chunk of the money went to his lawyers.

Given how much publicity had surrounded the case over the years, I fully expected our report would kick up some dust in the media, and possibly even bring it before the courts again. This was, after all, perhaps the worst crime of domestic violence in the history of the state of Florida.

But weeks went by after we submitted our report, and then months and years. There was no coverage on the evening news, no front-page newspaper stories to resurrect the case. The story simply faded away.

In time, I learned that, on appeal, both Frank Schaub and Frank Cline were eventually cleared of any wrongdoing. Beyond that, the only time that I heard anything about Richardson came some years after we finished our work on the case, when I read an article in the *St. Petersburg Times* about men who have been pardoned after spending time on death row. One of them was Richardson, who, at the time, was living at the ranch of his cardiologist in Wichita, Kansas, doing light work in exchange for room and board. The reporter never asked Richardson directly if he committed the murders he was charged with, or whether he had any idea who the real killer was. What he asked was if Richardson had any lingering memories of death row.

Yes, said Richardson, he did: "When I hear a bunch of keys shaking, I think they are coming to get me and put me in the electric chair. I'm trying to get over it. But it's something that a man can never forget."

Despite the best efforts of a string of dedicated prosecutors and law enforcement personnel, I believe that justice did not prevail in this case, and that was difficult, demoralizing knowledge to live with. As far as I was concerned, there was no satisfactory resolution to the terrible events on that long-ago day in Florida, and certainly no fitting commemoration of the victims. Just a memory, enshrined somewhere off the beaten path, in an overgrown cemetery in a place called Arcadia. A place in the sleepy backwaters, where seven small headstones stand in mute testimony to the truth.

CHAPTER EIGHT

REQUIEM

ALL THROUGH MY LAW ENFORCEMENT CAREER, I had my own way of dealing with the stresses of the work. It was called Sharon. For more than three decades, no matter what horrible things I saw in my work, no matter how many literal and figurative dark alleys I went down, whenever I came home, she was there waiting with a smile and some gentle reassurance.

It hadn't been easy being the wife of an FBI profiler. Every guy had a different way of dealing with the work, and their wives had different ways, too. Some tried to be a part of the dark world their husbands were seeing every day. Others tried to make the home a sanctuary. Some tried to be a listening post; others tried to be anything but. And there were more than a few who came to realize there really wasn't anything they could do about it when their husbands came home from work, distant and unavailable, either for them or their kids. As the wife of one original profiler put it, "Whenever he came home with that particular quiet mood, I just learned to give him a lot of extra space." Sometimes that was just what the job required.

Sharon had her own technique in handling it. First off, she was feisty. She took after her aunt Tricia, a pretty lady who worked in a neighborhood working-class bar in Detroit. One night her aunt was wearing a blouse with a little tie on each shoulder, when a big guy came in, already in his cups, demanding another drink. The guy motioned to her as if to whisper, and she leaned over the bar. Then he reached over, touched one of her ties and said, "What would happen if I pulled this little string?"

She looked him straight in the eye and said, "Did you ever get knocked on your ass off a bar stool?" That same blood ran in Sharon's veins.

Sharon also liked to have a good time. Our house was always filled with the kids, and with their friends and ours. We always threw a big Christmas party every year for all of my FBI colleagues, and we always had a great time. Her good friend Nancy Davis said her favorite of Sharon's looks was the smile she had after a couple of beers. And lastly, Sharon generally kept a pretty even keel, and she wasn't judgmental. Her mother's side of the family were McPharlins—Irish, and salt of the earth. Sharon's mother was one of eleven children, and she was the kind of person who just accepted you right away, no questions asked. And she raised her kids to be that way, too.

Still, I'm a traditional guy, a throwback, and I always believed that even though Sharon had no trouble whatsoever taking care of herself, it was also my job to keep anything bad from ever happening to her. It was a mind-set that went back to my own childhood and the way I was raised—the feeling that one of the main responsibilities of being a man was to protect women and children.

But one day, immersed in a case I was studying, I brought a few cassette tapes home from the office—the originals of our conversations with Edmund Kemper. They were one of the first products of Douglas and Ressler's prison interviews with a convicted serial killer, and I had good reason to be listening to them. Not only was I professionally curious about exactly what Kemper was disclosing and the kinds of information they were getting, but I also realized we were to some degree in uncharted waters, and as a manager, I believed in experiencing the same things my profilers were.

And so, I was sitting in my office in our house in rural Virginia, listening to Kemper tell how he removed the door handles in his car so the young girls he abducted wouldn't be able to open them from the inside, and how he told them why he had to kill them, and precisely how he was going to do it. Then I sensed I wasn't alone, and when I looked up, I saw Sharon standing in the doorway.

She didn't say anything, just stood there with a look of such sadness in her eyes. I never really knew if she was sad about there being such evil in the world, or because someone she loved was spending so much of his life pursuing it. But it was the last time I ever brought anything like that into our home.

By the time I founded The Academy Group, we were each going through changes. The kids were out of the house, and Sharon was deciding what she was going to do with herself, now that they weren't around all the time. She started by getting her real estate license, but in the end decided against hanging out her shingle. Instead, she learned all about painting and wallpapering, and started her own interior decorating business. She called it New Surroundings, and printed up business cards with her name on them, underneath a rainbow. Pretty soon, she had a thriving little operation going, and when our girls, Renee and Arleen, were home from college, they'd help Sharon out, the whole crew working away in pink jerseys and white overalls with their logo on the back.

Her friend Nancy Davis remembers the afternoon in 1991 when Sharon stopped by. She'd been dieting to lose weight, and it was working. Nancy says she never remembered seeing Sharon look more beautiful. The next day, when Sharon was working by herself, she fell off a ladder, blacked out for a few minutes, and couldn't get up. She hadn't broken anything, but that was the start of it. She started bleeding. Her doctor told us that she had a growth, and that she would need a hysterectomy and further examination. I was sitting next to her in the doctor's office, holding her hand, when he gave us the news. When Sharon had her surgery, they would need an oncologist in the operating room alongside the surgeon. Because Sharon had uterine cancer.

My friend and former FBI partner Joe Davis, Nancy's husband, was always a steady hand for me, and on the morning Sharon had her surgery, he and I were at the hospital together. The surgery was supposed to last two or three hours, but it ultimately went on for six. During it, I kept wondering what was going on, why it was taking so long. I got upset. I knew it must be bad, but I was glad to have Joe there with me.

Afterward, I learned the cancer had grown from her uterus into her stomach walls and muscles. It was a sarcoma that got into fibroid tumors. Bert Brown, former director of the National Institute of Mental Health and a true friend, told me, "Roger, there's one chance in three that she'll make it." I asked him how he could know with such certainty. She's otherwise in reasonably good health, I said. She might be the one who makes it. How could he know? He told me gently. The literature showed that most women with this extent of disease lived for no more than six months.

I couldn't accept it. I did what I'd done throughout my life whenever I was faced with something that seemed insurmountable. I fought back. I went to the library at the hospital, and searched computer banks. I spent many days. I couldn't find a single case of a survivor. I knew statistics. I'd spent my life compiling them and analyzing them, and learning from specific incidents to a general body of knowledge. I called friends who were surgeons for their advice. I researched and inquired and pounded the table. But in the end, none of it mattered. "This is what the disease is, Roger," Bert told me. "The outcome is not good." But now, I feared he was right.

Sharon fought it. There was radiation, then chemotherapy. She listened to tapes that were supposed to help her visualize her own body fighting the cancer. She kept exercising, and stayed on a healthy diet. And for a while, it looked like she was making headway against the disease. At one point, doctors did a CAT scan and all the tumors were gone. It seemed like a miracle. Then, two weeks later, she had three small tumors again.

We knew from the start that it was bad, and we fought back as hard as we could. But I think that even from the beginning, Sharon had an idea she wasn't going to win. One day, she looked up at me with tears in her eyes. "I just wanted to be a little old lady with you," she said. She was fifty years old.

Friends kept up a brave front for her, and out of her earshot, they tried to console me. Typical was Joe, my friend of many years, who quietly came up to me, put his arm around my shoulder, and said, "Look, I won't pretend to know what you're going through. But I know it's bad. I know you're hurting, and I want you to know we care about you. These aren't empty words. We've been through too much together for that. If there's anything that we can do for you, we're here. Anytime, day or night." Those were beautiful words, and he and many others stayed close to us, but even that couldn't take away the sense of impending loss, or the fear.

I thought of a much loved family dog, Spike, a Norwegian elkhound that my brother Gordon had given me for my birthday. A few years before, someone had shot and killed him. A neighbor called and said someone had found his body, and I went out to retrieve him and bring him home, so that I could bury him before the kids got home from school. I went out into the backyard, and starting digging his grave.

I kept digging the hole, deeper and deeper, far beyond what it needed to be. Then I took the dog and laid him in the ground. I arranged his paws, and patted him again. Sharon finally came out and said, "You know, Roger, that's a pretty deep hole that you're digging there. Why don't you finish up and come on in the house." She knew why I couldn't stop digging. I was doing it because I couldn't face what was coming next.

One night in the hospital, when Sharon got out of bed to go to the bathroom, she fell. I blamed no one. I knew that the nurse on duty couldn't be with her at all times. But I said, I can't go home anymore. I don't want her to fall again and not have anyone right there to help her. So from then on, I stayed in the hospital with her. I slept in a chair next to her bed.

Some time went by. Not much. But I realized I would have to be prepared. I'd spent my whole working life in the darkest realms of evil, and I'd long been haunted by the thought of the terrible fear victims must go through in their final moments. And I didn't want that for Sharon. I wanted her last hours on earth to be warm, and full of comfort and the people she loved.

I tried to anticipate what the experience of dying would be like for her. I thought she'd eventually slip into a coma, or at least be unconscious for a period of time. I figured if the last things that happened to her on earth were good, then maybe her last thoughts would be happy. The feelings were what was important. I didn't want her to feel alone. I talked to our kids, told them to remember the nicest times they had with their mother, and to talk about them to her. If there's anything you want to say to your mother, I told them, say it now.

I tried to do that for her myself. I sat with her in the hospital, and we remembered how, when we were first married, we tried to figure out what kind of a future we would have together, and we decided we wanted to go somewhere that was uncharted territory. We didn't want to stay in Michigan. We had big dreams. Our wedding was the start of an adventure, and we wanted to see the world. So we planned our honeymoon for New York City, where neither of us had been. I was from a big city myself, Detroit, and I'd been in the Marine Corps, so I knew how to handle myself, I thought. When we got into a cab after arriving at La Guardia, the cab driver took us to Manhattan via Ohio, miles out of our way. And I, the big-city sophisticate, not only didn't realize we were being taken, but gave him a big tip to boot.

On our honeymoon, Sharon and I did all of the tourist stuff. Went to Radio City Music Hall, and the Empire State Building, the Statue of Liberty, and the Hawaiian Room in the old Hotel Lexington. It's gone now, but it was something in its day—fancy dinner, dancing, and a floor show. At the front door, there was a big line of people waiting to get in. We didn't have reservations, and I realized we'd spent all night waiting to get in, so I turned to Sharon and said, "Do you want to try the exit door?"

"Sure," she said.

So that's what we did. Two kids from the sticks, sashaying right in the out door just like we knew what we were doing.

The floor show was great, the waiter was nice, everything went fine, and we had the best night. That's the kind of partner she was. Shoulder high, side by side. And game. Always game.

Sharon was a kid from Detroit, just like me, and we'd grown up together. She was the smart one who'd sit on the front porch and give me a smile when I delivered the paper to her house. Then, in high school, I started taking her to the movies, and later, out to dinner. By the time I got my first steady factory job, I asked her to be my wife, and for thirty-two years, that's what she was. It had all been a big adventure, just the way we'd hoped it would be.

We'd been lucky enough to have it all—falling in love, making a life together, having the kids. We had suffered through hard times, and celebrated good ones. And now we were going to see the conclusion together, as it all came full circle.

At the hospital, I held her hand. I stroked her hair. The nurses found me sleeping next to her bed. And when there was nothing else that could be done, I brought her home to die.

One of her nurses advised me against it. She said, "Do you know what you're doing? Do you have any idea what you're up against, and how difficult it's going to be to go through that without the hospital's support?"

I thanked her, told her we'd be okay, and went ahead and

arranged for an ambulance to bring Sharon home. The kids had set up a room for her at the house. Sharon and I had both volunteered at a local hospice, and now they helped us in turn, providing us with a hospital bed, helping set up the room with the equipment Sharon would need. When she came home, we put her to bed. She was gravely ill. An intravenous line gave her morphine for the pain, and she couldn't speak clearly anymore. But I felt that, from time to time, she understood me. I knew what was happening now. She was letting go.

Later that night, the home nurse stopped by the house to see how things were going. She was very gentle with Sharon, and then she took me into the kitchen. "You know that she may not make it through the night. You know that, don't you?" That night, I slept next to my wife and kept my hand lightly on her, the way I had in the hospital, the way I had for all of my married life. All night long, I touched her so she could feel the physical closeness of me.

It was in the month of May that Sharon came home. I had wanted her to see her flowers in the garden. I wanted her to feel the warmth of the sun as it rose through the east window at daybreak. Instead, she died the next morning as I held her in my arms.

I don't really have a memory of the funeral. A friend recalls that I was not myself, and that everyone was worried about me. I never had much experience with crying, but what I do remember is in the following weeks I was weeping so loudly, howling really, in the house that afterward I wondered if the neighbors heard it, the keening, like a wounded animal. It was a terrible condition for a human being to be in.

People came to the house, called, brought food. They sent beautiful notes. And none of it was enough. I was looking for answers. But I only had questions. I had seen so much of the Devil's handiwork in the deeds of serial killers and child molesters and in the sorrow of grieving parents. There seemed no end to the permutations of evil, and the depth of suffering it caused. I knew how to pursue criminals, even how to think like them and get inside their minds. I realized that all the work I'd done could not protect me from what felt like a new kind of evil. A loss so deep and profound it seemed to cut me loose from whatever moorings I had in the world.

Why had this happened to Sharon, to us? Why is one person saved from cancer and another is not? In the midst of my grief, one question began to take over my thoughts: How could a God who allows so much evil in the world permit a person of such goodness to be taken?

It made no sense. Inside me there was a tremendous inner struggle, an internal battle going on. I began to see something. I began to see the contradictions in life. I began to see that life is a paradox. That so many of the things we think are important—the money, status, a standard of living—are not what's most important.

My friends encouraged me to stay busy, to get out more, stay active, and try to see people. They thought I should get rid of Sharon's clothes, and sell the house and move somewhere else. But I couldn't. Grieving is a personal thing, and people do it in their own way. I wasn't ready to let go so soon. But there was so little to distract me. I couldn't focus on my work, and no matter how hard my colleagues at The Academy Group tried to get me interested in new cases, it just didn't work.

I saw an interview with a man who'd traveled widely throughout his life, to many faraway places. Then his wife died, and he was asked if that made his traveling easier, or harder. "Oh, much easier," he said. "All my things are there, and it's still 'home.' But now it doesn't matter when I come home, or if I come home at all. I have no home. It's just a house. A place to hang your clothes. Because the magnet isn't there anymore. The thing that anchors me."

I knew exactly what he meant. Once, when I traveled to an out-of-town meeting, one of the worst moments of grief hit me when I walked into that empty hotel room. I realized there was no one at home waiting to hear that I had arrived safely. I was in a strange place, alone. And I had no one to call.

Slowly, inexorably, the rage set in. It rose up in me with a strength I'd never experienced before, not even in the days when I was a street fighter as a cocky young man, or when I was in the Marines, or when I came face-to-face with the most heinous criminals. This was larger, deeper, more all-encompassing. "Mad at the world"? That didn't even begin to cover it. I wasn't just mad at the world. I was mad at whoever had created it, and all the unseen forces that comprised it. I became the guy you don't want to cut off in traffic, the person you didn't want to accidentally bump into on the street. All I needed was an excuse. I remember thinking that God must be merciful after all. Because now, I really didn't care if I lived or died.

I was in that state for nearly a year. Later, my friends confessed they weren't sure I was going to pull out of it. But in time, for some reason I finally began to ask myself: What am I supposed to learn from this? And what kind of lesson would warrant this loss and sacrifice? Was it an evil lesson that would leave me with only anger, hatred, and rage?

When Sharon was alive, we used to go to Hardee's for breakfast after Mass on Sunday mornings. And now, on Sunday mornings, I got a folding aluminum lawn chair and picked up some breakfast and went over to the cemetery where she was buried. A couple weeks after her funeral I was just sitting there, looking around. I would set the chair up at her grave, and just sit there and talk to her, telling her how much I missed her and about how it was so hard to let go. Once, I was crying and thinking about how much pain she'd been in before she died. I couldn't imagine she wasn't in heaven, but I'd seen so much of the way people suffer before they die, and I needed to know, somehow, that she wasn't hurting anymore. That she was at peace.

For some reason, I noticed two white butterflies fluttering around over her grave. They were flying in small circles around each other. For a while I just watched them, and then they separated. One went down toward the ground, and the other flew up into the air, out of sight. I would never say it was a sign. But sometimes, things like that feel as if they are. Those butterflies were telling me that even though Sharon was gone, I had to stay here, and it was all right.

Gradually, as the months passed, I began to try to decide how I would go on in life. The thought of more work with serial killers, violence, and hatred was an impossibility. To do that work, I'd needed ballast—strength from Sharon. Now it was gone. I began to think about the paradoxes in life, and they began to fall into a religious context. As a Christian, I believed God had allowed the greatest evil in the world so he could have the greatest good. He allowed people to kill his son, unjustly, so that he could rise again. Maybe what I was going through was the same kind of paradox.

I took stock of my life. What was I good at? Teaching, certainly. I had an academic bent, and loved formalized learning. Service was important to me. And a relationship with another woman was, I was certain, not a possibility. I started remembering my days back in high school at the Holy Ghost Fathers Mission Seminary. I remembered how it represented a new world for me. After all of the awful, dark things I'd seen, I needed to find a place that could reteach me that there was still goodness in the world. Maybe, I thought, I belonged in the priesthood.

C. S. Lewis said that God whispers in pleasure, and shouts in pain, and what I was experiencing felt like a clear message. I called the diocese of Arlington, and the vocation director told me the diocese did not accept people for admission into the seminary who were over thirty years of age. That amazed and astounded me. A lifetime of experience didn't mean anything, I guess. "So you're telling me that Jesus Christ himself wouldn't have qualified?" I said.

The Baltimore diocese had a cutoff age of fifty. I was fifty-six. But they told me about a place in Connecticut called Holy Apostles College and Seminary that specialized in late-life vocations. I called one afternoon, got a recording, and left my name and number. Told them that I was interested in signing up. "And another thing," I said. "I'm going to tell you this right up front. I'm fifty-six years old." I hung up, sure that I'd never get a call back. And then, ten minutes later, the phone rang. It was a secretary. I told her a little about myself, my history with the FBI and the Behavioral Science Unit, bad guys, and the death of my wife, and the profound questioning that was going on. "So I guess I'm probably not what you're looking for."

And she said, "As a matter of fact," she said, "you sound just exactly like the kind of person that we're looking for."

She connected me with Father Ray Halliwell, the seminary's

admissions director. This was in September. He said, "Well, we're going to start classes on Monday, so perhaps you can start next semester."

I explained that this was something that would not wait. He asked when I could come and talk with him. "Tomorrow," I said. He told me that first I needed to get a psychological evaluation for the admissions process, and I did, with a psychologist in Virginia who screened candidates for the archdiocese. I took the Minnesota Multiphasic Personality Inventory (MMPI), and the Thematic Apperception Test, and other ones, too. The big guy with his arm around the little guy: "What does that signify?" Apparently I was sane enough, as far as they were concerned.

I overnighted the test results to the seminary, and three days later followed up, as requested, with a personal visit to Holy Apostles. I talked with Father Ray and some of the priests there. I was also screened by a nun named Sister Joyce Ridick, a clinical psychologist for the seminary. After two hectic days of interviews, she submitted her report: "Candidate has intact self-esteem, an active spiritual life of prayer, and a capacity for reflective meditation. Notably intelligent with integrity of person, he seeks spiritual growth as well as orientation to serve others. If he perseveres in his studies, he could be an asset to the religious order of the Missionaries of the Holy Apostles or any diocese."

A short time later, Father Ray gave me the official word: I had been accepted for admission. Classes for the term had already begun, so I had to hurry. I made a quick trip back to Virginia to tell the kids and put a few things in order. Then I packed a suitcase and set out for the nine-hour drive to Cromwell, Connecticut. I was heading back to the seminary, this time for good.

1. *Me* (right) *and my two older brothers, Ken* (left) *and Gordon. The strife of the world seemed far away from our home in the Detroit suburb of Roseville.*

2. *Me as a freckle-faced tenth-grader at Holy Ghost Fathers Mission Seminary.*

3. *In the Marine Corps, 1957.*

Clare, Mich. Police Department I.D. Card

Name   Roger Leonard Depue

Street 5593 Wash City Clare

Employed by City of Clare

Address   202 W. 5th St.

Age   28 Height 6'1" Wt. 195

Wm Cotter
                              Mayor

Roger L. Depue
                    Chief of Police

4. *My ID from the Clare, Michigan, police department. At the age of twenty-seven I was the youngest police chief in the state.*

5. *In the evidence storage room at the FBI's Washington field office, early 1970s.*

6. *Undercover, disguised as a UPS deliveryman.*

7. *Sharon and I on our wedding day, August 20, 1960. Sharon provided the emotional ballast I needed to work in a world filled with evil.*

8. *Son Steven, flanked by his sisters, Renee (left) and Arleen.*

9. *Sharon* (center) *is surrounded by her daughters and grandchildren.*

10. *With my mom, Viola.*

11. *The five Depue boys* (left to right), *Gary, Duane, Roger, Ken, and Gordon, back up their parents, Viola and Alvoy.*

12. *They say the greatest compliment you can pay someone is to imitate them. Three generations of Depue men in law enforcement: my son, Steven, an officer in Virginia's Fairfax County; my dad, Alvoy, who served twenty-seven years in the Roseville, Michigan, police department and retired as inspector; and me, a retired FBI agent.*

13. *The FBI's first SWAT team training class, code-named Spider One, which I joined in 1973.*

14. *Me* (second row, far right) *and other members of the FBI's Behavioral Science Unit, including Ken Lanning* (first row, second from left), *Bob Ressler* (second row, far left), *John Douglas, Jim Horn* (third row, center), *and Jim Reese* (third row, far right).

15. *The logos on my father's cap and shirt identify him as a special consultant for The Academy Group, which I founded upon my retirement from the FBI in 1989.*

16. *The aftermath of evil: The final resting place of the seven Richardson children, dead of poisoning in 1968. Their father's conviction for the crime was vacated twenty years later, in what my Academy Group termed "a terrible miscarriage of justice."*

17. *A place that could reteach me that there was still goodness in the world: St. Peter's, one of the simple white stucco buildings serving as home to the Holy Apostles Seminary in Cromwell, Connecticut.*

18. *The grotto chapel at the seminary, which helped me to discover my true place in the world.*

19. *With two fellow seminarians after a visit to Israel and Palestine in 1996.*

20. *With Brother Art Kirby and Sister Joyce at the seminary.*

21. *God had allowed the greatest evil in the world so he could have the greatest good: With the former Sister Joyce, Joanne Ridick, whom I married in 1998.*

CHAPTER NINE

HOLY GROUND

I HAD BECOME A MAN I did not know. And because I was now a stranger to myself, for the first few days after arriving at the seminary I kept mostly to my room and spoke to no one. Instead, I occupied myself with surveying my surroundings.

The Holy Apostles College and Seminary in Cromwell, Connecticut, was hardly a medieval monastery. There were no stone buildings here, or high walls, or crenellated towers. Instead, what I saw was a set of simple white stucco buildings on a cluster of green hills rising from the grassy banks of the Connecticut River. A two-lane asphalt road ran parallel to the river, separating it from the campus, which was made up of the registrar's office, an administration building that also housed the kitchen and dining hall, and a couple of dormitories. Each building was named for an Apostle. There was nothing imposing about the place, and, except for a forthright sign at the entrance, nothing that even announced it as a religious institution. But it felt peaceful to me, unambiguous. That in itself was a blessing.

I was directed to my room in the two-story dormitory building, an eight-by-ten cubicle with beige cinder block walls, a plain makeshift desk, a narrow iron bed, a small sink, and a crucifix on the wall. It looked to me like a monk's cell, which struck me as a sort of private joke, given the number of men I had helped to put into cells of a very different kind.

At the heart of the seminary was the chapel. I wandered into it on a warm afternoon, and was struck by the cool stillness within. Wooden pews, no cushions, and no kneelers. Even the tabernacle on the altar was unadorned. I looked up at the chapel's walls and scanned the Stations of the Cross, renderings of the final suffering of Christ, from the Agony in the Garden at Gethsemane, to the Crucifixion on Calvary. On the walls between narrow vertical windows were stark depictions of those events, almost abstract in their simplicity. That's what this place is, I thought—a distillation. There is nothing extraneous here. It occurred to me that in a truly holy place, it is necessary to sweep away whatever is not essential, and this spartan chapel had only the basic fundamentals for a house of God. It was not defined by its aesthetics. It was about simplicity of the spirit.

I had come here after spending nearly my entire working life hunting down the most depraved and vicious criminals. I was immersed in their dark world for nearly thirty years. But during that time, I'd always had Sharon. Now that she was gone, it was as if the one barrier protecting me from the true enormity of that evil had crumbled, and the power of those black forces was threatening to engulf me. I was doing the only thing I could. I was trying to find a safe haven, a place of refuge from evil.

I was angry and bewildered, and so full of despair that I had actually come to believe there was no longer a place for me in the world. Now, I was hoping not just to exorcise the memory of some of the terrible things I had seen, but to see through my bitterness and understand why, with all of the evil in the world, God had taken Sharon. It was something I couldn't make sense of.

She had been kind and strong, and faithful, and full of humor. She had cherished her religion, and raised our children well. She was a person who had never intentionally done harm to anyone. She tried, always, to do the right thing. She was the opposite of evil. And God, in His infinite wisdom, had snuffed out her life.

On the third day, after the evening meal, there was a knock at my door, and when I answered it I found a trio of young seminarians. Later, I would learn their histories, and a little about what had brought them to this place. The first had been a Navy crew man on a submarine. The second was a former amateur boxer, now a monk wearing the brown habit of the Franciscan order. The third, before coming here, had worked as a cowboy on a cattle ranch in Wyoming.

"We thought we'd take a walk down to the garden to say a Rosary," the boxer said. "Would you like to come with us?" A month before, lost in grief, I probably would have turned them away. But now I was grateful for the overture. I walked out into the twilight with them, beyond the library and small chapel, until we came to a grotto. It was at the far edge of the seminary property, and largely out of sight. If they hadn't brought me here, I wouldn't have known it existed. From the outside it looked like nothing more than a grassy hillock. But as we lowered our heads to walk through the stone entrance, I saw that inside was a small chapel, and at its center was a statue of the Blessed Virgin standing on a pedestal, lit by a burning candle. We knelt on the ground and began to pray the Rosary together.

"Hail, Mary, full of grace, the Lord is with thee . . ."

Gradually, in that rough grotto, it occurred to me that the three men kneeling here were as intrinsically good as so many of the men I had locked away were inherently evil. I had been struggling since Sharon's death to try to understand my place in the world, and now I experienced, for the first time in a long while, something resembling certainty. The feeling was, "I am where I ought to be."

As we knelt on the stony ground, saying the Rosary, I looked into Mary's eyes. They were heavily lidded, world-weary. In the cool darkness, she was serene, but there was also an unmistakable sadness in those eyes. Yes, she knew something about grief, this woman, who had watched, so long ago, as her only son was nailed to a cross. Who in the jeering crowds had shown kindness to him that day? Who did anything but vilify him? And she, his mother, had witnessed it all.

The faint glow from flickering votive candles cast shifting shadows on the angles of her face. Its alabaster skin had a marked sheen, almost lifelike, but not quite. I had seen that plasticine-like skin before. My mind began to wander, trying to place the image. And then it began to filter through. A dark-haired young woman, in her early twenties, with skin so pale it looked as if blood no longer ran in her veins. The memory became more distinct. Her eyes, too, were heavy, only half open. It was because there was no longer any life in them.

She was lying on a cold industrial tile floor, still in her winter coat, her keys lying just out of reach. She had been midstream in life. Now, her arms were flung out to the side, gracefully almost, as the end result of a terrible struggle. Torn stockings, a broken fingernail, tangled strands of hair. And those half-open eyes. There was no horror in them, no last expression of fear or anguish. But it had not been a peaceful end. The look in those eyes was as eloquent as if she had spoken. "I have given up," they said.

She had fought with every ounce of strength to survive, to stay among the living. But it was futile. When she was found, the knife blade still protruded from her throat on that restaurant floor, and those eyes told of a final surrender. In my mind, the two images began to merge. The smooth alabaster skin of the Virgin, and the pale, lifeless form of that young woman.

"Holy Mary, Mother of God, pray for us sinners, now and at the hour of our death."

So many hours of death, over so many years.

The religious order known as the Society of the Missionaries of the Holy Apostles was founded fifty years ago by a Franciscan priest, Father Eusebe Menard, a Canadian who believed that part of the answer to a growing shortage of priests throughout the world was to expand the priesthood's borders a bit. If other seminaries wouldn't consider accepting anyone over the age of thirty, Menard decided to welcome them. The college and seminary that shared the order's name was a place for people who had found their vocation later in life. Many, like me, had already had full lives and careers by the time they decided to enter the priesthood.

It had taken nearly two years to work it out, but I had come to terms with my decision to leave my old life behind. The Academy Group could run itself without me. For the past year, I hadn't really been of much use there anyway.

Here in the seminary, things were simpler. I began to adapt to a new, pared-down routine. I woke every morning at dawn, said morning vespers, ate breakfast, and then attended Mass in the chapel. I took my meals in the dining hall, cafeteria-style, and sat at one of a dozen long refectory tables, each with eight chairs. Sometimes meals were eaten in silence, but mostly there was conversation. I served as one of the members of a rotating dish crew, and two nights a week I did regular cleanup duty, scrubbing pots and pans.

The head of the dish crew was a religious brother who suffered from a neurological disorder. He wore thick glasses, was subject to seizures, and could be a little anxious at times. But he was unfailingly good-natured, and a hard worker. "Hey, boss," I'd say at the end of chores, "I've finished up over here. What else have you got for me to do?" When Sharon was alive, I had helped out with the dishes at home, and I had certainly pulled KP in the Marines. But as I, the former chief of the FBI's Behavioral Science Unit, stood in a steamy institutional kitchen, scouring the broiler, I couldn't help but be struck by this sudden role reversal.

Friday afternoons were reserved for physical labor. I was assigned to various maintenance jobs around the campus. I painted, raked leaves, hauled brush, took out the trash. And because I was the only person in the seminary who knew how to operate heavy equipment, thanks to my experience in Detroit, it was my job to drive the dump truck whenever the garbage needed hauling.

I wasn't in charge here, and no one expected me to be. I wasn't making life-or-death decisions, and human lives didn't depend on the choices I made. I was part of an organization, and for the first time in more than a decade, I wasn't running it. It was a humbling experience, and also an unburdening.

Prior to the seminary, over the course of my academic career, I had taken philosophy courses, which I had always enjoyed. There was, for instance, the old conundrum about a sinking ship. There are eleven remaining passengers, but, my professor explained, room on the lifeboat for only ten. Who should have a place, and who should not? Should the weakest be eliminated because he has the least chance of surviving? Or should it be the strongest, because he has the best chance? The oldest, or the youngest?

What struck me about the way he posed those questions was that they ignored another very real alternative. It was the one practiced in Auschwitz, when Maximilian Kolbe, a cleric who was later canonized by the Catholic Church, saw the Nazis were about to execute a man who was a husband and father. Kolbe, who had no wife or child, stepped forward and offered himself instead. He acted with the same impulse of a Marine who throws himself on a grenade to save the lives of others. No greater love. That's the Christian philosophy of sacrifice, isn't it, which teaches that there are worse things than death?

At Cromwell, my days were filled with classes preparing me for ordination: catecheses, epistemology, metaphysics, and fundamental moral theology. Some struck me as almost impenetrable. A graduate offering in philosophical theology, for example, titled Lublin Existential Personalism, promised "an exploration of Christian metaphysics, insights into contemporary existentialism and the methodology of phenomenology," as well as a discussion of what it termed "the dynamization of the acting person as superseding the Boethian definition of man."

I preferred more practical areas, like the writings of Eric Hoffer, the so-called working-class philosopher. Hoffer was a former longshoreman and an admirer of the essayist Montaigne, and he wrote a string of critically acclaimed works including *The True Believer*. In 1982 this self-taught man received the Presidential Medal of Freedom, the country's highest civilian honor. I felt an affinity for Hoffer, partly for his ideas about social upheaval, and partly because, like me, he had blue-collar roots. "Whoever originated the cliché that money is the root of all evil knew hardly anything about the nature of evil, and very little about human beings," he wrote. Also this: "Compassion is the antitoxin of the soul: where there is compassion, even the most poisonous impulses remain relatively harmless." Hoffer, I mused, must have been an optimist.

I also read deeply in the classics, the seminal works of philosophical thought. I studied Plato's tree, which posits a hierarchy of value as a potential for human development, moving from the lowest, which is the material, to a higher plane, which is the spiritual. I read about the Aristotelian concept of the soul, which, when joined with the human body, forms a single nature—the being of man.

I studied the tenets of classical Christian and Catholic philosophy, which see evil not as a discrete entity, but as something that exists only to defile the good. I loved the first sentence of Aristotle's *Metaphysics*, which says, "All men, by nature, desire to know." I also pondered the ideas of Socrates, who in the *Protagoras* said that people will commit evil acts only if they are deluded into believing what they are doing is right—the apparent good versus the real good.

In the middle of a class one morning, I suddenly found myself overwhelmed with a feeling of gratitude. The questions posed by my professors were pointing me in a different direction. How many people, whose lives were harder and more painful than my own, were able to have this luxury, to meditate and pray, to ponder the most difficult questions of existence? The lecturer was speaking about the nature of good and evil, and how wise men through the centuries have tried to define and conceptualize it. St. Augustine was the first to develop the idea of the origin of evil in Christian thought. Were we all born with the innate capacity for evil? I wondered. Or is it something that we learn?

My mind drifted back to that small town in Florida, and to the Richardson children. I remembered Betty Jean, who was murdered the week after her eighth birthday. Just a little girl herself, she was already shouldering the responsibility of taking care of her little brothers and sisters. I thought about how she had been used as an innocent pawn, provided with the poisoned food, and instructed to feed it to the other children. Or how, as a neighbor testified at trial, the children's mother had once eaten barbecued chicken for supper herself, while they were left to forage for food in garbage cans. Did the souls of the Richardson children carry the indelible mark of original sin? Or had they, through their suffering, transcended it in death?

"It was Thomas Aquinas who said that no man willingly commits evil," the lecturer was saying. "That no one performs evil intentionally." The words cut the flow of my thoughts. "Man may use inappropriate methods to have his needs met, but he is attempting to satisfy good needs. Sexuality is an example. It is good and beautiful. It allows for the highest form of intimacy between members of the species, it allows procreation, and for the delight of physical pleasure. It can be made ugly, even evil, when perverted by the demands of selfishness."

I mulled the implications, trying to fit them into the framework of my own experience. *No man intentionally commits evil.* I knew that he was speaking on a different plane, about truth in the largest sense. But how did the acts of Leonard Lake and

Charles Ng, and the machinations of Ted Bundy or John Wayne Gacy fit into the paradigm? I thought of the screams of a young girl as she was being tortured, and the perpetrator, who derived such intense pleasure from her pain. What about the sadistic killer who enjoys nothing more than the fear of his victim, or the child molester, who can't be persuaded he has done anything to harm the child?

Weren't those perpetrators acting of free will? Or could their actions be explained away as the result of life experiences that had stripped them of true volition? I didn't know the answer to those questions. All I knew was that my instructor hadn't met some of the criminals I had. Life in the seminary, I began to realize, would not be without contradictions.

Every so often I was given the opportunity to travel, and during my second year at Holy Apostles, I signed up for a trip to the Holy Land, a chance to study abroad that was offered by the seminary to members of various religious orders. I went with a group tour of about twenty people, most of them seminarians, too. I was looking forward to this chance to broaden my knowledge about a part of the world that was new to me, and to see firsthand the actual places featured so prominently in the New Testament. But when we arrived, our destination didn't seem like anyone's idea of a holy land.

A few days after we arrived, a bomb exploded in Jerusalem, and a number of innocent civilians were killed. This, I knew, was only the latest sad episode in a conflict that has existed for centuries. But witnessing the aftermath of that terrorist act underscored the point. Hatred was serious business here.

Not long after, we were on a tour bus, and had stopped somewhere along the way. Some of the group got off the bus, but I stayed on board, looking out through dusty windows onto what passed for a playground. I saw what at first seemed like an apparition, but it was very real. It was a little boy playing with a gun.

It seemed an oddly familiar image, even though I knew I'd never seen him before. How many nameless children had I seen on television or in newspapers, who lived in one war zone or another? Here was a little Palestinian boy playing with his toy machine gun, a remarkably lifelike replica of an M-16. He was also carrying a toy hand grenade, and he had a small dagger attached to his canvas belt. He was running randomly in the street, playing by himself, peering around the corners of buildings, darting between parked automobiles, pretending to shoot.

From the bus, I watched him. As a boy, I shot empty tin cans with BB guns, fantasizing I was Wyatt Earp or a character from comic books or the radio. What images did this little boy conjure up? Jewish children? Israeli paratroopers? Or was he so inured to violence that his toy gun had no more significance to him than a stick or a broom? So this is how the violence is perpetuated, I thought. In this most ancient of places, I wondered, who will win—God or the gun?

Several days into the trip, we traveled through Galilee to the town of Caesarea Philippi at the base of Mount Hermon, near where the borders of Syria, Lebanon, and Palestine all converge. Many of the places we visited had historical or religious significance, but this place held a special meaning for me. It was where, according to the New Testament, Christ, realizing that people were debating his true identity, turned to his disciples and asked, "What about you? Who do you say I am?" Now, where Jesus had once caused his followers to reflect on the nature of his own di-

vinity, I looked out and saw the evidence of a centuries-old conflict—soldiers, barbed wire fencing, and the devastation caused
by bombs and sporadic street fighting.

By this time, because we were living in close quarters, all of the
members of our tour group had come to learn a little bit about
each other. Everyone knew I was a former FBI agent, though certainly not that I had been head of the Behavioral Science Unit.
As we were looking out onto that decimated street, one of the
other members of the group announced nervously, "Well, at least
we're safe, because as long as Roger's here, we have the FBI with
us."

Every muscle in my body instinctively tensed up. I glanced
around at a number of Arabs who were standing around on the
street, and who heard him, and might well have understood English. I had no idea who they were, or what their political affilia-
tion might be. It seemed incomprehensible that my traveling
companion could have been so stupid as to broadcast my identity. How could he be so oblivious to the potential danger of
making a remark like that in a place like this? I might as well have
been wearing a sign saying, "I'm a U.S. federal agent."

He may have thought it was a joke, but I didn't. He had said
similar things several times before on the trip, and this was the
last straw. I walked over to where he was sitting and said, "The
next time I hear you make a remark like that, you know what I'm
going to do? In a loud voice, I'm going to start telling everyone
you're CIA. I bet that anyone who might be interested in that information will find it a lot more fascinating than that I'm a former FBI agent. They might want both of us, but they'll take you
first."

It was the last time he made any remarks like that. In retrospect, I suppose I overreacted a bit, but that flip comment struck

a nerve. I may have been a seminarian, but my past in law enforcement was a big part of who I was, and something I still took very seriously. It was not to be treated with so little respect, especially by someone who had so little understanding of it.

After my first year in the seminary, and as a required step toward ordination, I earned sponsorship from the order of the Missionaries of the Holy Apostles. Sponsorship, by either a diocese or a religious community, is necessary for any novice beyond the first year, because it guarantees placement, i.e. a job, upon ordination. Not long after, I was also ordained a lector, which meant I was able to participate at Mass in a formal capacity, reading selections from the Old and New Testaments. Later, I took temporary vows and became a religious brother.

Then, at the beginning of my second year, I was sent to live off campus for six months at the Holy Apostles novitiate, about twenty-five miles away, at a bucolic retreat house in Moodus, Connecticut, near the Connecticut River. I lived in an apartment with two other novices, and my days were filled with manual labor, study, and meditation. Moodus was also a site for religious retreats and talks; participants were assigned quarters in a dozen cabins known collectively as "My Father's House."

Every Thursday, the rector, Father Bill McCarthy, and the assistant rector, Sister Bernadette, brought in guest speakers. Some focused on topics of spiritual growth, others on biblical themes, and sometimes the night was given over to an Irish tenor who came in just to entertain everyone. One Thursday, after I had been at the retreat house for about six weeks, a woman who claimed to have religious visions came to share her experiences with us. The two other novices and I were low men on the totem

pole, seated off to one side of the lecture hall, where we were expected to make sure the speaker's water glass was filled, and the
microphone was working.

In a spiritual sense, I believe there is such a thing as divine intervention in the human condition, and that religious miracles,
things we can't otherwise explain, are possible. But I had a
healthy skepticism about this woman's claims, and her behavior
only reinforced my gut feeling. How, I asked myself, would I
react if I'd been selected by God to carry a message to his people,
like the children at Lourdes or Fatima? What kind of person
would I become if I'd actually witnessed an apparition of the
Blessed Virgin?

If that were true, I'd be changed by the experience, I thought.
I'd likely become more devout, pious, humble, and committed.
I'd undoubtedly pray frequently, attend Mass at every opportunity, look for guidance in periods of quiet and solitary meditation. But this woman seemed to be doing none of those things.
She didn't participate in any of the scheduled public prayers. She
wasn't a regular at Mass. In fact, she didn't seem particularly interested in anything other than retelling her remarkable story.

One evening, she invited a group of visiting religious VIPs to
accompany her to a nearby creek, where, she promised, a vision
would occur. I wangled an invitation, brought a tape recorder
along, and caught a number of her conversations. Afterward, I
went back to my room and analyzed what I'd heard. This woman,
I was convinced, was a fake, and I wrote a few pages of analysis
on her behavior. I believed she was an inadequate, submissive
personality, perhaps mentally unstable, and had allied herself
with a correspondingly strong personality, with whom she'd developed a symbiotic relationship. The man who accompanied
her—it was unclear if their relationship was more than merely

professional—was an ex–police officer who clearly protected her from the outside world. She could afford to be petite and pious; he called all the shots about who she spoke to and what she did.

The analysis seemed as natural to me as breathing. I was just conducting the same kind of personality assessment I had done so many times of criminals and fugitives. There was nothing I could do to short-circuit her speaking tour, and I really had no interest in raining on everyone's parade. But I did pay a visit to the rector with my analysis. "I think the appropriate response is one of skepticism," I told Father McCarthy, dropping my report on his desk. "Let's just put it this way. If she asks you to build a chapel on the spot of the apparition, I'd advise against it."

Not long after, another guest was invited to the retreat house, this one claiming she'd been the victim of a satanic cult. The setup was the same. I was playing the role of gofer, sitting off to one side in the conference room. Only this time, there was no speaker actually present in the room. The whole event was shrouded in mystery and suspense. This woman had convinced everyone she was in such great physical danger, that she couldn't afford to show her face. So they all sat facing a small public address system hooked up to another location on campus.

As I sat in that room, listening to this woman talk about how her father had been the leader of a satanic cult, and she had been one of its ravished victims, I wondered how anyone could possibly buy this story. She talked about the systematic rape and abuse of children, and claimed she'd witnessed human sacrifice. And now, she said, if any members of this cult found her, they'd kill her to keep her quiet.

At one point, as the woman continued telling her story, adding embellishments at every turn, one of the other novices had to put his hand on my arm to restrain me. It was all I could do not to jump up and shout, "This is bullshit! This woman doesn't know what she's talking about! She's a fraud!"

Beginning in the mid-1980s, my colleague Ken Lanning, perhaps the world's leading expert on crimes of child predation, had studied satanic cults. We had certainly conducted research on all kinds of horrible, twisted cases, and had seen some pretty mind-bending things. Cult-related killings, yes. But Ken's exhaustive research had never been able to substantiate a single case of a bona fide satanic human sacrifice in the U.S.

This was my field, my area of expertise, and as I listened to this woman spouting her bizarre assertions, my bullshit detector was off the charts. I was enraged that someone could be so manipulative, so blithe about injecting this kind of poison into the psyches of all those sweet little old ladies in the room, who were buying it hook, line, and sinker, and who might very well have nightmares about it later. And for what? So that some needy crackpot could get off on being the center of attention?

After the question-and-answer session, I went to the rector and asked if I could interview the woman. He suggested I speak to Sister Bernadette, who'd arranged the booking.

"Excuse me, Sister," I said, stepping into her office. "But I have to know. Do you really believe that woman out there has seen what she claims to have seen, and that she's who she says she is?"

"Well, of course I do," she said, in a hushed tone. "Don't you?"

"Actually, Sister, I don't. Not for a minute. This happens to be my field of professional expertise, and in my opinion, she's a liar and a phony. And it's disturbing to me that she's being allowed to get away with it."

Sister Bernadette made it clear she wasn't interested in my professional opinion. "Excuse me," she said, turning out the lights in her office and heading for the door, "but it's time to go to dinner and our guest is waiting for me." That's when I finally lost my temper.

"Sister Bernadette, do you really think the appropriate response—when you've just listened to an hour's worth of detailed allegations about crimes involving murder, rape, and child abuse—is to *go to dinner*? Is that the way you plan to respond to this information? By having a meal with friends?" By now, I was almost yelling. "Get on the phone if you believe this. Call the FBI. Call the police. We should hunt these people down. This isn't fairyland. This is the real world. And if this is happening to people, then it has to be investigated and stopped."

It was obvious she wasn't going to do any such thing. "All right then," I said, lowering my voice. "Then, please, give me a half hour with this woman, so I can interview her. Give me just that much, and I'll tell you if she's for real."

Sister Bernadette wouldn't allow it. But she did grant my final request, which was for equal time. The next Thursday, armed with a copy of Ken Lanning's research report on satanic cults, I was given fifteen minutes to address the group, and I did the best I could to set the record straight and dispel their fears. I laid it all out, saying I didn't believe this woman, that the FBI had been looking into these kinds of allegations for at least the past decade, and they had absolutely no basis in fact. Satanic cults do exist, I said. I won't deny that. But babies being offered up at Black Masses as blood sacrifice to the Devil? That was bunk. At least in this country, not one case had ever been substantiated.

I had a hard time understanding why, with all of the very real horror taking place in the world, people seem to have such a deep need to conjure up even more. I knew I couldn't really blame Sister Bernadette, or the retreat house, or any of these good people in the audience for what had taken place. They, after all, had never lived in a world of serial killers, rapists, and child molesters. God bless them in their innocence, I thought.

I wanted to stay busy in the seminary, to take advantage of as many new opportunities for growth and change as I possibly could. One morning in the registrar's building, I noticed a posting of openings for pastoral counseling volunteers, including one request for a seminarian who would be willing to work with inmates at a nearby maximum security prison. At first, I dismissed the idea, but it began to nag at me, and when I saw the vacancy still hadn't been filled a week later, I decided to sign up for it.

I had been in a lot of prisons throughout my career, and this, the MacDougall Correctional Institute in Suffield, about thirty miles north of the seminary, had a dull sameness about it. The grim entrance, the sound of security doors closing behind you as you passed through each checkpoint into the cell block area. The distinct sensation of leaving one world, and entering another.

After announcing myself to a guard, I was escorted directly to the office of Rev. Anthony Bruno, the chief prison chaplain, an affable man who clearly had his hands full. I told him a little bit about who I was, touched on my law enforcement background, and explained that I had an undergraduate degree in psychology, a master's in society and the law, and a doctorate in counseling and human development.

"I tell you what, Roger," he said. "Why don't you stop by for Mass on Sunday at the prison and I'll introduce you around."

That Sunday, I was shown to the room where the service would be held, not in a real chapel, but one of those all-purpose rooms with movable dividers. There were folding chairs and about thirty inmates. They had put together a little choir, and inmates served Mass and read scripture, and some even read some of the prayers. The person in charge of organizing the religious service for Father Bruno was a convicted murderer.

After Mass the chaplain introduced me, and I stood up to say hello to everyone. I wasn't wearing a collar or cassock, just my street clothes. I didn't tell them I was a former FBI agent, let alone the former chief of the Behavioral Science Unit. I didn't want to create a negative image in their minds right off the bat: "Here's a fed, a cop." But that was only part of the reason I didn't fully identify myself. I wasn't working in law enforcement anymore. Being a former FBI agent, profiler, and chief of the Behavioral Science Unit really wasn't relevant here. I was no longer a member of law enforcement. Now I was a professional man of God.

I simply said that I was a seminarian from Holy Apostles Seminary in Cromwell, had a doctorate in counseling, and would be happy to speak with anyone who felt the need to talk. "You can come and talk with me about any kind of problem you might have," I said. "Emotional problems, spiritual or practical ones. My goals for you are the same I have for myself. Physical, intellectual, emotional, social, and spiritual growth." Afterward, about a dozen inmates signed up.

These were maximum security prisoners, hardened cases who included rapists, killers, drug dealers, and armed robbers. Some had committed brutal homicides. I intentionally didn't learn anything about their crimes before they came to see me, because I didn't want to know. If they volunteered to talk about what had gotten them into prison, I would listen. But I wasn't there to interrogate them. The past is history, I often said. I want to talk about the present, and, more important, the future.

It was a change, to say the least. I'd been locking up men like this for many years, and now I was interested in saving their souls. Was I experiencing some kind of remorse—an attempt to do something positive for the very people I had fought so hard to remove from society? I wasn't sure. It's one thing to be the part of a law enforcement process that begins with an investigation and ends with a conviction. It's quite another to walk in and try to provide advice and counsel in the aftermath.

All I knew was that I felt terribly unprepared. I'd been taking a lot of classes at the seminary, but I knew I didn't have real depth in theology. For all of my training in the social sciences, I still felt ill-equipped. So on the mornings before I went to the prison, I did what I could. I prayed for guidance and enlightenment. And when I met each client before the counseling session, I began by reading the familiar verse from Matthew 18:20: "Wherever two or more of you are gathered in my name, there I am in your midst."

Every week I met with at least a half dozen of the men in one of the private offices the chaplain made available to us. The men came in wearing their prison uniforms, tan jumpsuits like the kind workmen wear. There was a sad familiarity about it all. One prisoner told me his wife wasn't writing to him anymore, and she no longer visited. He was having a hard time getting a sense of any kind of future for himself. He felt completely abandoned. Another inmate was worried about his teenaged kids growing up without a father in the home or, even worse, with a stranger who would take his place.

They came to talk with me for many reasons. Some out of curiosity or boredom. Some to challenge me, to rail against the idea of any belief in God at all. Some because they needed to understand why they had done the horrible things they had. Some were trying to find a way to make it right with the victims and families on the outside who hated them. Still others, after so many years behind bars, were genuinely terrified of being released. "I know I'm going to go back to dope, Brother, I just know it," one said. "I've been in the drug rehab program for a year now, but every night I still dream about getting high."

If their families were falling apart on the outside, what, really, could they do about it? What chance did they have, while incarcerated, of influencing the outcome? Sometimes, the sense of futility, for them and for me, was almost overwhelming. The men who came to see me weren't having the kind of problems that make headaches for suburbanites—the kids' grades are dropping or the wife wants her own SUV, or the boss is giving them a hard time at the office. These were serious problems. Sometimes, even life or death.

One day, an inmate came to me, and said he needed my advice. He had arrived at MacDougall a few months earlier, from another prison. There, he had gotten involved in selling drugs to other inmates, and he owed money to his supplier that he expected to collect on sales. But when he learned he was going to be transferred out, he decided not to bother repaying the debt. The dealer would never find him, and he would never have to see the guy again. Why bother paying him?

Then one day at MacDougall, as a line of prisoners was being escorted to dinner from their cell block, he looked up and was stunned to see the dealer. Since his arrival here, the inmate had gained weight and grown a beard, and he knew the dealer hadn't recognized him. But it was only a matter of time.

There are codes of conduct within prisons, different from ones on the outside, but codes nonetheless. Child molesters are at the bottom rung of the social hierarchy. And drug dealers don't like to be stiffed. My client knew what the consequences would be. A shiv in the back, a slit throat in the showers. It could be anything.

That week, I thought long and hard about this convict's options. This certainly wasn't one of the topics covered in Pastoral Counseling 101, and I knew I'd have to be a little creative in mapping out a strategy. "Is there anyone on the prison staff that you know and trust?" I asked him the following week. Maybe one person, he said—a woman who was a social worker in his drug therapy program.

Then I put it to him. I told him he should contact the social worker and explain the whole situation to her. Then, I said, he should give her some suggestions. Could she get to the dealer and bring him into the drug rehab program? If so, then she could open up a dialogue. She could start talking with the dealer, convince him, maybe, that with his transfer to this new place, he was in effect beginning another life, or at least had the opportunity. Dealing drugs was something that happened in the old prison, but drugs weren't permitted here. MacDougall, after all, was more progressive, newer, with better policing and rehab programs.

She could tell him this was the chance to do what prisoners call "good time." Maybe even make a little progress toward a new life when he got out. Emphasize to him that the past is over, and he shouldn't resurrect something that was no longer part of his life. Then, she could bring up something like, "You may see people here in this prison who you have had relationships with in the past. But now, it's time to let that go. This is your chance at a fresh start, and you have to leave that behind." After she told him all that, she could watch his response.

This social worker was no starry-eyed kid just out of college. She was a professional, she'd seen a lot, and she had street smarts.

She heard the convict out and said, yes, she'd give it a shot. Evidently, she did. Because after that, I noticed a marked change in my client. The old tension and fear seemed to dissipate. For the first time since I'd known him, he started to relax. He finally ran into the former dealer, and while some words were exchanged, no violence came out of it, and, as far as I know, there was never any trouble between those two inmates for the rest of their incarceration. Terrific, I thought. Chalk up one for the greater good.

At night, alone in my room back at the seminary, I prayed for these men. I pondered what had brought them to prison, and how my own life, with a few simple turns, could have wound up not so very different from theirs. What if I had really blinded that guy I fought in high school? What if I had caught the guys who beat me up so badly in that gas station on New Year's Eve? Would I have wound up like these prisoners, abandoned and without hope?

I did have sympathy for some of the men I counseled. They had gotten bad breaks in life, and many just didn't have the support or wherewithal to make good choices. But that wasn't all of them. Some of the prisoners were as evil and manipulative as anyone I'd ever encountered at the BSU.

Throughout my career, almost every child molester we encountered looked like the guy next door. The neighbors would always say, "This guy's a child molester? Impossible!"

But one day at MacDougall, a man came to me who was a child molester, and I can honestly say he looked like one. He was in his late forties, five-foot-eight, slim with a potbelly and a scraggly beard. After even a couple of meetings with him, it seemed to me he was interested in the ritualism of religion, but not necessarily its depth or substance.

"I say my prayers every morning, Brother," he said. But he didn't tell me how he prayed, at least not at first.

When he talked about his crimes, he always emphasized that he had never hurt his victims. That was typical of guys like him. "I never hurt them," he said. "I love kids. And they love me."

"What do you mean, you never hurt them?" I thought to myself. "You may well have done something that will take away from these children any hope of ever having a normal sexual relationship with another human being, let alone establish any kind of real emotional intimacy. And you say you didn't hurt them?"

The more he talked, the more I learned about those victims, and how many there were. He was what the literature calls a fixated pedophile. There were particular little boys between the ages of eight and ten whom he really preferred, and had learned a great deal about. He was like a child psychologist. He was predatory. He would go to places where children congregated—video arcades, shopping malls—and establish relationships with them. Dozens of them.

We began to talk about his daily routine in prison. "Tell me, just how does your day go here?" I asked. "How does it begin? When you get up in the morning, what's the first thing you do?" He told me that after he got up in the morning, the first thing he did was say the Lord's Prayer. Then he'd go for breakfast, and come back to his cell and read the Bible for an hour or so. After that, he said, he began to pray for his victims.

"And how do you do that?" I asked.

"Well, Brother, I pray for each one of them, individually. I want to help these children. I pray for them because of what I did with them. I love them, and I want to have God care for them and protect them."

I asked him to elaborate, and then I began to notice a remarkable change in him. Where he had been sitting straight in his chair, now he leaned forward, eagerly, his whole face lighting up. This line of questioning clearly made him feel good.

"And how, specifically, do you pray for them?" I asked. "Do you pray for them by name? Do you say their name aloud?"

"Yes," he said, "and I remember how good those little boys were."

I could tell from his body language that he liked talking to me. It was because he thought he had finally found someone who understood. And I did. I knew full well what he was doing. He was remembering in precise detail what he had done to each of those little kids, and having sexual fantasies when he spoke their names. He was calling to mind each particular victim, selecting his favorites. This was a singular kind of evil. It was the antithesis of prayer.

"You know what you're doing, don't you?" I said, interrupting him.

"What do you mean?" he asked.

"Why aren't you praying for all of these children together, as a group? Why don't you say to God, 'Protect all of the children I have harmed'?"

At that, he suddenly got really agitated. He didn't like that suggestion. "No, they were individuals," he said, "and I want to pray for each one, one at a time."

That was when I lost my cool. I managed to keep my voice steady, but my true feelings were unmistakable. "I know what you're doing. I know the game," I said. "You're taking pleasure out of remembering each one of those little boys. I think you take pleasure at that memory, and fantasize about it so you can live it all over again, don't you? And you don't want to give up the fantasy, not for anything. 'I never hurt them.' That's really what you think, isn't it? You've done something to those children that will scar them for life, even in the best of cases. And maybe, if they're not lucky, you've destroyed any chance they'll have for a normal sexual relationship, ever, for the rest of their lives. And you say you never hurt them?"

He reared back in his chair, and anger flashed across his face.

"Well, you've come to me for pastoral counseling, and that's what I'm going to give you," I said. "In fact, I have an assignment for you. The next time you say your prayers, you ask God to bless all your victims, not individually, but all of them together. And then, after you've done that, you say another prayer. This time you ask God for mercy. But you ask it for yourself. You confess to God about what you really did to the lives of those little kids, and then you beg him not to send you to hell."

I thought back to Ken Lanning, and the research he'd done at the Unit into sex crimes against children. Two different child molesters who had each killed several of their young victims stated the reason they murdered those little kids was to avoid being identified. The only way society could have prevented those murders, they said, would have been to legalize sex between adults and children.

The monster sitting in front of me had no idea he was talking to someone who knew more about who he really was than the judge who put him away, or the jury that convicted him, or the jailers who were keeping him alive. And I suppose I knew more about this kind of offender than any priest. I often wondered what he would have said if I'd told him he was spilling his guts to a criminal profiler, former chief of the FBI's Behavioral

Science Unit. I never got the chance to find out. That was the last time he ever showed up for counseling.

─────────────

Anyone who knows about recidivism rates understands the odds of rehabilitating hardened criminals aren't good. Within prison populations are many people who are at the low end of the potential for change, but the idea that even a handful of them had been able to do it was intriguing to me. After a while, my experience at the Unit began to click in. I asked Father Bruno, "Is anyone keeping statistics? Someone ought to be following the ones who, in the opinion of the prison chaplain, have actually undergone a religious conversion." When he said he knew of none, I wondered why. Maybe it was just the academic in me, but if it really was possible for even one of these inmates to turn his life around, wouldn't it be worthwhile to try to find out how he did it?

I remember one young man in particular, serving a life sentence for murder. He could have done a lot of things in prison—sold drugs, gotten involved with gangs, continued on the downward spiral. Instead, he became a prison chaplain's assistant. I was struck by that, and one day I asked him about it. Why had he done that?

"I guess it's because I can't do anything else," he said. "I've lost my family. I'm never getting out. So I may as well do this. At least it might be a way, after what I've done, of giving something back."

Giving something back. Here was a guy whose life, for all intents and purposes, was already over. He could have become even more violent in prison; God knows, many did. But instead, when it almost seemed not to matter anymore, when he was past the point of being able to have any positive effect on a parole hearing or commutation, he was trying to find some small bit of service to perform.

It made me think long and hard about the inherent capacity for goodness in people, even after they had committed some pretty terrible acts. I knew that if I didn't at least try to focus on goodness, even in this prison, then I would sink into a despair I might never come out of. I believed redemption was possible. I had to, because what I was trying to do was keep my own hope alive.

But the hard truth was, here in this maximum security prison, redemption was the noteworthy exception. Not everyone could be rehabilitated. For some, no matter what they did to try to reverse the course of their lives, it was too late. Most were too entrenched in the criminal realm to change now, no matter how many one-hour counseling sessions I could provide. And some of them, like the child molester I counseled, were perfectly capable of going back out into society and causing terrible suffering again.

Evil truly exists. I knew that much. The question was, what was I going to do about it?

The Holy Apostles Seminary was home to men who were neither duplicitous nor violent. They had renounced the ways of the world, and had no motives other than to do good. Their main ambition in life, they said without embarrassment, was to become saints. They weren't ashamed of that. They would tell you if you asked.

I had needed a place like that, full of goodness, to wash away the ugliness I'd seen, both personal and professional. I had the opportunity to be renewed and to grow in another direction. To just be. And just being was enough. Nobody was looking at me to excel, or to begin something, or to supervise anything. I felt I was the least among the people there, that everything I'd done in my life was nothing compared to what these people were.

Now I thought back to the stories my father told about his early days, working as a child laborer and farm hand. It was in those days, cut off from family and living in whatever rough rooms he was given, that he began the habit of going to Mass every Sunday. Sometimes, when his boss told him he couldn't go, he'd sneak out a window and ride his bicycle miles to church.

Not everyone liked Catholics, and one memory that always infuriated him was the way some of the other workers teased him and made fun of his religion. "They'd take a statue of the Blessed Mother and stand her on her head," he said. "Then they'd defile her. They'd say to me, 'There, you ever seen a Virgin on her back?'"

My belief in God was something bred in me. My faith would always be with me, and would continue to be a comfort. It was true that I was now a religious brother, dedicated to the principles of love, forgiveness, and self-sacrifice. But I was also something else.

The priesthood represented one way to fight evil, and it was an infinitely noble one. The men I had met in the seminary were some of the strongest and most selfless human beings I'd ever known. But so, too, were the men I'd known in a small-town police department in Michigan, and in the remote parishes of Mississippi and Louisiana, and in the inner-city streets of Washington, D.C., and in the halls of the FBI Academy. I thought of people like Chip Shepherd, and Barry Colvert, and Joe Davis, and Doug Cannon, and Con Hassel. Their style was very different, but weren't they, too, like these good men in the seminary, fighting evil every day?

My father took his religion seriously, and I did, too. It had been a touchstone in my life, and I knew it always would be. But there were things I'd come to know, and things I'd seen. I had earned my experience, and received knowledge—unwillingly, sometimes—that not everyone has access to. Ultimately, I felt I'd been given a great responsibility. Evil has many faces, and there are many ways to fight it. Some pray, some carry a gun. Those who have a true religious vocation might take a vow of silence and live apart from the world in a cloister, or run a soup kitchen in the inner city, or work as a teacher in a religious school. For me, there was another path, and I knew it.

Something else was going on that had a significant bearing on my self-analysis. Her name was Joanne Ridick. Sister Joyce, which was her religious name, was a professor of psychology and on the admissions team at the seminary. We first talked early on, when I was making my application and she administered some of the psychological assessment tests that I had to take. Later, she taught a course called "Anthropology of the Christian Vocation," and we got to talking a little bit more about our respective backgrounds. Joyce was a clinical psychologist, scholar, and author, and had been the first woman with full professorship at the 500-year-old Pontifical Gregorian University, just outside the Vatican in Rome, where she'd worked for nearly twenty years before coming to Holy Apostles. Beyond those formal credentials, she was the first person I'd ever met who was able to integrate the study and practices of psychology and theology.

One day, while I was at the retreat house in Moodus, she called and asked for help with a staffing problem. One of the priests at Holy Apostles seemed to be experiencing some potentially serious psychiatric problems, and she figured I'd know who to call. I set her up to talk with Bert Brown. "This guy sounds high-risk to me," I said, "and you need to talk to the best."

Joyce did her follow-up, and I was struck by how calm and in control she was, how perfectly capable of handling the situation. I began to realize how much I enjoyed talking with her. She was a warm human being, very intelligent, and she understood a lot of things about psychology and my work. After a while, I started realizing something else. Watching her as she prayed at Mass, I found myself beginning to wonder if there might be a place in my life for a woman like this.

Joyce had a sense of humor. So did I. We had lunch a couple of times. She'd already planned a sabbatical. When I finally acknowledged to myself that I was attracted to her, whatever uncertainty there was disappeared.

The seminary had more than served its purpose. It had saved my life. But now that I'd gotten my strength back, soaked up a little wisdom, and deepened my spiritual life, I began to understand that Cromwell was no longer the place for me. I belonged in the outside world again, contributing what I could.

And so, in the fall of 1997, nearly three years after I'd entered it, I walked out the doors of the Holy Apostles Seminary, and came back again to a broken world.

CHAPTER TEN

THE BROKEN WORLD

NOISES SOUNDED LOUDER NOW, the ringing telephone more jarring. Movies looked a little more violent to me, magazine ads a little more risqué. And when I made my first Saturday afternoon trip to a suburban shopping mall, after walking around for a while, I had to sit down for a minute, just to get my bearings. The world doesn't seem like such a fast-moving place until you leave it for a while. Then, when you come back to it, all the colors are a shade brighter, and you realize that it's going at a pretty fast clip.

After leaving the seminary, some things made me a little nostalgic. I wasn't used to eating a meal alone, for instance, or functioning without the order and predictability I'd known at Holy Apostles. My whole day wasn't planned out for me, from morning vespers to my prayers at night. But there was a sense of freedom about being back in the outside world again, too. Everything was chaotic, open-ended, and exhilarating. Despite all that newness, I felt centered and at peace.

Something had changed in me as a result of my years in the seminary. Yes, I'd acquired formal knowledge in theology and philosophy. But that wasn't really what it was about. It was also about taking a sabbatical from evil.

I'd been lucky enough to get myself to a safe haven, to find a place that allowed me to step out from the cascade of horror I'd seen for most of my working life. I'd been given the opportunity to clear my vision and get a little distance on things. When I came back to the mainstream, I felt refreshed, clean, and restored. There was a sense of discovery in my everyday life that I hadn't felt in years. I should've known it wouldn't last.

Before leaving Holy Apostles, I'd already formulated a vague plan to return to The Academy Group and pick up where I left off, but I was going to do it on my own schedule. Take a few months to get settled back into the house, get everything squared away before jumping back into the fray. Of course, it didn't happen that way. Before I even had the chance to move back into my office, I got a phone call from my friend Bert Brown. He needed a little help, he said, another set of eyes, for a case he was consulting on. He wondered if I could take a look at the JonBenet Ramsey ransom note.

I knew about the basics of the case from news reports—on the morning of December 26, 1996, a wealthy Boulder, Colorado, couple, John and Patsy Ramsey, reported that their little blond six-year-old daughter had been kidnapped; not long after, she was found, murdered, in the basement of the family home. I certainly didn't have any inside knowledge of the case, but I had heard that a ransom note had been found in the house, and was the subject of a lot of speculation. Bert was working on the case as a consultant to the Boulder district attorney's office, and wanted to know what type of person might have written it.

He sent me a photocopy of the two-and-a-half-page note, written on a legal pad, and I began writing down my thoughts. I knew enough about the crime to realize there'd been a tremendous disturbance of the crime scene itself. The little girl's body had been moved by her father before the official examination and crime scene search, which meant the location was permanently tainted, destroyed as a pure evidentiary source. So what were we left with? The ransom note. The note was a crime scene in and of itself, hard physical evidence that remained as fresh as it was on the day it was found. And it could be interpreted. The written word *is* human behavior, like any other behavior, and it will betray the traits and characteristics of the writer. This is what it said:

Mr. Ramsey,

Listen carefully! We are a group of individuals that represent a small foreign faction. We respect your bussiness [sic] *but not the country that it serves. At this time we have your daughter in our posession* [sic]*. She is safe and unharmed and if you want her to see 1997, you must follow our instructions to the letter.*

You will withdraw $118,000.00 from your account. $100,000 will be in $100 bills and the remaining $18,000 in $20 bills. Make sure that you bring an adequate size attache to the bank. When you get home you will put the money in a brown paper bag. I will call you between 8 and 10 am tomorrow to instruct you on delivery. The delivery will be exhausting so I advise you to be rested. If we monitor you getting the money early, we might call you early to arrange an earlier delivery of the money and hence a [sic] *earlier pick-up of your daughter.*

Any deviation of my instructions will result in the immediate execution of your daughter. You will also be denied her remains for proper burial. The two gentlemen watching over your daughter do not particularly like you so I advise you not to provoke them. Speaking to anyone about your situation, such as Police, F.B.I., etc., will result in your daughter being beheaded. If we catch you talking to a stray dog, she dies. If you alert bank authorities, she dies. If the money is in any way marked or tampered with, she dies. You will be scanned for electronic devices and if any are found, she dies. You can try to deceive us but be warned that we are familiar with Law enforcement countermeasures and tactics. You stand a 99% chance of killing your daughter if you try to out smart us. Follow our instructions and you stand a 100% chance of getting her back. You and your family are under constant scrutiny as well as the authorities. Don't try to grow a brain John. You are not the only fat cat around so don't think that killing will be difficult. Don't underestimate us John. Use that good southern common sense of yours. It is up to you now John!
Victory!
S.B.T.C

To begin with, in two decades of analyzing written crime scene evidence, I'd never seen a two-and-a-half-page, hand-printed ransom note. Never. That was how unusual it was. Criminals who write ransom notes are trying to get across only the information that they need to. Anything else is superfluous, and only going to give more clues about their identity, and there's no need to write an opus. A real kidnapper has no interest in revealing the kind of telling information that this note did. According to my analysis, here are some of the telling characteristics:

The note begins with a formal salutation, followed by an exclamation point. The author wants the reader to *hear* the message, as if the material will be spoken or read to someone.

"a group of individuals"—this usually means one person trying to appear as a group.

"a small foreign faction"—foreign to whom? A meaningless phrase.

"respect your bussiness"—misspelled, but shows an awareness of John Ramsey's business.

"posession"—again, shows the author's proclivity for misspelling double S words.

"but not the country that it serves"—a political statement inappropriate to the goal of ransom.

"withdraw $118,000.00 from your account"—shows proprietary information, i.e. knowledge of the precise amount of John Ramsey's bonus, and that it is in a bank account rather than somewhere else, as in other investments.

"Make sure that you bring an adequate size attache to the bank" and "I advise you to be rested"—both maternal-sounding remarks. Shows motherly feeling. Also, why "attache" and not the more common "attache case"?

"You will . . . be . . . denied burial"—more likely to be said by a female than a male. Also, suggests the victim is dead. If the victim is still alive, burial would be the least of anyone's concerns.

"gentlemen" and "watching over"—again, more likely to be used by a female.

"fat cat"—an expression common in the 1950s and 1960s. Indicates a writer in the forty-something age bracket.

"Use that good southern common sense of yours."—a phrase not likely to come to mind from a Northerner. The writer is likely from the South, and knows that Ramsey is, too.

"Victory!"—inappropriate. Meaningless for a kidnap ransom note. A clumsy attempt to sound like a terrorist.

"S.B.T.C."—no known organization, and no explanation of the acronym.

"At this time," "to the letter," "hence"—habitual expressions.

In addition, the three exclamation points and other punctuation indicate a relatively educated, literate writer. The sophisticated vocabulary (faction, monitor, deviation, provoke, countermeasures, etc.) and grammar (largely correct) also point to an educated person.

The gradual shift from "I" to "we" in the second paragraph makes it doubtful that the writer is from a group, let alone a group of terrorists. In addition, the note doesn't demand enough money (considering the Ramseys' wealth) for taking a kidnapping risk. And its overall tone, which becomes more threatening throughout, suggests someone on intimate enough terms with John Ramsey to chide him. "Don't try to grow a brain John." My overwhelming feeling about this note is that there's too much

Hollywood in it. Good people make bad criminals, and the note smacks of inauthenticity. It shows a low level of criminal sophistication, and was most likely written to distract authorities from conducting an immediate investigation of the complete home, which it did.

There was certainly a lot of crime scene information, other than this note, to process. We knew, for example, that the killer apparently took the time to write a practice note on the same legal pad, which began: "Dear Mr. and Mrs. Ramsey." But sticking just to the written material available to me, I could tell a lot. My analysis indicated that, operationally, the note was prepared without much planning, and contained inconsistencies not expected in a bona fide kidnap demand note; psychologically the perpetrator was sane and stable, but distressed, and of low criminal competence. Furthermore, my profile of the writer revealed someone who was in all likelihood white, female, Southern, well educated, middle-aged, and who knew John Ramsey, his personal life and business, quite well.

So, who was the killer? In behavioral analysis of a written communication, we can never make that pronouncement. Profiling doesn't identify individuals—just types of people. We tell as much as we can about the kind of person who is most likely to have written the material, and then it's up to investigators to match up what they've learned with our assessment. That's how crimes get solved. In this case, of course, it wasn't. I gave my verbal report to Bert, who, I assume, submitted it to the authorities. From there, I imagine, it was thrown into the hopper with all the other information in the JonBenet Ramsey case file. Just one more piece in a large, unsolved puzzle.

Later, I had the chance to read the autopsy report on that little girl, and it wasn't an easy thing to do. By that time, I had nine grandchildren of my own—living, breathing little people who were, with a little luck, going to carry on a bit of my own genetic material. This little blond girl's life had been cruelly short-circuited. And though we had our suspicions, we, the pros, couldn't say with certainty who'd done this to her.

I don't know why that was so hard for me to admit this time, but it was. I'd worked a lot of cases in my career that had remained unsolved, and it was always part of the job. You win some. You lose some. You fight the good fight. But somehow, seeing photographs on the news of that little girl when she was still alive, I felt as if I was witnessing the beginning of a whole new era, the next generation of evil. To me, the photographs were a reminder of all the bad stuff I wasn't going to be able to stop.

This much was obvious: There was going to be no easing back in. The evil in the world hadn't stopped just because I'd left it for a while.

I kept on working, I guess, partly for the routine, partly from a sense of duty. At the Behavioral Science Unit, I'd been part of a team that was a court of last resort for law enforcement. But the cases coming to The Academy Group were usually ones that had already worked their way through the criminal justice system, and still hadn't reached any satisfactory resolution. Now, it was as if we were a court of last resort for human beings.

One day we got a call from a distraught middle-aged couple in Pennsylvania whose twenty-one-year-old son had died. One morning, the young Pakistani exchange student who was living with the family for the summer walked into the bedroom he shared with the son and found the young man, partially clothed, hanging from a necktie attached to the top of the bunk beds. From appearances, he seemed to have just let his body weight fall, and once the noose tightened, he lost consciousness. He looked as if he'd simply taken a step forward into death.

The Pakistani boy—I'll call him Kashif—ran upstairs and got the mother, who came down and tried to give her son artificial respiration. He was still warm, and for a moment she could have sworn she felt his heart beating. But it wasn't. He was gone.

The local police conducted their investigation, and officially pronounced the death a suicide, possibly as the result of auto-erotic asphyxiation. Then they closed the book. But the parents couldn't live with that. They knew their boy, and they knew there must be more to the story. He couldn't have ended his life like that.

Their son was mentally stable, they said, reasonably happy, and had been looking forward to the future. He had a girlfriend he planned to marry. He was from a good family that loved him and had more than enough money and a nice home. In any case, suicide is a difficult thing for a family to accept, and it wouldn't have been surprising if they were simply in denial. But after talking with these parents, we became convinced that maybe they were right.

It would be our job to conduct what we call an equivocal death analysis, a subspecialty that emerged in the Behavioral Science Unit. This technique weighs all available evidence to determine if a suspicious death is most likely the result of homicide, suicide, or simply an accident.

My colleague Don Bassett and I began, as we often do, by going to the local police who'd conducted the original investigation. They didn't want the case reopened, and they didn't want anyone else looking at it either. So we began by questioning the dead boy's family, friends, and girlfriend at length, and closely studying the tapes of those interviews. Our goal was to reexamine the last six months of the boy's life, and determine if any of the things typical of pre-suicide behavior were in his recent past.

In the vast majority of cases, people who take their own lives are feeling unhappy, sad, isolated, and depressed, no matter what their friends or relatives might think. Characteristically, the victims fantasize about ending it all, plan it, and even attempt it. They may write letters or a journal, make indirect statements to someone about it. Then, they sometimes suddenly come out of the depression, and the people around them think they're getting better.

In reality, that apparent lifting of spirit just means the decision has finally been made, and there is relief that the pain will be ending soon. At that point, they generally have a plan, and may start giving away personal possessions. It's not necessarily major or dramatic; they're just making sure to get things they've treasured all of their lives into the hands of the people they'd like to have them. "Hey, you know, why don't you take this wristwatch of mine. You've always liked it."

But what we found didn't match up with that scenario. In addition to what we'd learned about this boy's overall outlook on life, we saw more immediate signs counter-indicating suicide. He'd just taken a shower and was in the middle of changing clothes. He was going to work that day. He'd had a little tiff with his girlfriend, but it wasn't a deal-breaker. The whole theory of suicide just didn't make sense. But something else began to.

We learned that not long before the boy's death, he and Kashif had argued, and Kashif was informed he was going to have to move out. Far more telling was what the parents said happened after their son's death. Kashif began wearing the dead boy's clothes, had told the parents that perhaps death wasn't the worst thing in the world, and even though they'd lost their boy, they still had a son—him. They told him to get out, and never heard from him again.

We also learned that Kashif had a black belt in martial arts, as, it happened, Don did, too. We learned that there was a TV program that the dead boy liked, and sometimes he'd watch it before he went to work. If he was sitting, watching TV in the separate finished basement that he and Kashif shared, Kashif could have come in without being heard. Approaching from behind, he could have put a carotid artery chokehold on the boy that would have killed him within minutes.

We acted the whole thing out, to make sure it was plausible. I played the victim. When Don came in, he did it without my hearing him, and he got me in the chokehold, even though I was ready for it. I tried to struggle against it, and I have a belt in combat judo, but if you're seated and someone comes up behind you and pulls you backward against a chair, there isn't much you can do. In this case, I was in a sofa, which was impossible to tip over no matter how hard you tried. If the victim hadn't been able to break the hold almost immediately, he would have been unconscious within seconds, and dead in a matter of minutes.

From there, it would have been relatively easy for Kashif— drag the body down a short hallway to the bedroom, put the necktie around his neck, stage the death scene. There were a few *Playboy* magazines on the bedroom bookshelf, but no evidence of autoerotic asphyxiaton.

I thought about the dead boy's struggle, and the terrible injustice the police verdict had put on him, and his surviving family. He couldn't defend himself, but I wanted to vindicate him. There was only one problem. By that point, Kashif had outstayed his student visa and was now officially an illegal alien. But the Immigration and Naturalization Service had lost track of him, and apparently had no way of finding him. And we couldn't make a final determination without first interviewing him.

We worked with the INS in an effort to try to find Kashif, and even hired a crack former FBI fugitive investigation agent who had all kinds of contacts. We really went out of our way to track down this guy. But in spite of our best efforts, we couldn't find him. He'd fallen through the cracks.

As investigators, we'd done our job. We did the legwork, and came to a conclusion. Certainly there had been cases in the past ending without firm resolution. But this one hit me harder. This dead young man's parents now had some confirmation of what they believed to be the truth, yet they were powerless to do anything with it. There was no satisfaction for us in seeing these suffering parents left like that. In the end, we just helped them trade one kind of hell for another.

It wasn't our fault. We had done the best we could. We had just been too late. And that was the problem, as I began to see it. In so many of these cases, we were just too damn late.

Something was changing in me, and at first, I wasn't sure what. The seminary alone hadn't done it. But it was the first mile of a new journey. My time at Holy Apostles was my time in the wilderness, I guess. It was what broke down my defenses, my old way of doing things, and gave me the fresh eye.

For the first time in my life, I found myself wanting to work different kinds of cases. The vicious homicides just didn't appeal—if that's the right word—as much to me anymore. It wasn't that I found them more horrifying now. It was just that there was such a numbing, relentless familiarity to them. And I didn't want any morally ambiguous cases, either. No degenerate police chiefs looking for a break, or crooked corporate execs who'd dipped into the pension fund and were trying to get out of jail time.

As a result, I began venturing into other areas, defending a few people who, I felt, had been wrongly accused. I took on one case where a law enforcement officer had acted bravely and properly, and was now being accused of wrongdoing. At one hundred sixty pounds, he was trying to subdue a three-hundred-pound man high on PCP, who'd tried to grab the officer's gun while they struggled. The man was shot and killed; now the officer was being charged with use of excessive force. Another case I took on involved an officer fired by his department, sacrificed really, after he was forced to shoot a man while the guy was assaulting him.

These weren't cases of bad cops who'd crossed the line. They represented wrenching split-second decisions by men who'd literally risked their lives, and now felt discarded and betrayed. These were instances, as I saw it, where moral issues were at stake. In fact, it was as if, before the seminary, I saw the law as a function of the material order. Now I was seeing it as a product of the moral order. And where I'd once believed I could fight evil through brute strength and sheer force of will, now it seemed as if there were a lot of shades of gray in the world.

It was at about that time that a case came over the transom, involving a murder of a young woman in Montana in 1995. It had been a terrible killing, and the woman's family was left devastated. The killer had been convicted, and was put away for life. Now that he was safely off the streets, the victim's family was seeking civil damages because they felt her employer, the state of

Montana, had been negligent in providing for her security on the job. We all agreed we needed to conduct a prison interview with the killer, and decided that colleague Ken Baker, who had worked with me on the Moxley, Brooks, and Richardson cases, would handle this one, too.

The victim was murdered in the early morning, not long after she arrived for work at a state nursery. Now her assailant was serving one hundred ten years in prison, without possibility of parole. In his official written confession, he described the crime this way: "In the parking lot of the nursery I put a sleeper hold on her, and cut her neck back and forth with a knife. I then put her in the front of my truck cab. Once inside, I stabbed her. She doesn't move or seem to feel anything. She's dead."

He was thirty years old, wearing an orange prison jumpsuit, handcuffed to a chain around his belt when Ken first saw him, being escorted into the holding area by an armed guard. "Could you at least undo the handcuffs from the chain?" Ken asked. "And I'd like two cups of coffee, please." Then he turned to the subject. "How would you like your coffee, Russell?"

Ken knew it was critical to establish a rapport with the prisoner, and so he did. "This is an opportunity for you to tell me how the thing really went out of control, Russell," he said. "I don't know how other people have related to you, but you're a human being to me. I hope that in talking, maybe you'll leave this room today with a better understanding of why you did what you did. Maybe, afterward, you'll feel better about things."

Because he'd studied the crime, Ken knew it hadn't been planned. The killer had not buried the body, just covered it hurriedly with brush and leaves. He'd been drinking, smoking marijuana, and wanted sex. She was the one who happened to cross his path.

Over the next seven hours, Ken drew out the details of the prisoner's life. The poverty, brutality, the repressed rage. He'd been in trouble before, was a guy who got drunk and wanted to fight, but, until this, he had never killed. So Ken asked, "Just how did this happen, Russell? Can you tell me how it all went down?"

He'd been having trouble with his wife, he said, and went out and made several attempts to pick up women, but they ignored him. Then, in the predawn, he spotted his victim driving to work, and followed her there. The front door was unlocked, and he surprised her inside. At first, he pretended he would leave. Then, as she was escorting him out, he tackled her and hit her, hard enough to stun her.

"I grabbed her and she was screaming. I told her, 'Bitch, shut up or I'm going to hurt you,'" he said. He dragged her outside, toward his pickup, pulled a knife, and said, "I'll put it to your throat if you don't shut up." But she kept screaming. He got to the driver's side and opened the door. He told her to get in, but she continued to struggle. That was what finally set him off. It was then, he said, that "I just cut her."

She was hurt now, bleeding. He pushed her into the red and white truck, but still she continued to scream. An old man who lived a few hundred feet from the parking lot heard the struggle, and called out, "What's happening out there?" The prisoner drove out of the parking lot with his lights off and down the highway, taking the first dirt road he came to, up into the hills.

Ken was conscientious. He'd prepared himself well, poring over the crime scene photos, learning what he needed to. He knew how her body had been disposed of. He knew she had bruising around her ankles, and a severe contusion on the back of her head, consistent with a fall, but not a sharp blow. When she was found, one of her shoes was missing, and she had no clothing from the waist down.

"Russell, when you parked your truck, you opened the door to get her out, you grabbed her by the ankles, didn't you? You pulled her out, but you dropped her. You let go of her ankles, and you were shocked by the sound when her body hit the ground, weren't you?"

The prisoner looked at Ken, unsure. "How do you know that?"

"Because I've moved dead bodies around," Ken said. "And when you take a dead person, a body no longer moving, and you pull and tug on it, and then drop it from a distance as high as a truck seat, the upper body of a lifeless woman, and her head hits the ground, it makes quite a thud, doesn't it? A thud you probably weren't prepared for, because you'd never done this kind of thing before. In fact, the thud was so loud and surprising, it caused you to let go of her ankles, right out of your clenched hands, didn't it?"

The prisoner stared at him. It was as if this interrogator could see the images in his head.

"The movement was so violent it pulled her shoe off." More silence, an affirmative. (That must have been a whole small problem of its own, Ken thinks. What to do with that shoe? Dress a dead woman? Anyone who's tried to put a shoe on a small child knows how hard it is if they don't cooperate. And this woman could no longer cooperate.) "So you just took it and heaved it out into the field, didn't you? That was the only thing to do."

Ken was in the prisoner's mind now, standing on its horizon. He'd studied this crime, knew its deepest recesses. Had he really left so many clues, the prisoner wondered? How could this man know these things?

Ken continued. "You have blood all over you now, on your clothes. And you haven't brought any tools to bury her. You didn't plan to kill anyone, did you, Russell? I know that. So you did the only thing you could. You started dragging branches to cover her, but it's getting late now, and you know it's going to start getting light soon. You know someone will be looking for her, and the body will be visible from the air, maybe even by one of those damn rush-hour traffic helicopters. So you cover it with branches and leave her body there. You jump back into your truck but there's blood all over the seat. There was so much, it was dripping down onto the ground. Your heart was really pounding through all this, wasn't it, Russell?"

"I thought it was going to jump out of my chest."

Afterward, he had come back down that mountain road a murderer. Then he went to his family's house for a change of clothes and some money, and drove back to his own place, to wait for what was to come. He decided to plead guilty rather than go to trial. He admitted to the murder. It was all over now, settled.

Save for one remaining question. There was one other dark fact that Ken had discerned: By the time the prisoner had raped his victim, she was already dead.

"Just one more thing I'd like to know, Russell," said Ken. "She was already gone. You'd already killed her. You didn't mean for it to happen, but it did. Things were out of your control. But why did you do that one last thing? You could have just left her there. You hadn't meant to hurt her. So why did you do it, after she was dead?"

There was silence for a time, but when the answer finally came, Ken knew it was the truth. She wasn't really dead yet, the prisoner said. She wasn't moving, or breathing, but she was still warm. Still sweet-smelling and pliant. He wanted sex, and she couldn't fight it.

"I guess it's like when you shoot an animal," he said. "Once you've gone to all the trouble, you don't want to waste the meat."

Horrifying? Yes. Incomprehensible, even. But in talking with Ken about the case, it was as if I was somehow seeing this incident through a different lens. I knew all of the particulars, and yet the one question that kept floating up in my mind was, "Why?"

I thought back to some of the men I'd counseled in prison. Some were pure evil, through and through. But others, in fact a good number of them, were where they were because of one wrong turn. A wrong turn that may have escalated into many, on a course that began with one identifiable, if egregious, mistake.

We all make mistakes. I certainly had. I remembered that guy I'd pounded in a high school fight, and the way it nearly cost me my graduation. What if that punch I'd landed had actually blinded him, instead of just sending him to the hospital with a badly cut eye? What might have happened then? My first jail term? As it was, all I'd had to do was say I was sorry, have my parents go to school to plead my case, wash some windows, and the principal allowed me to graduate from high school with the rest of my class. But I knew full well things could have turned out very differently.

I remember talking to my old mentor, Barry Colvert, about this once. He was a master interrogator, the best of the best, and now he was a consultant with us at AGI, a polygraph specialist. What you had to do in an interview, he said, was take your time. There was no point in rushing it. You had to invest yourself in the process.

"You'll see the sorriest, most sadistic people on the face of this earth," he told me, "and somehow, after a few hours you start say-ing to yourself, 'My God, I can see where he's coming from. I'm beginning to understand it.' That empathy is what makes you a successful interrogator. But it's also what scares the living hell out of you when you go home at night—the flicker of recognition, the 'Oh my God, that's *me*.'"

This man in Montana had committed a murder, a terrible, chilling crime that not only ended the life of his victim, but caused unending, incessant agony for the family and friends who'd loved and depended on her. There was no way to minimize or excuse that. He was serving out the rest of his life in prison, and he deserved to. But I had seen worse.

This prisoner wasn't a serial killer. He hadn't done this kind of thing over and over again, without any remorse. I don't even be-lieve he had really planned it. He had done a monstrous thing, but he wasn't a monster. How was that possible? How could a person who in many ways seemed like a normal human being come to a point where he was capable of committing such an act?

In 1999, I was hired as a confidential consultant in the Columbine school shooting, where two kids, Dylan Klebold and Eric Harris, gunned down a teacher and twelve of their class-mates. It was my job to determine whether or not the police, who were being sued by parents of the dead children, had done their job properly. As part of my research, I looked long and hard at the fantasies spun out in journal entries by Harris and Klebold.

In the end, we found that there had in fact been problems with the police action. It wasn't perfectly clean. One teacher trapped in the school who might have been saved instead bled to death. And we learned that police had dropped an earlier investigation into complaints about the two killers. But was that really the whole story? Did that mean the rest of us were off the hook?

I thought back to the concept of leakage I'd developed at the Behavioral Science Unit, the idea that a person's strong fantasies, values, and beliefs will leak out of them, no matter how hard they try to keep them hidden. Had there been signs of leakage in these young killers presaging what was to come? Had we ignored the warning signs?

I'm way too smart a guy to even try to advance the argument that the responsibility for crime rests with society, mainly because I don't believe it's true. But that wasn't where I was going. I just got more and more interested in the idea of trying to work the front, rather than the back end of violence. Now, I saw myself focusing not so much on the horrible aftermath of crime, but on how to keep it from happening in the first place.

The crimes we saw at AGI were a reflection of what was happening in society at large. And over time, we began to get more requests for help from corporations who were worried about violence in the workplace, and from school systems worried about violence in the schools. Actually, they were more than worried. They were scared, and it wasn't hard to understand why. Every time you picked up the paper or turned on the TV, it seemed, there was some kid or disgruntled employee cutting loose with an AK-47 and causing the kind of carnage you see on a battlefield.

For the most part, these perpetrators weren't the psychopathic monsters we'd encountered in the Unit—people for whom rehabilitation and treatment were a joke. Many of these office and schoolyard killers, especially the kids, didn't have long track records of stupefying aberrant behavior. It seemed to me they had pre-existing chinks and vulnerabilities. And then, when something happened to overload the circuits, they veered off the road.

A few months later, at a speaking engagement in Oklahoma, a school resource officer came up to me after my presentation, and showed me an essay written by one of his students, a young boy. In a childish scrawl, the boy wrote about what he saw as mistakes made by the inept killers at Columbine. He'd do things differently, he said.

For three long pages it went on like this:

People maybe thinking well we can't get out the windows because when we open them we'll die a painful death in fire. But we'll have all the school doors chained, ha! So when people run down the school stairs trying to get out of the fire of the pipe bombs, they'll blow-up and die too.

Simple boyish bravado? No, I told the resource officer, I didn't think so. These three pages were far too specific, showed too many hours of careful thought. The fantasy was too advanced. This young man, I told him, might well be embarking on a plan.

———

One of the accomplishments I was most proud of as head of the Behavioral Science Unit was my lead role in helping found the National Center for the Analysis of Violent Crime, a national clearinghouse for unusual, bizarre, serial, and particularly violent crimes that gave local law enforcement tools to apprehend some of the country's most dangerous offenders. I also oversaw the Violent Criminal Apprehension Program, the brainchild of Pierce Brooks, the former LAPD detective of *The Onion Field* fame, which became the first-ever worldwide computerized databank of unsolved homicides.

I'd always thought of myself as a big-picture guy. Even in those early days at the BSU, I was interested in the idea of coordinating work by different agencies for a common goal, and taking the idea of individual profiling and expanding it to apply to entire segments of the population—say, terrorist groups, or the entire city of Rochester. A lot of people made a big deal of the fact that, a decade beforehand, I'd "predicted" the big crime wave of the late 1980s and early 1990s. Actually, all I'd done was look at statistics on who commits the most crime, see what size certain societal subgroups would be ten or twenty years hence, based on what we knew about baby boom demographics, and then extrapolated the statistics. It wasn't clairvoyance. It was just a matter of examining data, and adding a little bit of foresight and some good common sense.

In a way, that's what I was doing now. When I returned to AGI from the seminary, the very first speaking engagement I accepted was from a group of police executives on the topic of violent crime. Fifty percent of your job is tied up with the mechanics of law enforcement, I said: investigation, apprehension, prosecution, and incarceration. But what about the other fifty percent? What about prevention? It's no big mystery who commits two thirds of the violent crime in this country. We know from years of research: young males aged fifteen to twenty-five, most from broken homes who don't have jobs, fathers, or much schooling, and who've learned about violence from the back of a hand. We already know who they are, and what they're likely to do in the future, I told them. The question, I said, is what are you going to *do* about it?

Whenever I was hired by a corporation to advise them on reducing the likelihood of workplace violence, I made a point of pulling out of my briefcase a well-worn copy of the Constitution and Declaration of Independence. You can tell a lot about a country, or an organization, from its basic documents, I said, and these are ours. I told them I'd interviewed a number of workplace killers in prison, and almost every one mentioned how in some way, real or imagined, they'd felt shortchanged, denigrated, or demeaned by their employer.

The very first step in creating an environment where violence isn't likely to thrive, I said, isn't metal detectors, security cameras, and armed guards at the door. It's making sure the basic rights in our most revered documents are provided. The first step is to make sure you treat every employee with dignity.

After all my experiences, I'd come to some conclusions about human character. No one had to tell me that most serial killers were beyond rehabilitation. But I now believed there was true goodness in the world, and that it was at least as powerful as evil. In the seminary, for the first time, I got to know criminals as human beings, at least enough to see the potential in them, and feel sadness at how it had been lost. It wasn't just about catching the bad guys anymore. Now I was working the other side of the human coin.

There was also something else going on. Something inside me. For the first time in my life, I was able to admit to myself that my whole way of dealing with the world had been about being tough and invulnerable. Using your fists, your gun, your badge, your credentials.

Now, because of a process that began with Sharon's death, and continued in the seminary, I realized there were other things you could use. Your emotions. Your experiences. Your heart. I realized I wasn't doing anyone much good by being my old autonomous, competitive self. Now it was more important to me to be part of a team. And if someone on my team asked for advice, I tried to back up what I was saying by sharing personal experiences and feelings.

I was beginning to see The Academy Group from a different perspective, too. To me, it wasn't just a moneymaking operation. My colleagues and I didn't always have to be chasing the ugly aftermath of evil. We could try to get in there beforehand, as moral agents fighting for right and good.

I thought about how, as head of the Behavioral Science Unit, I'd sometimes kept the peace at contentious brainstorming sessions by raising my voice and slamming my fist on the table. Now, at AGI, whenever we all sat down in the conference room to start work on a case, we first took a minute to offer up a prayer. Nothing formal. The guys around the table were of almost every religious stripe. All we were doing was taking a moment to acknowledge the victims, make a request for a little guidance, and voice the hope that, in the work we were about to undertake, we might add something positive to the world.

Life has taught me that sometimes it takes a long time for the seeds you've planted to take hold. But once in a while, if you're lucky, something happens like those butterflies that day over Sharon's grave. Something that you know intellectually is just a random event, but nevertheless feels like a validation. It was in early August of 1998 that one of those remarkable things occurred.

That month, out of the blue, The Academy Group got a call from Bucks County, from a young detective, Nelson Whitney, in Falls Township, Pennsylvania. The township had just gotten a new police chief, he said, who really wanted his people to take a look at the cold homicides still on the books. The one that caught Whitney's eye was the Terri Brooks case—the brutal murder, four times over, of the pretty fast food restaurant assistant manager whose dying gaze still crept into my dreams.

Whitney apologized for what his colleagues had, or hadn't, done—wasting our time eight long years ago, and then dropping the ball. But this time, it was different, he said. He was serious. He'd read the profile we did on Terri's fiancé, Alfred Scott Keefe, and was more than intrigued.

Over the phone, Whitney started peppering me with questions. Why didn't we think this was an armed robbery? What made us think Keefe was good for it? How sure were we? So I told him. I talked about the violence of the crime, about the degree of overkill, and said I believed the killer had to have been someone who knew Terri. This time, he really listened.

Whitney asked if he and the young DA who'd been assigned to the case, Lori Markel, could come down to AGI to discuss it. We said, "Sure," and on August 12, 1998, they did. By this time, we had no official role in the case, we weren't on the clock, and we certainly weren't getting paid. But despite having spoken with Whitney for just a short while, he'd impressed me, and subsequently, so did Markel. Both were hard-chargers, they knew how to hustle, and they were sincere. I was convinced they wanted to solve this crime.

As Whitney leaned forward in his chair and fired questions at me, listened carefully to what I was saying and took notes, I saw something of myself in him, saw that eager young small-town police chief I'd been thirty years before—who had the sheer force of will to get things done.

Ken and I took Whitney and Markel into our conference room and had a really good discussion. Nelson later said he felt like he'd gone straight to the FBI Academy at Quantico. We laid it all out, reiterating the details of our investigation, and articulating our conclusions. We even gave them the full transcript of our interview with Keefe, which had been synopsized in the original report. "Scott Keefe is your prime suspect," we told them. "We're convinced that he committed this homicide."

In return, Whitney and Markel told us what they'd done from their end, and what they'd found. They'd conducted thirty-five interviews in all, and when they began putting their information together with ours, the fit was stunning.

They learned that Keefe had been heavily into methamphetamines, and even dabbled in dealing. That information dovetailed nicely with an excerpt from our interview with him eight years before: "Scott, this [murder] was a terrible thing. What kind of person do you think could have done it?" we asked.

His reply: "He had to be stoned out of his mind."

Whitney also learned that in 1990, Keefe's live-in girlfriend, by then his ex-wife, woke one morning to find a goodbye note from Keefe, saying, in effect, "I'm going out into the world to take my own chances." What was interesting was that, now that we were all putting our heads together, we realized he'd written it exactly when the noose began to tighten—on the very day we first contacted him for our interview.

Within a short time, Whitney and Markel were as convinced of Keefe's guilt as we were. The problem was making a case that would hold up in court. That was where fate intervened. Because now we had an investigative tool that wasn't available back in 1984. It was called DNA.

Nelson took all the remaining crime scene evidence that might contain genetic material into the lab, and within a month, crime lab technician Diane Lichtenwalner called him with good news.

She'd found the DNA from an unknown subject—a male—in three places: a stray pubic hair found on Terri's gray slacks, a scraping from underneath her fingernail, and on the kitchen knife used in her murder.

But what could they try to match it with? In mid-October, Whitney conducted a trash pull, grabbing garbage discarded from Keefe's house. It wasn't exactly a pleasant task, but in all the muck he found, among a lot of other things, Newport cigarette butts, which, his investigation confirmed, were Keefe's preferred brand. Whitney sent the butts to Lichtenwalner, and a few weeks later, she called back. "I got the results," she said. "The DNA on the butts is a match to your crime scene evidence."

As it turned out, the three unknown DNA samples were all from Keefe—his blood on the knife, his skin cells under Terri's nails, and his pubic hair, which had been transferred from his pants to Terri's, we surmised, when he was straddling her and beating her head against that kitchen floor.

Everyone knew we couldn't afford to have any possible loopholes or uncertainty in front of a jury. The DNA evidence had to be rock-solid and crystal-clear. And it was. Lichtenwalner worked nights and weekends to individualize the DNA samples to the exclusion of the entire world's population, many millions of times over. When she finished, Whitney remembers feeling like it was Christmas: "Right then and there, you knew this guy was on borrowed time."

Still, even though they had enough DNA evidence to prosecute Keefe, it's always better if you can get a statement from the accused with even more detail or, hope against hope, an actual confession. Now, Whitney was going to interview Keefe, and he called us for advice.

We started discussing investigative strategies. The first time around, a lot of things weren't done properly. The police interview with Keefe, for example, had been far too sympathetic. In the initial questioning, they, quite appropriately, had treated the grieving fiancé with kid gloves. They didn't lean on him, which may have been fine for the first interview. The problem was they'd never gone back to interview him again. No follow-up. Incredible. Someone should have waited a decent interval, then gone back and been more confrontational. That was all so much water over the dam, we said. The important thing now was not to spook the guy, or he'd run.

Whitney and Markel dug up as much information as possible to help prepare the interview strategy. They subpoenaed Keefe's school and employment records, did surveillance on him, kept on doing interviews. Then they came back down to AGI.

This time, Ken Baker, Dick Ault, and I laid out the scenario for the all-important interview. This was in December, and the anniversary of the murder would fall on February 4—fifteen years to the day after the crime. As I well knew, the anniversary of their crimes often holds special meaning for killers. Pick Keefe up on that precise date, I said. It'll only increase the likelihood he'll crack. And interview him the same way we did, under the pretense of needing his help. Once you convince him of that, and hear his litany of lies, you can move in the direction of confrontation.

Also, I said, make sure you interview him not at home, but at the police department, which will take him out of his comfort zone. Then, at the end, make sure you provide him with a ready-made face-saving scenario. Let him tell you that she was partly at fault for her own death. Be sympathetic. Then, apply the coup de grâce: talk about how Keefe is the only one who can give closure to Terri's father.

Whitney added his own natural interviewing skills, followed our advice to the letter, and it worked. Keefe's story was that Terri had wanted to call off the wedding. She'd taken stock of him, and realized he was never going to amount to much. It was bad timing on her part. He went to the restaurant to see her, and when she gave him the bad news, everything erupted.

Whitney and Markel got the brass ring—a signed confession. In his statement, Keefe wrote that when he went to pick Terri up from work that night, he learned that "She didn't want to be around me anymore and she hated my guts. I turned away, when I turned around she was holding a kitchen knife. I went toward her and she swung the knife, I grabbed the knife. She came after me. That's all I remember till I got in the car."

The interview went on for hours, and lasted until two in the morning. Now, without any sleep, the first thing Whitney and Markel did was jump in the car and head for Warminster. They'd worked hard to keep everyone in the dark about their investigation, including Terri's family, so there was no chance that Keefe, or anyone else, could be tipped off. But now the local DA had called a press conference for 9:00 a.m., and they wanted to give Terri's father the news in person before all hell broke loose in the media.

When they got to the Brooks home at 5:00 a.m., and knocked on the door, George's wife answered it in her bathrobe.

"Betty," Whitney said gently, "there's been a development in the case."

Her voice broke. "Okay," she said, "let's go up and tell George."

George Brooks hadn't been a well man for quite some time, and his illness was one of the things that lent a special urgency to the case. As Whitney knew, Mr. Brooks's prognosis wasn't good. He was dying of liver disease.

The three went upstairs to where George was lying in his hospital bed, and Betty woke her husband. He opened his eyes, took a few moments to focus, and realized it was Whitney standing at the foot of his bed.

"Mr. Brooks, we've made an arrest," Whitney said softly. "It was Scott. He confessed."

You can make all the brilliant, insightful suggestions in the world, and if no one follows up on them, what good are they? It was true—I pushed over the first domino, began the reexamination process, and reported our findings. We got the ball rolling again, but we didn't solve the case by ourselves.

For that to happen it took the efforts of an earnest young man, someone who was interested in playing by the rules. Someone who cared about justice and wanted to make sure that the record was set straight. Whitney's efforts didn't ingratiate him with a number of law enforcement personnel in Bucks County. They weren't very happy about his second-guessing their initial investigation. But Whitney stuck to his program anyway, and on June 6, 2000, sixteen years after Terri Brooks's murder, Alfred Scott Keefe was sentenced to life in prison without the possibility of parole.

There was one other piece of information I later learned—the kind of thing I call a pot-sweetener. Whitney himself never came right out and said so, but the Terri Brooks case was his very first homicide investigation.

About a year later, when things had settled down, Ken and I were invited up to Bucks County to receive a plaque from the

City Council. It was quite a moving ceremony. George Brooks had since died, but Betty was there, and so were Whitney and Lori Markel, who are now engaged to be married. Everyone had tears in their eyes, and they talked about how nice it was that George learned the truth before he died, because it had given him some peace.

Sometimes, out of nowhere, I find myself thinking about Martha Moxley, or JonBenet Ramsey, or the seven dead Richardson children, or Terri Brooks. I know their murders were unrelated, but in my mind, if you put them all together, there's a lesson to be derived. The lesson is that evil is sometimes evanescent, capable of appearing, disappearing, or hiding itself for years. Evil exists in individuals and in institutions, in well-meaning laws and bureaucracies. Sometimes, most dangerously, it even masquerades as the good.

Goodness, too, can remain dormant for long stretches, but unlike evil, it doesn't change. Truth is immutable; it never goes away. And it doesn't need to be reconstructed or refurbished. Mark Twain put that very simply once. When you tell the truth, he said, you don't have to remember anything.

As I see it, if the Richardson murders represented a coalescence of evil, then the solution of the Terri Brooks case represents a convergence of the good. If it weren't for the fortitude of a few dedicated people—a detective, a prosecutor, a family that wouldn't give up hope—the outcome might have been very different. And no one understood or appreciated that more than the people who loved Terri Brooks.

Not long after her killer was convicted, Whitney and Markel

received a letter from Terri's family. "Words can never express our gratitude for what you have done," it read.

Below that, the family had all signed their names. And, since Terri wasn't alive to do it for herself, there at the bottom, they signed her name, too.

Our office is located in a standard professional plaza in one of those stretches of suburban strip malls that pock the landscape now in Manassas, Virginia, bookended by furniture outlets and drive-thru fast food chains. From the outside, there's absolutely nothing remarkable about it. Out in the rear of the building, where there's designated parking for an ophthalmologist's office and an insurance company, you have to look hard to even see the small brass-colored sign that says, "The Academy Group."

Through an unmarked door, at the top of a set of carpeted stairs is a second-floor landing, on a plain white wall, hangs a bas relief of our corporate logo—a red dragon, with clawed feet, a trident tail, and a single spiked dorsal wing. I chose that symbol, a satanic icon from the Book of Revelation, for a reason. I wanted that image, the same one that's on our letterhead and business cards, to serve as a constant reminder of the enemy that is ever before us.

In my office, the shelves are lined with mementos, books, and reference tools—*Catechism of the Catholic Church*, Teilhard de Chardin's *How I Believe*, and *Favorite Poems of Emily Dickinson*, next to *The Sexual Trafficking in Children* and *Practical Aspects of Rape Investigation*. On a corner credenza is a dimestore mannequin bust, staring blankly from her perch. She has some painted ornamentation on her bald head, what looks like a petaled flower, and four small parallel lines. The flower actually represents tissue-splitting blunt-force trauma, the lines signify four rapid-fire blows from a golf club. The mannequin is the model we used as a graphic illustration of the rage wounds inflicted on Martha Moxley.

There are other, happier, mementos, too. Certificates of merit, letters of commendation, a bulletin board with someone's scrawled paraphrase of the seventeenth-century English essayist Joseph Addison: "We cannot ensure success, but we can deserve it." All of these things are, in one way or another, artifacts from my law enforcement career. But none is more meaningful, I think, than the one that sits collecting dust at the back of a top shelf, almost out of view.

It's a small commemorative plaque, the kind you might get for winning a local bowling tournament, that I received a few years back when I went down to Bucks County at the invitation of the city fathers there. Inscribed on it are the words, "In Recognition of Personal and Professional Dedication to Serve the Interests of Justice," and the following salutation: "The Community of Falls Township, Bucks County, Pennsylvania, Extends Its Sincere Thanks for Your Efforts in Providing Investigative Assistance and Behavioral Analysis in the Terri Brooks (Cold Case) Homicide Investigation."

What it means, I guess, is that sometimes, just when you've about given up hope, it's still possible that something will come along, as if out of nowhere, to say, "This time, you win."

CHAPTER ELEVEN

THE DIVINING

FOR YEARS I HAD THE DREAM. I would wake, thrashing and chilled by a cold sweat, not knowing where I was. Sharon tried to calm me, reassuring me I was safe. But I wasn't, in the dream. I remember darkness, glistening pavement, a labyrinth of urban streets, and a sense of undefined foreboding. In the distance is a faceless child. Boy or girl, I cannot tell.

In the dream I am running, sweeping the buildings with my eyes, watching for what—a rifle barrel in a window, a stray bullet, the arc of a lobbed grenade? I am not afraid for myself. I fear for the child. Whatever this impending evil is, I know that it wants the innocent. He is wandering, aimless and unaware. I know this much: He does not know the enormity of the force pursuing him.

In the dream, I am running, but why? To shield him from the danger? Catch him in my arms? Somehow, to rescue him? Those things are never clear. All I feel is panic, the terror that I won't reach him in time. And when I wake, I am breathless from the running.

I live on the side of a mountain in rural Virginia now, not far from a hallowed place where, more than a century ago, soldiers by the thousands in blue and gray shed their blood on cornfields and pastures. Today, the suburbs are encroaching on this land. But at the bottom of the mountain where I live is a small farm where, every morning, a man whose family has worked this land for generations still comes to tend his cows and feed his horses. I feel here the same way I did in that little grotto in the seminary. This is a healing place.

I wanted to take some of the goodness I experienced in the seminary out into the world with me, and I did. In the summer of 1998, I married Joanne Ridick, the former religious sister who was the clinical psychologist at Holy Apostles Seminary. It wasn't done lightly, but after a period of soul-searching, we realized it was the right decision, for both of us. The wedding pictures show us at our reception, beaming and surrounded by kids and our friends. I won't say the transition to this place wasn't difficult. Joanne and I sold the house that I'd lived in with Sharon and our kids for twenty years, and emptying it out was one of the most bittersweet things I've ever had to do. But I said goodbye to my past.

Joanne and I live what most would consider a quiet life, but it has a rhythm of its own. We've moved into our new home and she's done most of the decorating, with flowers and soft pastels. Our house is filled with cherished relics from our past lives, and the basement is stacked to the rafters with volumes that will serve as the resource library for the books of philosophy and theology we plan to write together. Somehow, we've managed to make a new life for ourselves. When I look back on it all, it seems like a miracle to me. But Joanne has brought joy into my life again.

Here on the mountain the sky is ever-changing. In the spring the rains come, turning the winding dirt road to our house into a muddy trail, and in the winter, it freezes into an icy slick. But even on the days when I don't venture out, I'm content. From the sun room, with its wall of glass, I have a view for twenty miles, and I can see the great storm fronts approaching, gathering strength as they rise up over the foothills. Sometimes, when they reach the high ground, they unleash torrents of black rain that cause the small stream that passes our house to overflow its banks. And sometimes, they pass by.

It seems inconceivable that evil could find its way here. But, from time to time, it does. Five years ago, not far from my home, two young girls, ages twelve and eight, suddenly disappeared. Some days later, their bodies were found in the swirling currents of a local river, lying side by side, almost fully submerged, their hands floating up in the water, nearly touching.

Perhaps the most difficult job in all of law enforcement is delivering that kind of news to a victim's family. But one investigator who had become personally involved in the case now felt that it was his responsibility. When he went to the family's home, he gently sat the mother down, and chose his words carefully. "No one will ever hurt them again," he said.

The mother did not flinch, or lose her composure. She just kept her eyes on him. "Were they underwater?" she said. Then again, "Tell me that they were underwater."

The investigator had seen people mentally dissociate when confronted with grief too great for them to handle. He knew that it is a way the human mind tries to protect itself from what it cannot process. But this grieving mother was in control of herself, and coherent.

She could not possibly have known the details from the scene. "Why are you asking me that question?" he said.

"Because last night I had a dream that God came for my girls," she said softly. "And when He came down for them, they were underwater. And I saw them holding hands."

I know there are unseen forces in this world that we cannot fully understand, because I have witnessed their end result. At this stage in my life, I ponder not just what is visible in this world, but what has yet to be revealed. These things are what consume my thoughts now, on this mountainside in Virginia.

In the course of researching this book, I have gone into my closed case files, to help me recall specific events. But sometimes, images from those early days return to me, vivid and unbidden. A simple walk through the grocery store can conjure up terrible scenes from the past. Not long ago, standing in front of the roasts at the butcher's counter, in my mind's eye there floated up a roadside scene from a distant night in a small Michigan town. Of a dead man whose random body parts I put into a sack like so many pieces of holy rubbish.

But human beings are more than blood and bone. We are intellect, emotion, the product of our experience, and of free will. We are also of the spirit. I have seen enough corpses to recognize the ineffable look that a body has after the life has gone out of it, and I know through personal experience that we are more than just a physical husk.

I believe that a life well lived is a journey toward selflessness. It begins with the importance of self, and ends with the importance of others. Good moves humanity toward harmony and perfection. Evil, which loves chaos, seeks to destroy it. But the tension between those opposing paths is complicated by what we human beings bring to it. There is a difference between reality and our perception of it, because our own life experiences color what we know of the world.

A boy who has been beaten and abused by his father may come to believe that he himself is bad. Overwhelmed by the memory of abuse, he may even forget there were those who once loved him—a mother, a brother, or an aunt. That is why it is so necessary to reflect on our experiences, to be aware of how they influence what we see. Children who are emotionally damaged in their early years can put up self-protective walls that, later on, are almost impossible to break down—whether by a therapist, a teacher, or a priest. Our own elaborate defense mechanisms can distort our perceptions. That's why childhood is so very critical. It is the time when the map is being drawn for a journey, and what is lost during it is sometimes lost forever.

Not every victim of abuse turns into the abuser, of course. Some children who suffer terrible deprivation and violence become loving, complete human beings, and their achievement merits our attention. But we also know too well what the odds are for the susceptible child, whose complex genetic and environmental handicaps are fanned by cruelty and neglect. As the poet W. H. Auden once wrote:

> *I and the public know*
> *What all schoolchildren learn*
> *Those to whom evil is done*
> *Do evil in return.*

In his study of serial rapists, my colleague Roy Hazelwood learned that seventy-six percent had themselves been victimized as youngsters, and in the Behavioral Science Unit's survey of sexually oriented serial killers, we found fully half had their first rape fantasy between the ages of twelve and fourteen. By self-report, thirty-six percent of those criminals described killing and torturing animals as children. We believed that the real figure was much higher, but some of the offenders might not have been willing to admit to it.

Two years ago, researchers in New Zealand reported their study of four hundred forty-two boys, one third of whom had an odd genetic variation—a single, weakened gene. Remarkably, that gene seems to be activated by one specific trigger—extreme mistreatment in early childhood. Of the boys who had both the unusual gene and a history of abuse as youngsters, fully eighty-five percent went on to exhibit criminal or antisocial behavior. The "evil gene"? Perhaps. But even if it is, just knowing about it isn't really going to solve anything.

When I first began in law enforcement, we didn't really know much about where evil comes from. Now we do. It comes from past experience—a complex mix of genetics and the socialization process. We can't do much about the former. But we can do a lot about the latter.

It is a difficult thing to admit, but I know from professional experience: Some damage to the human being is irrevocable. Once the normal sexual urge becomes intertwined with violence, for example, it cannot be separated again, and my colleagues and I have spent our professional lives tending to the tragic result. A book called *Ghosts from the Nursery,* an examination of how experiences in infancy affect the lives of children who commit violence, speaks eloquently to that point. The title of the book, say authors Robin Karr-Morse and Meredith S. Wiley, is an acknowledgment that "murderers and other violent criminals, who were once infants in our communities, are always accompanied by the spirits of the babies they once were, together with the forces that killed their promise."

Human beings do not exist in a vacuum, and it's important to see the overarching context of our lives. When I was a boy, our 1930s house had a big front porch that was often filled with friends and family. The next generation of houses in the same east side Detroit neighborhood had smaller porches—concrete squares with room for just two chairs. Eventually, the houses of the 1980s didn't have front porches at all. People isolated themselves on backyard decks and patios, surrounded by landscaped backyards and high fences. Today, with everyone working high-pressure jobs and long hours, no one's home except the dog, and he's angry and alienated, too.

At the turn of the century, seventy percent of the population earned its living from agriculture. Today, the number is 2.7 percent. In just one century our entire socioeconomic structure has undergone tremendous change. But of all the shifts, whether in government, business, or industry, the death of the extended family and decimation of the basic family unit is the most significant of all. Some observers like to say that women's entry into the workforce is what has caused all the problems. I think the most damaging change came when men went to work. Men who were engaged in agriculture were physically present at home. Now, the job of providing for their families, and the commuter lifestyle it engenders, has taken them physically away.

In the face of tremendous loss, nothing has come to replace

that center of family life. We've all discussed the growing isolation in our culture, especially among kids. Parents work, schools are overwhelmed, and we're all tempted just to throw up our hands. But we cannot. The stakes are too high.

My attitude about fighting evil has changed since those early days hunting fugitives in Washington, D.C., and my instinct is no longer to go after one bad guy at a time. Police administrators today need to broaden their scope. We cannot leave our problems to a system of fragmented agencies. The criminal who is a robbery fugitive is likely to be wanted by the Drug Enforcement Administration, and the same one wanted by the family court for payment of nonsupport. Is this really the best we can do? Isn't there a better way?

The kind of coordination I'm talking about isn't a pipe dream. We did it with the National Center for the Analysis of Violent Crime. Pierce Brooks did it with the Violent Criminal Apprehension Program. Why was the Behavioral Science Unit so successful? Because the right group of people came together at the right time, in the right place. At a point in our country's history when there was a tremendous surge in violent crime, the FBI was concerned with trying to understand and prevent it. Were we mind readers? No. But we were visionaries. And despite the dark message of that vision, we were fortunate enough to be heard by people who recognized the value of what we were doing.

I am proud of my role in helping establish the Behavioral Science Unit, and the National Center for the Analysis of Violent Crime. But I would never claim I did all of the work myself. So much of what we accomplished was a team effort by brave men and women who banded together for the common good.

In 1962, when I was a police officer back in Michigan, the

number was around nine thousand homicides annually, and we solved ninety-two percent of them. Today, there are sixteen thousand homicides a year in this country, and only two thirds of them lead to arrests. That should rightly alarm the American public. But we shouldn't be overwhelmed by the ten percent of the population who are the evildoers. We need to focus on the ninety percent who are good.

I always tried to see that new agents kept a balanced perspective in their work. When you go into someone's house, I told them, look at what's taped up on the refrigerator. Homework assignments, the kids' dental appointments, a note about when the plumber's going to show up. "They're the same people you are," I said. "And they want the same things—a nice place to live, enough food to eat, and a better life for their kids." It was a way of trying to give these lawmen some context, to keep them from being consumed by the evil we all saw every day.

It wasn't always easy. The memory of victims is something that will stay with me forever—the mental image of a young woman whose life is about to be taken by a predator, calling on God to intervene. He does not answer her, no one comes to save her, and so her life on earth ends. I've often wondered: Does she die in despair? Does she lose her faith at the last instant? Those are the questions that haunt me. They are the things that can shake a man's foundation, even force him to question his commitment to a cause.

Still, over the course of my life, I have come to believe that good pre-exists evil, rather than the other way around. Evil corrupts and perverts the innocence that precedes it. In the natural order of things, good is apparent and primary; evil is the predator in the night.

I have thought long and hard about the battle between good and evil. And what I want to impart, more than anything, to readers, is that they are not helpless players in this grand, eternal struggle. They have more power than they realize, which is what C. S. Lewis was driving at when he said, "Good and evil both increase at compound interest. That is why the little decisions you and I make every day are of such importance."

I believe that the mystery of life is hidden in its opposites—challenge and complacency, presence and absence, acceptance and rejection, love and disregard. But the tension created by those contradictions isn't necessarily a bad thing. Sometimes, our own confusion and suffering is what propels us forward, toward a higher state of being.

There are events in this world, forks in the road, that force us to make decisions, to choose a path. We can go either way at these moments, and the repercussions can be small, or enormous. Stanley Hauerwas, one of the country's leading moral theologians, used the terrible events of September 11, 2001, as an example of such a crossroad. What we witnessed in the aftermath of the terrorist attacks, he said, was nothing less than an entire culture suddenly attempting to come to terms with death.

The sad reality of sudden, violent death is what I have had to confront nearly every day of my working life. To many people, the phrase "sanctity of life" is an abstraction. For me, it is not, and the words of the poet Rabindranath Tagore, the Nobel laureate for literature in 1913, hold a special meaning for their description of the marvelous wonder that is ordinary human existence:

> *When I think of this end of my moments*
> *The barrier of the moment breaks*
> *And I see by the light of death*
> *Your world with its careless treasures.*

Friends who were in New York City on September 11, 2001, told me about two separate incidents that occurred that awful morning. The first came when a terrified young mother made her way to Ground Zero to retrieve her two small children, who were in a school not far away. She recalls onlookers standing, stunned, in the minutes after the second plane hit the World Trade Center. They looked to the sky, and saw dark blots that began hitting the sidewalk, and realized, in horror, that they were people. She remembers a group of kids, standing in baseball caps and baggy jeans, who were watching things unfold. But as the bodies hit the pavement, those teenagers shouted out and cheered.

Another friend, a psychiatrist who practices in Manhattan, volunteered for one of the emergency counseling units hastily set up in the days after the attacks. Not long after, a young professional woman who had moved to the U.S. from South America came to him, with a remarkable story to tell. Her sister, a single mother, had worked as a housekeeper at the Marriott hotel, which stood between the Trade Center towers. She'd arrived at her job before dawn on that fateful morning, as she often did, with her seven-year-old daughter in tow, intending to drop her off at school when class began a few hours later. When the towers fell, the hotel was completely destroyed, and the mother was killed instantly. The little girl, critically injured, was not expected to survive.

Now, doctors had approached the young woman because of her status as the little girl's aunt and only living relative. They needed a family member to grant them permission to harvest the little girl's heart after death, for purposes of an organ transplant. The young woman, broken and distraught, was overwhelmed at the prospect of having to make that decision. Alone in the world, she felt she had no one to turn to for advice. But she soon came to realize that there was in fact one option, albeit a very difficult one, available to her. She went to the pediatric intensive care unit, and, as gently as she could, explained the situation to her niece.

"So, would you like to do that, Maria?" the woman asked. "Would you like another child to have your heart after you're gone?"

And the little girl, six hours before she died of her injuries, gave her reply.

"Yes," she said. "You can give them my heart."

Why does God allow evil to prevail in this world? It's an eternal question, which means that it's not likely going to be answered in our brief lifetimes. But in the end, I believe, the question itself is not as important as deciding what role each of us is going to play in the struggle. No human being is totally good—or totally evil. I remain convinced that, at least in some cases, we have the opportunity to alter the path of a child who has all the telltale signs of going bad. The hand is dealt, the cards are stacked, the forces are ready to come into play. Then, into that scenario, comes another human being.

In that sense, I do believe that one individual has the potential to alter the course of human events, through something as simple as a single act of kindness. Sometimes, it might be a matter of paying attention to just one neglected soul. How much damage might that one minor intervention prevent? How many horrible, unspeakable things might that keep from ever happening?

We all face choices, every day. And we can choose either to respond or to turn away. The eighteenth-century statesman and philosopher Edmund Burke put it simply: "All that is necessary for evil to triumph is that good men do nothing." In the pages of this book, I have tried to tell the stories of men I have known who, every day, risk their lives and sense of well-being in the pursuit of evil. There is no need to lionize them, but we should honor their victories, especially in these uncertain times. Find strength in their bravery. Take heart from their courage.

Not long ago, I spoke at an international conference on violent crime in Toronto, to a group of law enforcement officers—members of a criminal profiling community that exists because, some years back, one of them attended the fellowship program that we began at the FBI Academy. Today, hundreds of profiling units exist all around the world, offshoots spawned by methods and practices the Behavioral Science Unit pioneered. When I visited, I spoke to them about some of the things I believe the future holds.

I ended by saying that I have a dog who can recognize me as his master, even under the most extraordinary circumstances. He can detect my presence in the darkness, or even after I've left a room. He can distinguish my scent from that of any other human being, even if he's blindfolded. Aren't we highly evolved human beings at least as smart as that animal? I said. Shouldn't it be possible for us to do the same thing? I wanted to challenge them, to push them to imagine things that are no longer beyond imagining.

Fifty or a hundred years ago, there was no technique called profiling, and it was inconceivable that we would one day identify a perpetrator through microscopic traces of his DNA left on a cigarette butt or the rim of a water glass. Today, those techniques of detection are commonplace, and they have revolutionized law enforcement. I see no reason to believe they will be the last such advance. In fact, I envision the day when we will be able to walk into a recent crime scene, and simply take a sample of air to help us identify the unique scent of the perpetrator, or another microscopic signature—perhaps the bacteria left behind by a particular human presence. We will identify the killer, without ever having seen him.

We are already aware, thanks to the pioneering work of men like Robert D. Hare, that electrical impulses generated by certain parts of a psychopath's brain register abnormally on MRIs. What about the final moments that a victim experiences before dying a violent death? Is it impossible that a moment of such intensity creates a burst of energy that is somehow locked into the brain's neurochemistry, and is stored there as a kind of permanent record that, someday, we may be able to peer into and "read"?

I foresee a time when all of the brave, remarkable work the Behavioral Science Unit performed nearly a quarter of a century ago will become a vestige of the past. Its insights will be antiquated, its practices outmoded. Those in law enforcement research will move on to other frontiers. And when that day comes, I will welcome it. Because it will mean that we have taken one more long stride toward the vanquishment of evil.

At this point in my life, I've achieved a certain level of comfort. I know what my contributions have been, and what I yet have to offer. One part of my career is over now, and another has begun. I no longer work for the government. I'm in private practice. And though I still carry a heavy schedule, I have some control over how I choose to spend my time.

Twice a week, I drive down the mountain to a little town about thirty miles from here, to a small pastoral counseling center, where I work as a volunteer. There, I deal mostly with kids who are angry and confused, or who are having trouble in school.

Many of them come from tough family backgrounds, and for some, this is the only place they have to talk and unload. Some have pretty run-of-the-mill problems; others have experienced deeper, more profound damage.

I am, above all, a realist. I know that sometimes I can make a difference in these kids' lives, and sometimes I can't. But that doesn't change the fact that every week, I still take a few hours to make the drive anyway, to that white frame counseling center, with its donated furniture and scuffed wooden floors.

Because it is my way of restoring my own faith, and of giving something back. It is my way of attempting to short-circuit perhaps just one small path of evil in a world that, as Hemingway once wrote, is a fine place and worth fighting for.

ACKNOWLEDGMENTS

THIS BOOK HAS BEEN THE JOURNEY of my life-
time. It has come about by the methodical review of my life: the
events that have shaped it and the people who have played major
roles in it. So many people come to mind. I am full of gratitude
and appreciation to the kind, competent, and supportive people
who have helped me to recall some of the more important aspects
of that journey for inclusion into this manuscript, but also to
those beautiful people who guided me though the difficult times
of my life, enabling me to accomplish whatever achievements I
have been able to bring about.

It is impossible to acknowledge every person who gave me a
push, pull, or jolt, causing me to move to a better place in my life.
I will try to at least pay homage to some of them who have made
a contribution to the compilation of data for this book.

First, I owe a debt of gratitude to my good friends and colleagues of The Academy Group, Inc. (AGI). The current members who helped in large and small ways include forensic behavioral scientists Dr. Dick Ault, Stephen Mardigian, Larry McCann, Mike Napier, Ken Lanning, President Pete Smerick, Chief Operating Officer Martin Rehberg, Office Manager Elaine Fox, and ITT experts Marilyn Ruland and Barbara Juedes. Special thanks go to Roy Hazelwood, who read the manuscript and offered helpful suggestions, and to Ken Baker, who has been my partner and co-analyst in so many cases over the years. Former AGI members who also deserve credit include Don Bassett, Dr. Tom Strentz, and Howard Teten, the godfather of profiling. This book has relied largely on the memories and editorial comments of Dr. Bert Brown, former director of the NIMH, and Conrad Hassel, Esq., my good friends and fellow founders of AGI.

Those special agents and support personnel of the FBI, both former and current, rank near the top of the appreciation list for their interest and guidance. These include people like supervisor Ernie Porter of the FBI Public Affairs Office, polygraph examiner Barry Colvert, FBI photographer Nancy Soberg, researcher Jean Caddy, Unit chiefs Dr. John Douglas and Bill Hagmaier, and Cindy Lent, technical assistant and researcher of the FBI National Center for the Analysis of Violent Crime (NCAVC).

I am especially indebted to the members of the FBI Behavioral Science Unit, including Chief Dr. Stephen Band, supervisor Harry Kern, homicide experts Art Westveer and Win Norman, researcher Sandy Coupe, retired Unit chiefs Jack Pfaff, Larry Monroe, and Tony Rider; former BSU supervisors and members Dr. Jim Reese, Jim Horn, Blaine McIlwaine, John Minderman, Bob Ressler, Joe Harpold, Dr. Dave Icove, Pat Mullany, Bill Peters, Dick Harper, Tom O'Malley, Dr. Bill Tafoya, and Joe Conley; and FBI Academy academic deans Dr. James O'Connor and

Dr. John Campbell, assistant directors Jim McKenzie and Jim Greenleaf; and I cannot forget the unselfish help of former secretaries Kathy Meadows and Bernadette Cloniger.

Especially good Bureau friends who helped me through tough times were former assistant director Joe Davis and his wife, Dr. Nancy Davis; and supervisor Doug Cannon and his wife, Dot.

Caring persons who provided spiritual guidance during melancholy periods of my journey were Fathers Phillip Mijka, Marc Pollard, Mike Bazan, and David Martin; Br. Tom Walbroehl and the men and women of the Fr. Veger Council of the Knights of Columbus in Warrenton, Virginia; and at the seminary in Cromwell, Connecticut, were Fathers Ray Halliwell, vice rector, Pat Tagliercio, dean of students, Tad Hallock, spiritual director, Bill McCarthy, novice director, and friends such as Fr. Paul Lamb, Br. Art Kirby, Fr. Stanley Grove, Fr. Jim Downs, and Fr. Tony Bruno, chief chaplin, McDougal Correctional Institution, South Windsor, Connecticut.

Those professional persons and law enforcement officers who assisted me in collecting facts about cases were Lyndi Gordon, Esq., investigator Rick Hart, reporter John Lawhorne, and Dawn Krebs, (the barefoot) editor, the *Sun and Daily Arcadian* newspaper, and Eugene Hickson, former mayor of Arcadia, Florida, in the Richardson Case; Greg Sturn, Esq., investigator Nelson Whitney and assistant prosecutor Lori Markel in the Teri Brooks case; and former FBI assistant special agent in charge Jim Murphy and NYPD detective Willis Krebs in the Martha Moxley case.

I also thank my friends and readers Ann Rule, Robert Hare, Stephen Michaud, Ron Kessler, William Petersen, Joe Pistone, Lawrence Schiller, Dennis McDougal, Thomas Groome, and Rabbi Harold Kushner. I owe a debt of gratitude to editors Rick Horgan and Beth de Guzman of Warner Books for keeping me focused, and to Frank Weimann, my agent, who took my story to them.

I must acknowledge the help of the man who is my hero, mentor, co-worker, benefactor, and, most of all, my father, Alvoy I. Depue, retired inspector of the Roseville, Michigan, Police Department. Many thanks for the contributions of my always supportive brothers—Gordon, Kenneth, Duane, and Gary—and to my wonderful children, Renee, Arleen, and Steven, who is a master police officer with the Fairfax County, Virginia, Police Department.

Sometimes an author may feel the need to acknowledge a person he has never met because that person played an important part in forming his or her direction in life. For me, Franco Imoda, S.J., author of *Human Development: Psychology and Mystery,* is such a person.

It is probably a bit unusual for an author to acknowledge his co-author, but I must pay homage to Susan Schindehette, who did me a great service by causing me to reflect on my life so that I could pull out thoughts, feelings and experiences, some of which I had never put into words. Then she decorated them with the beautiful vocabulary and style of the talented writer and wordsmith she is.

Most of all, I acknowledge the invaluable assistance of my wife, Joanne, who remained married to me through these years of writing, re-writing, adding, deleting, and changing this story, and who stayed lovingly at my side through the many moods of anger, outrage, grief, sadness, and finally joy and happiness. She is the wind beneath my wings.

INDEX

ABOUT THE AUTHORS

A former Marine, **Roger L. Depue** began his law enforcement career in the late 1950s. In 1962 he became chief of the Clare Police Department in Michigan (one of the youngest chiefs in the nation). Six years later, he was a special agent for the FBI, posted in New Orleans. He was an original member of the FBI's first SWAT team, Spider One, and served as chief of the FBI's Behavioral Science Unit from 1979 to 1989, a time when the Unit's pioneering work in criminal profiling first came to prominence. In those same years he was the administrator of the FBI's National Center for the Analysis of Violent Crime (the precursor to VICAP). In 1989 he founded The Academy Group, Inc. (AGI)-an elite forensics group that served as the basis of the Fox television show *Millennium*. In 1995, after the death of his first wife, he became a religious brother and seminarian at the Holy Apostles College and Seminary in Cromwell, Connecticut, and counseled prison inmates. He returned to AGI in 1999 and has since served as a consultant on several high-profile cases, including the Martha Moxley murder, the JonBenet Ramsey murder, and the Columbine shooting.

Depue has a BS in psychology, an MS in society and law, and a PhD from American University in counseling and development. He has won over twenty law enforcement awards, testified before Congress, conducted White House briefings, and delivered hundreds of lectures to professional organizations. He has been interviewed on all the major networks, A&E, and the BBC, and been profiled or quoted in periodicals ranging from the *Washington Post* to the *New York Times* magazine and *Vanity Fair*. He has served as consultant for novels, television shows, and motion pictures, including *Silence of the Lambs* and *Red Dragon*.

Susan Schindehette is a senior writer at *People* magazine, where she has authored several cover stories and appeared numerous times on network television. She previously worked at *TIME* magazine and is the co-author, with John Walsh, of the *New York Times* bestseller *Tears of Rage*.